THE POLITICS OF ECONOMIC CRISIS

The Politics of Economic Crisis

Lessons from Western Europe

Edited by

E. DAMGAARD

P. GERLICH

J. J. RICHARDSON

Avebury

Aldershot · Brookfield USA · Hong Kong · Singapore · Sydney

Published by
Avebury
Gower Publishing Company Limited
Gower House
Croft Road
Aldershot
Hants GU11 3HR
England

Gower Publishing Company
Old Post Road
Brookfield
Vermont 05036
USA

British Library Cataloguing in Publication Data

The politics of economic crisis: lessons
from western Europe.
1. Western Europe. Economic conditions,
Political aspects
I. Damgaard, E. (Erik) II. Gerlich, P.
(Peter) III. Richardson, J.J. (Jeremy)
John), *1942-*
330.94

ISBN 0 566 05517 1

Printed and bound in Great Britain by
Athenaeum Press Limited, Newcastle upon Tyne

Contents

Figures

Tables

Contributors

Erik Damgaard University of Århus.
J. Will Foppen Erasmus University.
Peter Gerlich University of Vienna.
Edgar Grande University of Konstanz.
Gunnel Gustafsson University of Umeå.
Volkmar Lauber University of Salzburg.
Wolfgang C. Müller University of Vienna
Ben Pijnenburg Erasmus University.
J. J. Richardson University of Strathclyde.
Joan Subirats University of Barcelona.

Preface

Since the 1970s new and increasing challenges are facing democratic governments. Stresses and strains have been felt in all European countries. Political science has reacted only slowly to this new situation. It has, however, increasingly turned from structural concerns towards analyses of political processes, legislation and policy styles. These studies have mostly been conducted on the level of single countries.

Under the auspices of the European Consortium for Political Research (ECPR), a research group was formed in order to analyse the responses of Western European states to the post-1974 economic crisis. Meetings of the research group were held in Florence in 1984, Barcelona in 1985, and in Gothenburg and Vienna in 1986. Our approach has been to analyse the selected individual countries according to a common format – dealing with such questions as perceptions and definitions of the crisis, economic strategies, other issues and policies, and the results of crisis management. Our hope is that we have produced a volume which is genuinely comparative in its approach and which contributes to an understanding of the western European polity and its capacity to meet challenge.

We wish to acknowledge the support of the ECPR; of Fonds zur Förderung der wissenschaftlichen Forschung, Vienna; Österreichische Forschungsgemeinschaft, Vienna; Webster University, Vienna, and its Director Dr Robert Brooks; and the Department of Political Science, University of Gothenburg. We are also grateful to Grace Hunter and A. M. Robinson for assisting in the preparation of the manuscript.

E. D. P.G. J. J. R.

1 From the politics of abundance to the politics of scarcity: strategic options

Introduction

The purpose of this volume is to analyse the ways in which Western European democracies responded to the economic crisis of the mid-1970s. How were the new economic challenges perceived in various countries? Which political and policy responses followed from the perceived economic problems? How successful in economic and political terms have European democracies been in their attempts at crisis management? By describing and comparing the experiences of nine European countries since the early 1970s, we hope not only to answer these difficult questions but also to arrive at some general lessons with respect to the governance of modern democratic societies.

From prosperity to crisis

During the past fifteen years most European democracies have faced new economic and political challenges. In the early 1970s the liberal democracies of Western Europe were noted for their reliance (although in varying degrees) on corporatist policy-making arrangements and their goals of economic growth and welfare state expansion. Despite signs of new forms of mass political participation (Barnes *et al.*, 1979), and the emergence of new political issues (Inglehart, 1977), the ''European Polity'' Model (Heisler, 1974) appeared rather stable and capable of handling political problems and difficulties. At the risk of oversimplification, one might argue that the routinized integration of organized interests in policy-making functioned fairly smoothly within a growing economy.

In the mid-1970s things had changed in most Western European countries. The politics of abundance of the 1960s and early 1970s gave way to the politics of scarcity. Economic indicators began to look gloomy after 1974. Many countries experienced sharply increasing rates of unemployment and soaring inflation. Economic growth decreased markedly while balance-of-payments deficits and public sector deficits increased. In several countries the combination of such unfortunate developments justified the use of the overworked term 'crisis'. As the downturn of the economy was not a short-term phenomenon, it called for policy adjustments to prevent further deterioration and possibly a threat to the democratic welfare state.

Slow growth and scarcity would seem to demand limits on public expenditures that could not continue to expand as in the past. Yet the big public sectors appeared to be resistant to change, not least because various types of producer, client and professional interests have been built into the governmental and administrative systems. Throughout western Europe we find strongly sectorized systems organized around particular political, administrative, and organizational interests. Consequently, cross-sectoral policy-making and coordination had become difficult at a time when it was needed more than ever. Would immobilized stalemate societies perhaps emerge? (Crozier, 1982.)

The need for change was also felt with respect to the private sector of the economy. Did not 'Old Europe' need innovation, industrial modernization, and adjustment to high technological developments? And had not government regulation of citizens and firms been carried too far? Would governments none the less introduce more regulation to solve new problems?

The new economic problems had to be managed in an era with important changes in the social and political environment. First, a number of new issues and demands were placed on the political agenda. While some of them were not really 'new' in the sense that they had been known before, they were new in the sense that they mobilized significant numbers of people for political action, thus challenging established patterns and solutions. The new types of demands concerned such issues as environmental problems, equal treatment of sexes, minority rights, peace movements, and anti-nuclear movements. Some of these new problems could perhaps be solved by money, though at great cost, while others clearly could not. Secondly, alongside the changing political agenda, we see an increase in the number and forms of unconventional political behaviour: grass root activity, demonstrations and so on, as well as demands for more direct participation of affected interests in decision-making. This development is to some extent explained by an increasing level of education which seems to produce a more active and critical citizenry. To this should be added that, in several countries, the electorate became more volatile (Pedersen, 1983), implying that political parties could not rely on their voter support to the same extent as in the past.

What could be done in these circumstances, and what was actually done, to solve or at least reduce the scale of the new economic problems? The answer seems to depend upon a number of factors, one of which is how the economic crisis was perceived in the various countries.

Perceptions of the post–1974 crisis

If measured by standard economic indicators, the economic problems of the mid-1970s did not hit all countries in the same way or to the same extent. For example, Austria and Sweden appeared to be less vulnerable than Britain and Denmark. Hence one should not expect exactly the same responses in all countries. However, what matters in politics is not just 'objective facts' but how the facts are perceived and interpreted by decision-makers, who at the same time are influenced by certain values or ideologies. A socialist or social democrat may not agree with a liberal or conservative on the nature or implication of some brute facts – unless the facts are so compelling that they leave no doubt as to the appropriate response. Generally, however, we would expect political ideologies to influence the perceptions of economic problems, which therefore are likely to vary within and across democratic countries.

The importance attached to the perceived economic problems is affected by the possible existence of *other* serious problems on the political agenda. For example, the Belgian political élite is bound to pay more attention to ethno-linguistic cleavages than the French élite, and one would certainly understand if the leaders of the new Spanish democracy were preoccupied with the consolidation of a democratic system of government in the late 1970s.

The first task in the country chapters that follow is to describe how important actors perceived and defined the economic crisis. While the perceptions may vary according to different 'objective' circumstances, political ideologies, and the existence of competing problems, there may also be some common features across countries. Thus, for example, it might be that some countries perceived and defined the crisis in terms of a temporary world phenomenon which could be 'ridden out' with short-term measures. Others perhaps perceived and defined the crisis in terms of structural changes in the world economy, and related this to the need for structural change in national economies. In addition one might expect the smaller countries to think, at least initially, about the crisis as being a cyclical phenomenon generated from the outside and over which they had no control, whereas the larger countries could perhaps think of counteracting the crisis by their own independent policy initiatives (cf. Katzenstein, 1985).

General responses to economic crisis

The second task in the country chapters is to give an overall account of the reactions to the economic crisis. The purpose is basically to characterize the period under study in important respects. First, how did public budgets develop in terms of growth in expenditures and changes in the balance between programmes? Secondly, how were governments and political parties affected by economic and electoral developments? Thirdly, which (if any) broad policy strategies were developed to combat the economic crisis?

The latter question is presumably related to the crisis perceptions mentioned above. Therefore the broad strategies developed are likely to vary in similar ways within and across countries.

Key issues and policies

A third major task is (against the background of the broad policy strategies) to analyse a number of selected key issues and policies, that is, what governments actually *do* in order to deal with the economic problems.

From a substantive policy perspective the list of possible key measures is long. It is likely to include some kind of fiscal austerity, such as incomes policy or wage restraint, tax increases, cuts in welfare benefits, and so on. Such measures might simply appear 'necessary' in an economic crisis situation. Others may reflect political ideologies, such as Conservative privatization in Britain and Socialist nationalization in France. The same may (although not necessarily) be true for efforts to modernize or reorganize the public sector, to simplify or abolish public regulations, and to stimulate the development of key sectors of private industry.

The country reports on key issues are expected to be rather different in view of the national variations with respect to governmental structure, party system, interest group structure, economic and industrial structure, and so on. However, we also expect a certain similarity, given the pressure placed upon all the systems by the economic crisis, and perhaps also because possible solutions may be imported from other countries through a process of diffusion or imitation.

Leadership styles

An important aspect of the analyses of perceptions, general responses and key issues is the range of policy styles available to governments and political leaders. If governments are able to manage the economic crisis, the question is how, that is, by which methods, they go about doing it. Here we are not thinking about specific, substantive proposals of the sort indicated above, but rather about the ways in which governments manage to cope with the challenges stemming from serious economic problems.

In principle there is a wide range of leadership styles. One obvious strategy is that governments *decide to govern* in response to challenges – what in Britain may be termed 'toughing it out'. Such a strategy will no doubt increase conflict; but governments do, perhaps increasingly, deliberately challenge entrenched interests in order to secure policy change. They are thereby introducing 'non-negotiable' policies and appear determined to push them through at all costs. In some cases such a style may be successful in actually *reducing* conflict, as the participants come to accept what may be called a 'shut up' decision. This leadership style is presumably most likely to be chosen in countries with strong majority governments. Minority governments as well as strong corporatist structures would seem to make this approach to governing less likely.

In contrast to the 'toughing it out' style of governing is the willingness to let an issue 'stew' for a period with apparent governmental inactivity. The objective of this strategy is that once an issue has been 'stewing' for long enough, a situation will emerge which is propitious for policy change to take place. In effect the participants will be either exhausted with the debate or come to recognize the 'reality' of the situation.

A variant of allowing the participants, or even the general public, to recognize the reality is for governments to actively seek to *manage* people's perceptions of reality. As Schattschneider (1960) argues, the definition of alternatives is the supreme exercise of power. Thus, in response to challenges and problems, governments may seek to create a situation in which only one solution is seen as possible. Modern communication skills can be used to shift the ground of debate in such a way that even the opponents seem forced to accept underlying premises when advocating policy options.

A closely related strategy is the manipulation of the *definition* of the problem to be solved. For example, the size of a problem can be influenced by the way in which statistics are collected and presented. It may be possible to define problems away to some degree, or even to avoid their appearance on the agenda.

A different, but common, strategy to meet difficult challenges is to resort to structural change. It can be summed up in the view that 'if we can only get the structure and organization right, our problems will be solved'. Thus many western European nations have seen big reorganizations of existing structures before, such as local government, the health service, central departments, nationalized industries, and even cabinets.

As challenges increase in intensity and complexity, leaders may come to recognize either their inability to act, or that action would be too costly. Thus they may resort to symbolic (or placebo) policies (cf. Edelman, 1964). They know the policies are unlikely to 'work' (in the sense of solving problems) but they are presented in such a way as to give the appearance of action. In the short run at least, the issue is removed from the political agenda. It may never return, or when it does, different perceptions and attitudes may have emerged, leading to different solutions.

Finally, it should be mentioned that a government can sometimes 'solve' a problem by just revising its stand on it. Thus it sometimes happens that governmental parties make U-turns after realizing the untenability of their original positions. For example, parties may demand and promise lower taxes and yet do exactly the opposite.

These different strategies are not of course mutually exclusive. In politics we expect mixtures to occur in a synchronic as well as a diachronic perspective.

In most policy areas, whatever the leadership style adopted to meet new challenges, there remains the very important question of how to deal with the interest group network which has been expanding greatly during recent decades. Today the interest group network presents a complex picture of a great and increasing variety of demands being addressed to the government.

Four main strategies may be used in dealing with the challenges originating from the expectations and behaviour of interest groups. First, as part of a decision to govern, leaders may deliberately attempt to bypass or outflank entrenched interests. Secondly, leaders may resort to 'sham' consultation, that is, making the effort to 'consult' as many interests as possible but with little intention of actually listening to the representations made. In effect the original policy proposal is adhered to notwithstanding the consultation process that has been gone into. Thirdly, leaders may resort to 'inner circle negotiation' with those whose interests are thought to really matter, including those who have a capacity to influence the effectiveness of the policies at the implementation stage. Fourthly, inner circle negotiation may take the form of institutionalized tripartite or even corporatist structures for determining policy change.

It is important to note that the economic crisis and political challenges can also be seen as *opportunities* for some leaders to introduce their personal ideas for policy change. The more skilful leaders may be able to so manage and manipulate the process that policy change does indeed take place. Such changes may have been overdue but perhaps only feasible in a situation of impending or actual crisis. We hope to identify the conditions in which such 'entrepreneurship' can take place.

The results of crisis management

The final task of the country chapters is to summarize and evaluate the economic and political results of crisis management. This is done by means of various economic indicators and through assessments of the impact of crisis management upon the respective political systems, individual governments and other main actors.

The concluding chapter attempts to summarize and assess the main findings concerning similarities and differences in the political management of economic crisis in western Europe. What can be learned about success and failure in various economic and political conditions?

Nine countries have been selected for this project. They were all affected by economic crisis in the period studied, and although they have rather different historical records they are all democracies. Apart from that they tend to differ in respects that are important to our analysis. Some are small states (Austria, Belgium, Denmark, Holland, Sweden), and others larger (Britain, France, West Germany, Spain). In some countries minority governments are often formed (Denmark, Sweden) while majority coalitions or single party majorities prevail elsewhere. The degree of corporatism (however measured) varies, but Austria and Sweden head that list. Furthermore the nine countries provide varying governmental party constellations for analysis. In short, these countries furnish rich material for comparative analysis of our main questions.

References

Barnes, S. H., *et al.*, (1979), *Political Action: mass participation in five western democracies.* Beverly Hills, Cal., Sage Publications.

Crozier, M. J. (1982), *Strategies for Change.* Cambridge, Mass., MIT Press.

Edelman, M. (1964), *The Symbolic Uses of Politics.* Urbana, Ill., University of Illinois Press.

Heisler, M. O., ed. (1974), *Politics in Europe.* New York, David McKay.

Inglehart, R. (1977), *The Silent Revolution.* Princeton University Press.

Katzenstein, P. J. (1985), *Small States in World Markets.* Ithaca and London, Cornell University Press.

Pedersen, M. N. (1983), 'Changing patterns of electoral volatility in European party systems 1948 – 1977: explorations in explanation' in Daalder, H. and Mair, P., *Western European Party Systems.* London, Sage Publications.

Schattschneider, E. E. (1960), *The Semisovereign People.* New York, Holt, Rinehart and Winston.

2 Britain: changing policy styles and policy innovation in response to economic crisis

J.J. RICHARDSON

Main political events

February 1974	Conservative government defeated in general election (during a coal miners' strike) and Labour government elected
October 1974	Labour government re-elected with increased majority
Late 1976	Labour government responds to IMF pressure and introduces tough economic measures including expenditure cuts
May 1979	Conservative government elected under Mrs Thatcher as Prime Minister, after 'winter of discontent' under Labour government
June 1983	Conservative government re-elected under Mrs Thatcher
June 1987	Conservative government re-elected under Mrs Thatcher

Introduction

The UK policy style and crisis management

In discussing Britain's response to the post-1974 economic crisis, it is important to emphasize that crisis management is not new to Britain. In many respects British politics since the end of the Second World War can be characterized as primarily concerned with the civilized management of economic decline. Indeed some observers have suggested that the British economy has been in a steady long-term relative decline since the latter part of the nineteenth century. In contrast to countries like Denmark where, as Damgaard notes (see ch. 5), the period prior to the 1974 world economic crisis had seen a very healthy economic growth, Britain's economic position had been worsening steadily in comparison to her competitors. That the decline had not been in *absolute* terms, and that inflation and unemployment had been kept within politically acceptable bounds prior to 1974, no doubt facilitated the political management of Britain's relative decline. Without the tremendous financial benefits of North Sea oil, Britain's economic plight would have been desperate and her political problems possibly unmanageable. Rather than a debate on how to manage a post-industrial society, Britain's debate in the 1970s and 1980s has been more concerned with the accelerating de-industrialization and how it might be reversed.

Although this chapter is devoted to the *politics* of crisis management, we should note that it is at least possible that political factors may have little to do with the decline itself, although the priority given to the value of sterling in the 1950s and 1960s almost certainly increased the rate of decline. Stanislow Gomulka has argued that one of Britain's central problems is the rate of industrial innovation which has been significantly lower than in Japan and western Europe since the beginning of this century (Gomulka, 1979, p. 169). In particular he suggests that: 'The phenomenon of wide and still increasing relative gaps in productivity (especially) and technological levels between the UK, and Western Europe and Japan is essentially unrelated to postwar government policies' (p. 170). These conclusions are echoed in the Brookings Institution study, published in 1980, which also highlights the differences in productivity between Britain's industries and those of its main competitors. Taking a pessimistic view of the likelihood of this situation changing (but see below for a slightly more optimistic view), Caves has pointed to the role of the political system in *managing the political and social consequences* of the economic situation, rather than in changing the economic situation itself. Thus he suggests that:

> because the productivity problem originates deep within the social system, one needs an optimistic disposition to suppose that a democratic political system can eliminate that problem. Perhaps the most useful advice the economist can offer policy-makers is for them to recognize the constraints on economic change and progress found in British society . . . and to try to hold Britain's aspirations for consumption in line with what the system is willing to produce. (Caves, 1980, pp. 185-6; see also Davies and Caves, 1987)

We must therefore be especially careful to note that the economic crisis after 1974 was merely an *intensification* of what had gone before. The post-1974 world economic situation highlighted and exacerbated long-standing structural (and cultural) problems, it did not create them, although its new intensity forced important political changes, both in the style of government and, in some cases, in the nature of policies adopted.

Notwithstanding that the word 'crisis' is more than usually dog-eared in Britain, the main actors in the political process prior to 1974 had, by their actions, if not by their rhetoric, indicated little disposition towards radical policies which might affect the adverse economic forces at work. This is not to suggest that policy change did not take place or that institutional innovation was avoided. For example, the 1960s saw Britain institute a wholesale shift from an education system based upon selection to a system of comprehensive schools; it saw experiments in 'indicative' economic planning; and in the 1970s Britain became absorbed in changing the actual institutions of government – central and local. Indeed Britain has often seemed to believe that if it could only get the correct *institutional* arrangements, the necessary policy change would follow.

A closely-related phenomenon is the tendency to enthusiastically adopt new theories (and hence 'solutions') explaining the country's decline. As King notes, the 1970s saw what he terms a 'change of mood', so common in Britain. This was based upon the theory that the non-marketable sector (essentially public) was too large to be supported by the existing marketable (essentially private) sector. The theory quickly reinforced a developing and conventional wisdom amongst politicians and commentators, reflecting as it did, the development of a much more broadly based new orthodoxy (King, 1985). This new orthodoxy has been a feature of both the perception of and reactions to the post-1974 crisis.

While it is not possible here to detail the nature of the policy process and norms which influence and shape the responses, it is worth quoting Hayward's now famous characterization of Britain's attempt to institute a French style system of economic planning in the 1960s as 'toothless tripartism' (Hayward, 1974), as a perceptive comment on the *style* of government. This style has elsewhere been characterized as based upon consultation and negotiation with the 'affected interests', with a predilection for the avoidance of policy change unless it is based upon some broad consensus in the relevant policy community (Jordan and Richardson, 1982; Jordan and Richardson 1987. For a criticism of this view, see Rhodes, 1985a, and Hogwood, 1986).

Without entering into the debate about the usefulness of the concept of the British 'policy style', it is reasonable to argue that the intensification of the crisis, post-1974, presented the most severe peace-time test of established policy procedures, existing relationships, and political attitudes and behaviour. Not only did the world economic crisis produce a sharp *intensification* of those factors already working to Britain's disadvantage, but also the bulk of the period since 1974 has been under a Prime Minister determined to challenge what she herself saw as a very damaging style of government, based upon consensus and compromise. To Mrs Thatcher, the old policy style was best described as 'fudging' issues rather than resolving them. One of the central themes of this chapter is therefore an examination of the degree to which the Conservative government, first elected in 1979 and re-elected in 1983 and 1987, developed its own distinctive style of government as a response to the crisis. Before concentrating on the Thatcher governments, however, it is important to describe the post-1974 perception and definition of the crisis as it affected Britain.

Perceptions of and reactions to the economic crisis 1974–9

The arrival of the 1974 oil crisis coincided with one of the most turbulent periods in post-Second World War British history – the 1973–74 miners' strike under the Heath government. Some would see this conflict as a confrontational style of government deliberately introduced by the Prime Minister Edward Heath, just as a decade later Mrs Thatcher's dispute with the miners was seen as deliberately confrontational (Scammel, 1986). Suffice it to say that in the event Mr Heath was replaced in February 1974 by a Labour government (with a small parliamentary majority) led by Harold Wilson, which was re-elected with a more comfortable majority in October 1974. The arrival of the Wilson government saw perhaps the remnants of the old style politics (often characterized as 'beer and sandwiches' politics, from Mr Wilson's habit of calling trade union leaders to Number 10 Downing Street for discussions over beer and sandwiches), in which discontent could be bargained away or bought off by increased public expenditure. By 1976 however, the financial and economic crisis was such that the IMF could dictate terms to the Labour government in return for international financial support for Britain. By now it is reasonable to argue that there was some degree of practical working consensus (in terms of actual policies rather than party rhetoric) across the political spectrum, about both the perception of the crisis and necessary remedies. As always the demands of adversary politics gave the appearance of great confict, and pressure groups such as the Trade Union Congress disputed individual policy responses, but we should be careful to concentrate on what actually happened in policy terms.

In this context, the reaction of the Labour government (1974–9) in the latter half of its term of office, is worth dwelling upon, if only to emphasize the basic similarity of some of the economic policy responses between the Labour governments 1976–9 and the Conservative governments under Mrs Thatcher, 1979–present, based as they were on a surprisingly similar perception and definition of the central problems facing Britain. As Rose suggests, it may be reasonable to see the period since 1976 as the Healey-Thatcher years, reflecting the fact that 1976 – rather than 1974 – was the turning point in British economic history (Rose, 1986, p. 13). Thus is was in

1976 that the monetarist economic strategy, for which Mrs Thatcher has become so famous, was first instituted, albeit under the threats of the IMF and against a rather reluctant Labour Cabinet. Prior to the mid-1970s public expenditure financing appeared to play a subordinate role, as it was assumed that borrowing would fill the gap between expenditure and resources. After 1974–5, the size of the Public Sector Borrowing Requirement (PSBR) became one of the key issues in the public expenditure process and in the determination of economic strategy (see Wright, 1980, p. 92).

Emphasis on the PSBR ('those four damned letters', as a Labour Financial Secretary to the Treasury called them (see Barnett, 1982)) began to epitomize the broad political consensus on how to face the economic crisis. It was as though a new 'middle ground' had emerged from the crisis – a new 'synthesis' resulting from the realization that the economic crisis facing Britain had taken on a new dimension. (Interestingly, the 'consensus of reality' was not especially British, although in the context of western Europe Britain was perhaps the first to adopt it). For example, in July 1976 the Labour Chancellor of the Exchequer, Denis Healey, announced that the growth in public sector borrowing would be limited to £9 billion and that cuts would be made in public expenditure on industry, defence, health and social services, food subsidies and local authority loans. In addition all new local authority housing contracts were to be frozen. By September that year, following additional credit of £2.3 billion from the IMF, Healey was introducing public spending cuts of £2.5 billion over two years. By the time of the 1978 budget the Labour government was looking even more like a Conservative government with tax cuts of £2.5 billion in an attempt to increase incentives and encourage pay moderation. The surprisingly 'monetarist' philosophy of the Labour government was most evident in July 1978. It blamed an 'accommodating monetary policy' under the Conservatives in 1972 and 1973 for contributing to an acceleration in inflation. Drawing upon the lessons of this period of rising inflation the Labour government stated that:

> *the focus of monetary policy is now specifically the control of the money supply,* for which a formal target . . . was announced in 1978. Control of the money supply, in helping to rebuild a climate of confidence and stability in financial markets and to reduce expectations of future increases in prices, *is now seen as one of the two main strands of counter-inflation policy,* the other being policy on pay and prices. (*Economic Progress Report,* July 1978, emphasis added)

Thus it is worth reminding ourselves that by 1979 (the year the Conservatives came to office) public expenditure was 1 per cent lower in real terms than four years earlier. It is important to note however that although a major continuity between Labour and Conservatives is being identified here, in that 1976, not 1979, is the major turning point in terms of attitudes to public expenditure, the Healey version of monetarism was more a part of an intended *policy mix* than emerged later under the Conservatives. Healey was to some degree still a Keynesian, adopting monetary *policy* as one of the responses to crisis, whereas the early Thatcher years were to be characterized by monetarism as a *strategy* in itself, albeit not implemented as intended. At that time, the Labour government was committed to close cooperation with the unions – in the rather corporatist 'social contract' which eventually collapsed (see below), and to the development of 'planning agreements' with industry. Thus the Labour government, facing the early years of the world economic crisis, was still searching for a way of solving unemployment – by spending and by industrial policy – and solving inflation by incomes policies and monetarism.

As we shall see below, the Conservative government which was elected in March 1979, decided to give a very strong push further in the direction of monetary policy started by Labour, elevating it to its central strategy and combining this with a desire to introduce a range of potentially radical policy reforms, more related to its philosophy for dealing with an ever-ailing economy. The Conservatives were certainly more willing to sometimes (by no means always) challenge entrenched interests, in contrast to the normative values of consensus and negotiation suggested by the prevailing policy style of the 1950s, 1960s and early 1970s. Yet here too we can see the beginnings of this change in the dying years of the Labour administration under Prime Minister Callaghan.

It was Callaghan, having become Prime Minister after Harold Wilson's surprise resignation in 1976, who signalled to the Labour Party conference that the 'spending party' was over (Rose, 1986, p. 13), and who ran into widespread conflict with what were then regarded (especially after the miners' 'victory' over Heath in 1974) as the most powerful interests with whom governments had to deal – the trade unions and also the local authorities. Chancellor Healey's introduction of cash limits on some public expenditure programmes, and the government's strong desire to control public sector wages, led the Labour government into the so-called 'winter of discontent' in 1978–79, ending in defeat (on the issue of devolution to Scotland and Wales, as it happens) in the House of Commons for Callaghan's Labour government, and the subsequent election victory for Mrs Thatcher. The failure of Labour's 'social contract' with the unions to produce more than a temporary lessening of inflation and hope of economic growth (Clark *et al.* 1980), having seemingly discredited the old style bargaining between government and the trade unions as key economic actors, paved the way for a much more full-blooded attempt to manage the economy along monetarist and market-orientated lines.

Thus before turning to the most prominent political feature of the UK response to the post-1974 crisis – namely Mrs Thatcher's three governments, we should note (a) that some of the core economic policies of Thatcherism (for example monetarism, the control of public expenditure) were not particularly new by 1979; and (b) that what many saw as a deliberately confrontational style of policy-making and implementing was not by then unique either. What did turn out to be new was a willingness to place the attack on inflation clearly above the attack on unemployment, as political and economic priorities; a desire to tame the unions, with whom Labour had tried to co-operate; and an intention to emphasize market forces rather than developing further sectoral industrial policies.

In emphasizing some key similarities, however, we do not wish to imply that there was no dissent from the growing conventional wisdom that the public sector could not continue to grow, that incentives had to be increased via tax reduction, and that Britain had to become more competitive and entrepreneurial, with greater emphasis on market forces. In particular, Callaghan's shift to the right caused deep divisions within the Labour Party, with a strong fight by the left for more say in the party's affairs. The apparent success of the left in gaining a stronger foothold within the party ultimately led to the departure of a few leading individuals to form the Social Democratic Party (SDP) in 1981. The growing strength of the left in some constituency Labour parties seemed to be matched by the ascendancy of the right in the Conservative Party, eventually opening up electoral space for the new SDP and the existing Liberal Party to form the Alliance (though retaining their separate identities). In terms of party politics we have seen fierce battles in the Labour Party between the centre and the right on the one hand and the left – especially the Militant Tendency – on the other. On the Conservative side the divisions have been equally serious, with constant battles between 'wets' (who wanted more public expenditure) and the 'dries' (who wanted less public expenditure). Hence the crisis has split the two major parties and assisted the creation of the new SDP. (At the time of writing, late 1987, the Liberal/SDP Alliance is passing through a period of turmoil as the two parties negotiate full merger terms).

Conservatives and the crisis: macro-economic policy 1979–present

The attempts to be more radical and sometimes to govern in a different way, which we have seen from the three Thatcher governments (1979–83, 1983–7; 1987–present), may have been made slightly easier by a general realization, by 1979, that the world economic crisis had really laid bare the fundamental weaknesses in the British economy. The harsh world climate after 1974 had quickly eroded the rather thin layer of protection which a hitherto buoyant world economy had afforded Britain. To some degree the British electorate appeared to accept the dictum that when the going gets tough, the tough get going.

The explanation for the shift in attitudes towards change in the face of economic pressures is complex. It would be misleading to claim that there had simply been a shift to the right in electoral opinion. The economic crisis arose when electoral behaviour had already become destabilized. As Franklin has suggested, there had been major changes in the strength of party allegiance from 1964 onwards (Franklin, 1985), opening up the possibility for dramatic changes in the party system. But he has also demonstrated that Mrs Thatcher's resounding electoral victory in 1979 (with the greatest swing in votes at any election since 1945) was not really a resurgence in conservatism. His analysis suggests that rather than a simple resurgence of conservatism (after all, the 'landslide' victory of 1983 was despite a *decline* in the number of Conservative votes as such), there has been a rise in the importance of issues not traditionally associated with either the Conservative or Labour parties, and that the Conservatives have been more effective in adapting to the new climate of opinion. If this is the case the Conservatives have gained support despite Mrs Thatcher's conservatism rather than because of it (Franklin, 1986, p. 3). In effect, by 1974 'the old collectivist mould of British politics could no longer contain the diversity of issue concerns of importance to British voters', a very similar phenomenon to the 'particularization' of voting choice noted in the USA (Franklin, 1986, p. 7).

Of special importance is the fact that the post-1979 Conservative government's response to crisis was a determined attempt by the government itself to shape perceptions of the causes of the crisis and of possible solutions to it. Much effort was put into building on the image of the Prime Minister as the 'Iron Lady' (as the Soviets had dubbed her), with clever speech-writers coining phrases such as 'the lady is not for turning' and 'I'm right, you turn' (a pun on Mr Heath's famous 'U'-turns, so despised by Mrs Thatcher). Even more emphasis was placed on convincing the electorate that 'there is no alternative' to the government's chosen strategy for dealing with the crisis – hence the TINA nickname for Mrs Thatcher. As Miller suggests, the 1983 election victory may well have owed much to the success of that strategy, no doubt assisted by the strengthening of Mrs Thatcher's image for leadership after the Falklands War (Miller, 1984). (No doubt her even more remarkable victory – gaining a third term of government in 1987 – was also a reflection of a public mood sceptical of an albeit well-presented Labour alternative).A related 'issue management strategy' was to blame the crisis on the decline in the world economy. This twin track approach for managing the *political* effects of the deepening economic crisis was especially successful in mitigating the potentially disastrous political consequences of rapidly rising unemployment (Richardson and Moon, 1984). Thus one of the more remarkable political milestones in post-1974 crisis Britain was Mrs Thatcher's electoral victory in 1983 (repeated in 1987), despite 12 per cent (approximately) unemployment and the fact that it had trebled under the Conservatives. The government could however point to a major success, namely the reduction of inflation to single figures by 1983 (it had reached 24 per cent in 1975). Not only did Mrs Thatcher demonstrate that governments could on occasion govern, but she also demonstrated that: '. . . the government of the day commands immense power to shape the terms in which political discourse is carried on.' (Franklin, 1986, p. 2).

The government also demonstrated that crisis could present policy change *opportunities,* in that a sense of crisis and doom could be used to introduce fairly radical change when normally powerful interests, such as the unions, were at a disadvantage. High unemployment certainly made it much easier to introduce reforms of trade union rights and duties (see below), and to increase the pace of some tough industrial restructuring policies (already started by Labour, in steel, for example) in the old declining publicly-owned industries. Similarly, a tough business environment forced private industries to be more efficient (and forced them to *manage* their businesses).

The backcloth against which specific policy initiatives were played was the government's macro-economic policy as outlined in its Medium Term Financial Strategy (MTFS), the central objective of which was to reduce the rate of inflation. The strategy, published in 1980 and preceded by the 1979 budget – which cut direct taxes, raised indirect taxes and reduced planned increases in public expenditure – was based on a belief that strict control of public expenditure, and of the money supply, would both reduce inflation and facilitate a reduction in the size and importance of government itself. Jackson suggests that the Conservative government's objective 'ended the post-war social democratic consensus which had placed the stabilization of employment top of successive governments' macro-economic objectives' (Jackson, 1986, p. 5). However, as we have noted earlier, this policy could hardly be claimed to be entirely new. What was perhaps new was the seeming *determination* of Mrs Thatcher to pursue this strategy and a more open decision to accept the 'inevitable' rise in unemployment (it had actually doubled under Labour). This determination, and the often hectoring and unpleasant political style with which she and some of her closest followers accompanied it, created much confict on the political stage, nowithstanding the elements of *continuity* referred to earlier. To Mrs Thatcher's government inflation was the key evil, not just because it eroded the value of the savings of the middle classes, but also because Britain could not hope to become more competitive until her costs could be brought into line with her competitors. Factors such as exchange rates and interest rates were to be determined more by the market than by government intervention. In the event the government did (and continues to) intervene heavily in both, forcing a policy of very high interest rates and eventually being active in the foreign exchange markets.

There has been much debate about the path of the governments's monetary strategy. Initially emphasis was placed on the conventional definition of 'sterling M3' as a measure of the state of the money supply. By 1985 this measure had been virtually abandoned by the government as 'unreliable'; although critics argued that it was abandoned because it showed that the government had *not* stuck to its monetary strategy, blaming both the government's stern monetary policy for Britain's high unemployment (eventually reaching over 13 per cent), *and* claiming that monetary policy had been a failure because sterling M3 had nearly always exceeded the set targets by wide margins. Certainly by 1985–6 the Chancellor of the Exchequer, Mr Lawson, was engaged in some unseemly juggling as he searched for a more 'appropriate' technical measure of money supply. For example, the House of Commons Select Committee on the Treasury and the Civil Service criticized the Chancellor for failing to clarify how the government was conducting its monetary policy – describing the government's explanation as ambivalent. Thus sterling M3 had been reinstated as a measure in the 1986 budget, but the committee expressed doubts about the significance of a strategy in which one of the important elements – sterling M3 – was targeted for only one year ahead (Select committee, Fourth Report, 1985–6). These doubts were also echoed by the Governor of the Bank of England, no less, in October 1986. Thus Sir Robin Leigh-Pemberton admitted that 'It cannot be said that our expertise with our chosen framework for operating monetary policy has been satisfactory'. In particular, he argued, only two of the last six annual target rates for sterling M3 had been achieved, while the rate of inflation had fallen sharply over the same period (*Financial Times*, 23 October 1986).

In fact, for whatever reason, the rate of inflation had fallen to around 3 per cent in 1986 – as Mrs Thatcher put it in the Spring of 1986, the inflation dragon had been slain. But the figures for unemployment were exactly the reverse. Thus at the same time the unemployment figure was stubbornly refusing to fall below 12 per cent, with a steady increase in the number of long-term unemployed within the total. Only by mid-1987 did Britain begin to see a long-awaited fall in its unemployment.

In reality the government had faced enormous difficulties in cutting public expenditure, partly because it was committed politically to increasing public expenditure considerably in certain key policy areas (notably defence and law and order, but also in health, as it turned out), and partly because the kind of constraints faced by all governments did not disappear simply because Britain had a right-wing Prime Minister committed to reducing public expenditure. Just as in the past, when Mrs Thatcher was in charge of a big spending ministry (Education), so now her own spending ministers fought hard to defend – and even expand – their budgets. Other budgets could not be controlled in any case – particularly the welfare costs of unemployment – unless benefits were to be lowered or removed at impossible political costs. Similarly the inherited problem of how to control local government expenditure presented major political obstacles. Economic crisis or not, the spending game looked much the same as ever, with ministers fighting their corners in the usual way against a Treasury keen on restraint.

As with monitoring the money supply, it is not easy to give a simple answer to the question 'what acutally happened to the Conservative government's determination to cut public expenditure?' As Jackson suggests, it is useful to divide expenditure in a number of ways in order to assess trends. Thus there has been a great deal of stability in public sector *current* consumption, a rapid rise in the cost of *transfer payments* under the social security system, and a relatively rapid decline in public sector investment expenditure (Jackson, 1986, p. 12). By deflating public expenditure totals by the appropriate price index, Jackson has calculated that the public sector's *relative* claim on resources has changed little over the last twenty years. Table 2.1 shows that public expenditure actually increased by 10.3 per cent in real terms between 1979/80 and 1984/5, indicating that the overall object of reducing public expenditure was not achieved by the Conservatives. They did, however, manage to change the distribution of that expenditure. In particular, housing, and trade and industry suffered big reductions. (Overall expenditure is still rising, with the January 1988 White Paper on Expenditure allowing for real growth of one and a quarter per cent per year. See CM 288-1.)

Table 2.1 Public expenditure trends 1979/80–1984/5 (1984/5 prices)

	1979/80 £ (billion)	1980/85 £ (billion)	% change 1979/80–1984/85
Defence	14.70	17.2	22.9
Agriculture, fisheries, food and forestry	1.5	2.1	60.9
Trade and industry	3.4	2.3	−32.4
Energy	0.9	1.8	100.0
Employment	1.9	3.0	57.9
Transport	5.0	4.8	−4.0
Housing	6.9	3.1	−55.1
Law and order	3.9	5.1	30.8
Education and science	16.6	16.8	−1.2
Health and personal social services	16.8	19.7	17.3
Social security	29.5	37.9	28.5
Miscellaneous	18.2	16.7	−8.2
Total public spending	118.4	130.6	10.3
Special sale of assets	−1.5	−2.0	33.3
Debt interest	5.2	8.5	63.5

Source: Jackson, 1986, p. 25.

The shift in the pattern of expenditure reflects in part the political preferences of the Conservatives, but also the political necessities of office, with the biggest cuts falling on the area easiest to cut – capital expenditure. An added complication in assessing the government's public expenditure strategy is that the apparent rise in expenditure has been reduced by big sales of public assets in the privatization programme. For example, the 1985 budget estimate of £2.5 billion of assets sales was later increased to £4.75 billion. As Jackson points out, this allowed the government to spend an extra £2.25 billion more than planned while keeping within its spending target of £139.1 billion (Jackson, 1986, p. 17). On the taxation front, taxation actually *rose* as a percentage of GNP between 1979 and 1984 (from 37 to 42 per cent, Jackson, 1986, p. 6). The Institute of Fiscal Studies has calculated that only 6 per cent of the population have actually benefited from tax cuts under the Conservatives (quoted by Jackson, 1986, p. 13).

In practice the government has steadily changed its objectives (though surprisingly, almost never being accused of making the dreaded U-turns) from reducing public expenditure in volume terms, to holding the level constant in real terms, to lowering the share of public expenditure as a percentage of GDP. The record is 'inferior' to that of the previous Labour administration.

Policy style and policy innovation

It is clear that the Thatcher government developed a *rhetorical* style of a different order to its predecessors, even if some of the general economic messages and the fundamental outline of broad economic strategy bore similarities to those expressed by James Callaghan as Labour Prime Minister. However, as Kavanagh notes (1985, p. 545), there was 'a major change of style' post-1979 which was not all rhetoric. Even so, much of the business of governing remained firmly rooted in consultation, bargaining, and consensus-seeking (Jordan and Richardson 1987). Thus it is difficult to accept Kavanagh's contention that Mrs Thatcher rejected the tripartite style of decision-making (Kavanagh, 1985, p. 545) when the evidence suggests that for many policy areas and many policy decisions, consultation, if not tripartism, remained in place. There is no doubt that tripartism and consultation went out of fashion in the field of macro-economic policy-making – indeed in 1987 the government enforced a considerable diminution in the role and status of the National Economic Development Council (NEDC) – but the TUC, for example, remained on over 100 governmental bodies (despite a temporary withdrawal from NEDC) and the CBI sat on a similar number. Even in those areas where we see fairly radical policy change, we should not overestimate the unique contribution that the government has made. Thus Moran's fascinating study of changes in the financial sector is worth quoting; he writes of the changes in the regulations governing the financial institutions of the City of London:

> a close examination of the City's revolution soon reveals puzzling features. We might naively expect that competition and deregulation would cause the state to

> retreat, and controls to disappear. The contrary has happened . . . what has happened to regulation is only marginally the result of individual design. The Government, and the great and the good in the financial community, are not in control of events. They are more or less hapless agents of deeper social forces: the changing structure of the world financial services industry the changing balance of domestic financial interests and the changing political environment of the industry. (Moran, 1987, p. 1)

Yet clearly the government was on occasion willing to confront entrenched interests (most visibly the miners' strike of 1984–5). It also broke the monopoly of solicitors over the conveyancing of houses, and the monopoly of opticians in supplying spectacles, and introduced other deregulating measures, such as a major liberalization – the so-called 'big–bang' of the City of London. More important the government did embark on examples of what can only be described as radical (or heroic, in Hayward's terms) policy change. Space prevents a full discussion of the whole range of policy responses, but five key policy areas illustrate the government's policy innovation thrust and illustrate the degree to which the Thatcher governments have, *cumulatively,* developed both a differing style and an unusual amount of policy change. Trade union legislation is perhaps the most obvious policy area where consultation and negotiation were not practised, but privatization, employment policy, education policy and central/local relations, all illustrate major shifts in policy either as a response to the crisis or as opportunistic moves in response to specific crisis situtations.

The legal framework for trade unions is a good example of the government seizing the initiative in relation to those interests already weakened by the effects of crisis. Its initiative was aided by the fact that there was generally agreed to be a backlog of overdue reform. The policy changes have taken place in stages against a background of extremely high unemployment, which has seen a considerable decline in the power of unions as interests groups. In no sense have these policy changes emerged from a process of consultation and consensus. On the contrary, they have provoked considerable conflict with the trade union movement. The changes have also brought about conflict *within* the union movement. In addition, employers have been more aggressive in dealing with unions, again using the high unemployment and changed climate of opinion to their advantage. The government itself, as a direct or indirect employer, in addition to new legislation, has been 'tough' on one or two specific issues, for example the miners' dispute of 1984–5, and in banning trade unions from GCHQ (the secret governmental communications headquarters).

The three Employment Acts introduced (1980, 1982, 1984 – more are planned) are said by Gennard and Lockyer (1986, p. 10) to constitute a significant change in public policy, namely:

1 A new set of individual employment rights have been established in relation to non union membership in a 'closed shop' situation.
2 There has been a narrowing of the boundaries of lawful strike action.
3 There has been a significant increase in the financial penalties to unions which stray beyond these new limits of lawful action.
4 The mandatory balloting of members of unions over a number of issues has been introduced.
5 Some of the long-standing props to support and supplement collective bargaining have been removed.
6 There has been a relaxation of individual employment rights in certain areas, particularly unfair dismissal rights.

Even these fairly radical and hard fought changes, however, may be seen as some kind of moving consensus. Much debate preceded these changes and earlier legislation had been either mooted or introduced by previous governments, and so there was a sense that changes were necessary. Moreover some elements of the policies are likely to remain under a Labour government (for example the retention of statutory balloting provisions), indicating a possible permanency to the stress on individualism, and intervention and constraint on trade unions (Gennard and Lockyer, 1986, p. 16).

Privatization has by now become a second major policy innovation, with massive privatizations either carried out or planned. For example, Britoil, British Aerospace, National Freight Corporation, Cable and Wireless, The Trustee Savings Bank, British Telecom, British Gas and British Airways have been privatized; and current plans are to privatize the electricity, steel, coal and water industries. The Thatcher administration has become the benchmark, in comparative terms, for the privatization process, which has been imitated to some degree elsewhere in the world. (There has also been a significant degree of liberalization – in telecommunications especially, but also in long distance and urban bus transport, financial services and building societies. See Table 2.2.)

The motivation is no doubt complex. In part it is related to the Conservative's perceptions post-1974 crisis in that they felt that a liberalized and privatized economy was the only way for Britain to meet the intensified world competition. In part it has been purely financial and pragmatic. Just as the previous Labour government decided to sell off some of its holding in British Petroleum in 1976 in order to raise cash for the public Exchequer (Barnett, 1982), so then the present government's increases in public spending have in part been met by its huge sales of public assets – 'selling the family silver' as former Prime Minister Harold Macmillan put it. Thus the total assets sales for 1986–7 equal £4.75 billion. (Following Labour's albeit small example, the government has also sold off its remaining 32 per cent share in BP in order to raise up to £3 billion.) The effects of privatization are as yet difficult to determine (Heald, 1986), but there is no doubt that the financial benefits to the Treasury have been of major significance and that there has been a major shift from public to private ownership of industry. It is worth noting however that privatization cannot be seen as a big extension of market forces. The government has been careful to bargain with the key interests, for example managers and financial institutions, in designing its privatization policies. As a result there has been criticism of the shift from public to private monopolies with little increase in competition.

Table 2.2 Privatization proceeds 1979–April 1987

	(Net of costs, £m)
Amersham International	64
Associated British Ports	94
British Aerospace	389
British Airways	415
British Gas	1796
British Gas Debt	750
British Petroleum	827
British Sugar Corporation	44
British Telecom	2598
BT Loan Stock	105
Britoil	334
Cable and Wireless	1015
Enterprise Oil	382
National Enterprise Board Holdings	294
National Freight Consortium	5
North Sea Oil Licences	349
Miscellaneous	510

Source: *The Thatcher Years: the politics and prospects. Financial Times*, 1987.

'The politics of unemployment' has also been a key feature of the post-1974 situation. Much policy change has taken place but there has been as much policy succession (Moon, 1983), and interest group accommodation as radical policy change. There has of course been conflict, especially between the government and the opposition parties, and between the government and the trade unions. The politics of unemployment, post-1974, is best described as a government (a) determined to 'tough it out' in accepting very high levels of unemployment in its attempt to reduce inflation, increase competitiveness, and restructure the economy; (b) determined to bring about a shift in perceptions and expectations; and (c) willing to increase public expenditure and develop policy initiatives as a means of 'responding' to unemployment without changing its broad economic strategy. The evidence suggest that in *political* terms this has been a rather successful strategy (Richardson and Moon, 1984), and that some fundamental shifts in values and perceptions have resulted.

Education policy too has seen attempts to bring about a change of values, conflict (for example teachers' industrial action for over a year), and a new determination after the 1987 election victory to bring about major policy change. Again we could not see education policy resulting from a well-tried and established process of consultation and negotiation. In essence the government has its own view of what education policy should be, and is forcing through curriculum and examination reforms affecting schools, giving schools the right to opt out of the local government system and be funded directly by central government. It is also strengthening its role vis à vis the universities and polytechnics, reflecting a rather strong centralizing tendency under the Conservatives. The style has been to press for radical change, if possible via the established negotiating machinery, but to force change through if agreement could not be reached.

The turmoil in education policy has been excelled by that in central/local government relations. This has been a major area of 'crisis' and change on two points: (1) the financing of local government, with ever-increasing central controls over local authority financing; (2) the abolition of the big (Labour controlled) metropolitan counties and the Greater London Council (GLC). Thus the usually well 'managed' area of central/local relations has been a major area of controversy and conflict. As Rhodes notes, 'If one single theme permeates recent developments, it is the search by central government for more effective instruments of control (not influence) over the expenditure of local government . . . the Government has also sought to restrict the size of the public sector by divesting local government of some of its functions' (Rhodes, 1985b, p. 11). This, he argues, has been accompanied by a change of style of decision-making, shifting from a consultative style to a more unilateral style. Recalcitrance has replaced consultation (Rhodes, 1985b, p. 11). Recalcitrance on the part of local authorities has been met by further policy change – in the direction of greater control by the centre. Even here, however, we need to exercise caution in seeing change as due to post-1979 conservatism. Change was already under way and the crisis has *intensified* these changes, with Mrs Thatcher's government more willing to tolerate the conflict that these changes inevitably provoked. As Rhodes puts it, 'The most disturbing features of recent trends in inter-governmental relations are *not* therefore recent legislative changes, but the continuities . . . If the ship of local government is heading towards the rocks, the hand on the rudder is as likely to be Labour as Conservative' (Rhodes, 1985b, pp. 31, 33).

Conclusion: capturing the national mood without courting consensus

These five policy areas perhaps illustrate the paradox of Britain's response to the 1974 world economic crisis. Just as the crisis itself was not new, then initiatives in even the most radically changed policy areas were sometimes the result of the recognition, prior to 1974, of a problem and of possible solutions. The policy changes themselves may have become in some cases part of a new synthesis or 'moving consensus'. Britain's broad response to the crisis has been, as Kavanagh suggests, to abandon 'like a paradigm, the old Butskellite optimism and Social Democratic and Keynesian policies . . . as more and more anomalies have crept in' (Kavanagh, 1985, p. 545). He predicts that there might be, over time:

> an uneasy synthesis between some elements of the old consensus and some parts of the present economic thinking, one that will have more to do with holding the line on state welfare provision and government intervention in industry, than with 'rolling back the state'. In particular, it will include the social and welfare elements of the old consensus and some of the economic thinking of Thatcherism. (Kavanagh, 1985, p. 546)

The post-1974 situation in Britain has seen the emergence, consciously encouraged by Mrs Thatcher, of a more mixed policy style. At times the government has appeared to place as much emphasis on consensus as ever – for example when it tried to reform the engineering profession (Jordan and Richardson, 1984) – and at others has been openly *dirigiste*, such as in dealing with the miners (having initially tried to negotiate a solution) or in banning trades unions at GCHQ (after negotiations produced what most observers felt was a very satisfactory solution from the government's perspective). In areas where fairly *dirigiste* policies were already started by Labour – such as the drastic slimming down of the steel industry – Mrs Thatcher's governments have been willing to force the pace still further and to withstand the increased political obloquy and financial costs on the Exchequer.

At the end of this process, which saw an increase in the bitterness of the traditional adversarial party battle, Britain is probably more divided than ever. The 85 per cent or so in work have done well – wages keeping well ahead of inflation – in the presence of an increasingly deprived poor. Thus the gradual postwar trend towards greater equality of incomes has been reversed with the rich gaining a progressively larger proportion of the national cake since 1979 – the top 10 per cent on the income scale raising their share of the nation's income from 21.6 to 29.5 per cent. Massive slimming down of traditional industries has occurred, for example the steel industry now employs under 70,000 people compared with over 270,000 just prior to the 1974 crisis; similar phenomena have occurred in shipbuilding, motors, and heavy engineering. Reforms (whether sensible or not is not for us to judge here) have been started in bastions of interest group power such as trades unions and the financial institutions of the City of London.

Time will tell whether the post-1974 world economic crisis did cause such a shock to Britain's political, social and economic institutions as to represent the spark of real and lasting change, and whether the Thatcher governments – which have so dominated our own perceptions of Britain's response – heralded a permanent change of style of politics and policies. Predictions are unwise. For example, in 1986 it seemed to many observers (including myself) that the tide was turning against Mrs Thatcher and her attempted new style of governing. It seemed then that the electorate had grown weary of tough crisis management and yearned for the years of consensus politics to return. Thus Kavanagh wrote that 'By 1986 the tide of opinion seemed to have turned against the government' (Kavanagh, 1987, p. 317), yet Mrs Thatcher went on to win a third successive term and to become the longest continuously serving Prime Minister this century. Part of the explanation for this remarkable achievement must lie in some of the rather positive performance indicators which have emerged in Britain over the period 1986–8; unemployment has finally begun to fall and at the end of 1987 was at its lowest for five years. Economic growth continues at historically high levels for the UK. Thus during 1971–80 Britain's annual growth rate was 1.8 per cent compared with the OECD average of 3.1 per cent. During 1981–7 it was 2.4 per cent compared with the OECD average of 2.5 per cent, with 1987 being the best year for growth in GDP since 1973 (at between 4 per cent and 5 per cent). These remarkable figures are even causing fears of overheating, the Treasury believing that the sustainable growth rate is approximately 3 per cent. Sterling M3, the initial centre-piece of the government's Medium Term Financial Strategy, actually grew by a phenomenal 22.8 per cent during 1987 – indicating a major U-turn in government policy since 1979. The most remarkable statistic of all, at the end of 1987, was the emergence of a budget *surplus* for the government – itself presenting a problem as demands for increased expenditure – especially on health – became even more pressing when it became known that a surplus was available. As national income has been rising since 1981 (especially so in 1987), public expenditure, though continuing to rise from its post-IMF low, has been falling slightly as a percentage of GNP. As the tax system is designed to generate tax revenue even faster than rising incomes (that is, the real burden of taxation increases as incomes rise) then the government has been in the lucky position of having very buoyant revenues in recent years. In essence the government is able to claim to be increasing public expenditure in real terms (which it is) *and* reducing public expenditure as a share of national income (which it is). Essentially, not only has sterling M3 been abandoned as a means of controlling macro-economic policy, but the government has abandoned its hopes of stopping the growth in public expenditure. The 'presentational' argument is now centred upon public expenditure's declining share of national income and even there, one needs to be careful in noting the enormous financial benefits to the government of its privatization programme. For example, its current target for privatization sales is £5 billion per year. Other beneficial indicators for the government now include enormous overseas assets owned by Britain, following surpluses earned on North Sea oil. These overseas assets have trebled in the past four years and now stand at approximately £114 billion; excluding gold, they are now probably higher than those of West Germany and Japan. Whether the underlying structural problems referred to above have been solved remains to be seen – but for the government it would claim success in terms of the indicators cited above (and would also emphasize productivity gains) despite growing poverty and inequality.

Finally, how can we characterize, in general terms, Britain's response to crisis? As the *Independent* observed (4 January 1988), Mrs Thatcher's government – in charge of Britain's affairs for all but five of the post-crisis years – has captured the national mood without courting consensus. In our terms, the style of governing had changed to a more mixed style, in phases. The period 1974–6 saw a Labour government not willing to face the reality of the situation. It was followed by the mixed strategy adopted by Chancellor Healey after pressure from the IMF in 1976. This period saw the beginnings of some elements of what became known as Thatcherism. The period 1979 to 1981/2 saw the Conservatives emphasize macro-economic policy, especially monetarism. The period 1981/2 to 1985/6 saw greater emphasis on micro-economic policy, especially privatization and the potential encouragement of market forces. The period since 1985/6 – and particularly since the 1987 election victory – has seen a determined attempt to tackle the social agenda, areas such as education, and now possibly health, as the Prime Minister's confidence in radicalism has grown.

One concluding hypothesis now presents itself as the government struggles to regain the initiative on health policy. Writing in the *Financial Times*, Peter Riddell observed that Mrs Thatcher's personal style has come to dominate the government's response to problems. Thus we see 'an initial dithering and uncertainty in response to crisis, departments waiting for a lead from Mrs Thatcher, and then a decisive initiative leading to radical change' (Riddell, 1988). Writing specifically on the health service he notes that 'historians may see recent events as the carefully contrived creation of an opportunity to restructure the National Health Service. But to participants, and current observers, Mrs Thatcher's latest move looks more like a rushed attempt to regain the political initiative'. Britain, it seems, has muddled through much better than anyone believed possible, not by adopting a grand design but by adapting its style of politics, when necessary, albeit with much good luck and not a little indecision. Bulpitt describes the Thatcher government's approach somewhat more politely, suggesting that there was rather less muddle and rather more 'statecraft' than we might concede. Thus he describes Mrs Thatcher's 'statecraft' (by which he means 'understanding and working within the limitations placed upon élite activity by the many changing structural constraints arising from within and without the polity') as a 'successful élite operation in damage control' (Bulpitt, 1986, p. 39). In essence, this has left many of Britain's deep seated problems unresolved.

Note

1 The author wishes to acknowledge the helpful comments and criticisms made by E.A. Sochart, J. Stringer, and E. Grande. The views expressed remain the sole responsibility of the author.

References

Davies, S. and Caves, R. E. (1987), *Britain's Productivity Gap.* Cambridge University Press.

Barnett, J. (1982), *Inside the Treasury*, London, Deutsch.

Bulpitt, J. (1986), 'The discipline of the new democracy: Mrs Thatcher's domestic statecraft', *Political Studies*, XXXIV, no. 1, pp. 19–39.

Caves, Richard E. (1980), 'Productivity differences among Industries' in Caves, R. E. and Krause, L. B., *Britain's Economic Performance.* Washington DC The Brookings Institution.

Clark, J., Hartmann, H., Lau, C., Winchester, D. (1980), *Trade Unions, National Politics and Economic Management*, Anglo-German Foundation, London.

Cm 288–1, *The Government's Expenditure Plans 1988–89 to 1990–91,* vol 1. London, HM Treasury.

Economic Progress Report, July 1978. London, HM Treasury.

Franklin, M. (1985), 'The new right and the particularization of British voting', Strathclyde Papers on Government and Politics, no. 49. Glasgow, University of Strathclyde.

Gennard, J. and Lockyer, C. (1986), 'Reversing the ratchet? Policy change under the Thatcher government 1979–86: industrial relations policy'. Paper presented to the PAC 16th Annual Conference, University of York, 1–3 September 1986.

Gomulka, S. (1979), 'Britain's slow industrial growth: increasing inefficiency versus low rate of technical change' in Beckerman, Wilfred (ed.), *Slow Growth in Britain: consensus and consequences.* Oxford, Clarendon.

Hayward, J. E. S. (1974), 'National aptitudes for planning in Britain, France and Italy', *Government and Opposition*, 9, no. 4, pp. 397–410.

Heald, D. (1986), *Public Expenditure.* Oxford, Martin Roberston.

Hogwood, B. W. (1986), 'If consultation is everything, then maybe it's nothing', *Strathclyde Papers on Government and Politics,* no. 44. Glasgow, University of Strathclyde.

Jackson, Peter (1986), 'Economic briefing' in Mayston, D. and Terry, F. (eds), *Public Domain: the public sector yearbook.* London, Public Finance Foundation, and Peat, Marwick, Mitchell and Co.

Jordan, A. G. and Richardson, J. J. (1982), 'The logic of negotiation' in Richardson, J. J. (ed.), *Policy Styles in Western Europe*, London, Allen & Unwin.

Jordan A. G. and Richardson, J. J. (1984), 'Engineering consensus: from the Finniston Report to the Engineering Council', *Public Administration,* 62, no. 4, pp. 383–400.

Jordan A. G. and Richardson, J. J. (1987), *British Politics and the Policy Process.* London, Allen & Unwin.

Kavanagh, D. (1985), 'Whatever happened to consensus politics?', *Political Studies,* xxxiii, no. 4, pp. 529–46.

Kavanagh, D. (1987), *Thatcherism and British Politics: the end of consensus?* Oxford University Press.

King, A. (1985), 'Governmental responses to budget scarcity', Policy Studies Journal, 113, no. 3, pp. 476–93.

Miller, W. L. (1984), 'There was no alternative! The British General Election 1984', *Parliamentary Affairs,* vol. 37, pp. 364–84.

Moon, J. W. (1983), 'Policy change in direct response to UK unemployment', *Journal of Public Policy,* vol. 3, pt. 3, pp. 301–30.

Moran, M. (1987), 'Corporatism, the Thatcherite state, and the city revolution', Paper presented to ESRC Workshop on *the State and the Professions in British Industry and Commerce,* London, 7 January 1988.

Rhodes, R. (1985a), 'Power-dependence, policy communities and intergovernmental networks', *Public Administration Bulletin,* no. 49, pp. 4–31.

Rhodes, R. (1985b), 'Continuity and change in British central-local relations: the Conservative threat', *Essex Papers in Politics and Government,* no. 2. University of Essex.

Richardson, J. J. and Moon, J. W. (1984), 'The politics of unemployment in Britain', *Political Quarterly,* 55, no. 1, pp. 29–32.

Riddell, P. (1988), 'Out of dither into decisiveness', *Financial Times,* 27 January 1988.

Rose, R. (1986), 'Changing the prescription', *The Times Higher Education Supplement* (6 June), p. 13.

Scammel, Margaret (1986), 'The enemy within: the Conservative government and the miners' strike 1984/5', *Strathclyde Papers on Government and Politics,* no. 45.

Select Committee on the Treasury and Civil Service, Fourth Report (1985–6), *The Budget,* HC 313.

The Thatcher Years: the policies and prospects (1987). London, Financial Times, Business Information Ltd.

Wright, M. (1980), 'From planning to control: PESC in the 1970s' in Wright, M. (ed.) *Public Spending Decisions: growth and constraint in the 1970s* (London, Allen & Unwin), pp. 88–119.

3 Belgium in crisis: political and policy responses 1981 – 1985

BERT PIJNENBURG

Belgium in crisis

As far as Belgium is concerned, no doubt one of the most important and most dramatic challenges the government and the political leadership in general have had to face during the last decade are the problems of economic recession and decline. The extent and impact of the economic crisis in Belgium seem to have been so considerable that it has almost completely dominated political life these last few years – and, as such, at every level of the system: public opinion and pressure-group interests, the decisions taken by parliament, governmental and public administration policy-making.

Economic decline

As far as the postwar evolution of the GNP is concerned, the indications prior to 1980 had been rather positive. Despite a rise in unemployment, the crisis of the 1970s, oddly enough, did not cause a sharp decline in economic growth. The GNP continued to grow at a rate of over 6 per cent in 1970 and 1973, 4 per cent in 1974, still 2.75 per cent in 1978, and also for 1979 the results were not unfavourable.

However, better productivity results were nearly always obtained via labour-saving investments and a thorough rationalization of business structures. And this was no doubt an important element contributing to the fact that by 1980 there were already almost half a million unemployed. The crisis had made the government speed up its efforts to create new jobs. In 1974 it invested approximately BF 128,000 per job; by 1980 creating one new job cost nearly five times as much.

The trade balance figures (billion francs) in 1970 were slightly positive (an excess of 0.72); ten years later (1982) they showed a 21.6 deficit. During the same period the net foreign position also declined dramatically, as the debt to commercial banks increased by more than twenty times: from 38 billion in 1970 it soared to 774 billion francs in 1983.

The country's rate of inflation for 1973 was already 7 per cent; it reached its peak in 1975: 12.8 per cent. Then it steadily declined and by the end of 1978 it stood at 3.7 per cent. After 1979 the inflation rate once again worsened, climbing to 5 per cent and then to 9 per cent.

From 1980 increasingly darker clouds gathered over Belgium's economic situation. The number of factory closures and bankruptcies, particularly in the weaker and often more labour-intensive sectors, was rising sharply. It was estimated that by 1985 the public deficit (already BF 230 billion) would have more than tripled. Even if a moderate growth rate of the GNP was maintained, and at the same time inflation did not exceed 6.5 per cent, there would be 600,000 unemployed in 1985. On the other hand, it was clear that Belgium's welfare-state system had continued to expand. Public expenditure as a percentage of GDP had more than doubled between 1950 (26 per cent) and 1979 (53.7 per cent). This was mainly due to a constant rise in social sector expenditures (including pensions, unemployment benefits and family allowance provisions, education, health care and public housing). By 1981 Belgian households were absorbing 81.8 per cent of the national income – a record figure in the country's history and, for example, some 15 per cent higher than the comparable level in West Germany. At the same time public and corporate spending had reached approximately 25 per cent. It was therefore no surprise that Belgium was building up a huge public sector deficit. The treasury's deficit for 1981 reached 12.6 per cent of the GNP. Adding the problems of local government spending and the social security system, the total public sector deficit amounted to 16.5 per cent.

Moreover the external current account deficit was 4.5 per cent of the GNP. According to a study carried out by one of the country's leading institutions for economic and financial research, the Belgian economy in 1981 was only 65 per cent as competitive as the average of six comparable European countries. Profits in industry were abnormally low. New foreign investment had declined dramatically and was only a tenth of the annual level of the early 1970s.

Crisis policies in Belgium

Probably the main reason that a new government came to office in 1981 (the two previous ones had lasted less than a year before they collapsed) was an 'enough is enough' acknowledgement that all the traditional solutions and remedies used to combat the economic decline of the country had failed miserably. The only alternative that seemed to be left was to embark on a tough and more 'Thatcherite' austerity programme. This required the possibility of imposing hard and unpopular decisions, as well as enough autonomy to take swift action at all levels of the governmental and public administration apparatus.

Indeed the new government's perception of the far-reaching and increasingly debilitating economic crisis which held Belgium in its grip focused on the endemic weaknesses and chronic failures of the system of top level political agenda-setting and decision-making, as well as its basic mechanisms for the implementation, management and control of policies. Such questions as whether the crisis was a temporary worldwide phenomenon requiring only short-term measures or, in contrast, whether international developments meant a need for a structural change in the national economics, were considered as no longer really relevant or of primary importance. International economic developments had merely exacerbated and highlighted the poor state and the vulnerability of Belgium's economy. They had operated as a catalyst and an intensifier, but by no means could these factors be deemed *the* cause of the economic débâcle in Belgium. To have argued in terms of an international recession and an economic emergency situation worldwide would merely make a correct, salutary and, above all, workable diagnosis of the Belgium variant of post-1974 crisis that much more difficult.

In fact, according to prevailing perceptions and definitions, only the weaknesses and shortcomings of the country's own economy had really caused the crisis in Belgium – it was no more complicated than that. Ultimately the disastrous state of the country's economy was something for which the political leadership, national policy-making agencies and the governmental/public administration apparatus were responsible (and for which they were thus to blame). By the end of the 1970s everyone (politicians, experts and advisers, the unions and employers' organizations, the media, public opinion – both within the ruling majority and within the opposition parties) to a considerable extent agreed on the remedies and solutions that were most likely to regenerate Belgium's economy in the short run. But prior to 1981 little or nothing had actually been done. The major reason for this was both a lack of political will, and insufficient 'operational manoeuvrability' or 'tactical resources' within the government, particularly within the Cabinet.

For example, the usual process by which political leaders and the government had conducted decision-making and policy affairs since the Second World War (especially when major economic issues were concerned), resulted in a long series of consultations and negotiations with every possible interest group, as well as in a considerable amount of time and energy spent on virtually endless parliamentary debates. These highly complex mechanisms of political representation were, of course, far from ideal for imposing tough policies and decisive action. Therefore, given the drastic austerity programme it had in mind, in 1981 the government demanded powers to rule by decree.

According to the Prime Minister, W. Martens, (interview with *Time Magazine,* 15 March 1982) the situation was tragically simple. 'This is the tenth time in Belgian history that the Government had been given special powers. . . Many of the other occasions were in times of war, and I consider this period to be war in terms of the economic problems we face.'

Postwar developments in Belgian politics

Recent changes at parliamentary and governmental level

Table 3.1 Party composition of the Belgian parliament (Kamer van Volksvertegenwoordigers): elections 1971–85

Party*		Number of seats (total 212) 1971	1974	1977	1978	1981	1985
–	Christian Democrats						
CVP	Christelijke Volkspartij (Fl.)	47	50	56	57	43	49
PSC	Parti Social Chretien (Fr.)	20	22	24	25	18	20
–	Socialists						
BSP	Belgische Socialistische Partij	61	59	62			
SP	Socialistische Partij (Fl.)				26	26	32
PS	Parti Socialiste (Fr.)				32	35	35
–	Conservative Liberals						
PVV	Partij Vrijheid Vooruitgang (Fl.)	20	21	17	22	28	22
PRL	Parti Reformateur Liberal (Fr.)	14	12	16	15	24	23
–	"Linguistic/Regionalist"						
VU	Volksunie (Fl.)	21	22	20	14	20	16
FDF	Front des Francophones (Fr.)	10	9	10	11	6	3
RW	Rassemblement Wallon (Fr.)	14	13	5	4	2	0
–	Minor/small parties						
	Communists, Ecologists, etc.	5	4	2	6	10	12

Note: *Fl. = Flemish, Fr. = Francophone.
**For the period 1971–8 the PRL score is a sum of the seats obtained by the Brussels and Walloon Liberals who operated as two separate parties (PL/PLP) until 1979.

Until the mid-1970s the differences between political parties (apart from the Communists) on the socio-economic left versus right dimension remained rather moderate and often seemed either vague, only marginal, or too subtle to be noticed. In the past decade there have obviously been some changes in this respect. Under the impact of the economic crisis, the left versus right profiles of the political parties diverged and their positions became much more clear-cut or polarized (Figure 3.1).

Left	—	Communists
	—	Socialists (BSP, SP, PS)
	—	Ecologists
	—	RW (Rassemblement Wallon)
	—	VU (Volksunie)
	—	FDF (Front des Francophones)
<Centre>	—	Christian Democrats (CVP, PSC)
Right	—	Conservative Liberals (PVV, PRL)

Note: Ranking is based on merely ordinal measurement. No indication of the (ratios of the) distances between parties has been intended.

Figure 3.1 Ideological party profile in socio-economic matters

Between 1971 and 1985 there were thirteen different Cabinets (Table 3.2). Invariably these were formed on the basis of a coalition majority. Seven times a change of government (either complete or partial, but in each case more than just a reshuffle of portfolios) occurred without new parliamentary elections being held; this happened in January 1973, June 1974, November 1978 (a transitional and merely 'caretaker' Cabinet), January 1980, May 1980, November 1980, and April 1981.

Table 3.2 Governing coalitions in Belgium since 1971

Duration	Majority parties
January 1972–January 1973	CVP-PSC-BSP
January 1973–April 1974	CVP-PSC-BSP-PVV-PRL
April 1974–June 1974	CVP-PSC-PVV-PRL
June 1974–June 1977	CVP-PSC-PVV-PRL-RW
June 1977–November 1978	CVP-PSC-BSP-VU-FDF
November 1978–April 1979	CVP-PSC-SP-PS-VU-FDF
April 1979–January 1980	CVP-PSC-SP-PS-FDF
January 1980–May 1980	CVP-PSC-SP-PS
May 1980–November 1980	CVP-PSC-SP-PS-PVV-PRL
November 1980–April 1981	CVP-PSC-SP-PS
April 1981–December 1981	CVP-PSC-SP-PS
December 1981–December 1985	CVP-PSC-PVV-PRL
December 1985–December 1987	CVP-PSC-PVV-PRL

'Partycracy' and neocorporatism

Originally Belgian politics corresponded completely to the traditional pillarization and consociational-democracy model (Lorwin, 1966, 1974). After the Second World War the pillarized and consociational-democratic system in Belgium became dominated by the political parties. During the 1960s this party politicization increased constantly, and eventually it resulted in a total 'partycracy' (De Winter, 1981). Parties completely controlled all major decisional and policy-making processes, at the expense of parliament, the public administration and even the Cabinet. The government-making, as well as the legislative and supervisory powers of parliament were gradually transferred to the respective party headquarters. Party leaders dictated the composition of the Cabinet and the designation of its ministers. Through the programme which was imposed each time a new cabinet came into office, and through special extra-parliamentary agreements, they increasingly determined the government's future policies. Ministerial staffs executed control over the public administration system on behalf of the political parties. The recruitment of civil servants and their careers depended highly upon institutionalized patronage of political parties.

Then came the 1970s and certain unmistakable signs of de-pillarization could be perceived (Billiet, 1984; Huyse, 1984). An increasing number of political problems and important issues emerged which had no links with the traditional (religious-philosophical, socio-economical, ethno-linguistic) divide between the pillars. These were problems and issues that did not enter the political arena in the usual way. They were, therefore, unpredictable and, as far as the political leadership was concerned, they considerably increased the burden of making decisions and policies. At the same time, more and more organizations and interest groups either acquired a greater freedom of movement or seemed simply to drift away from the pillarized conglomerates. They now directed both their demands and support (or protest) straight to the government and the public authorities. This led, inevitably, to flourishing of 'neo-corporatism' (Heisler, 1974; Huyse, 1984).

The ethno-linguistic cleavage and its centrifugal effect

The erosion of the central role and power of the parties is also the result of a second fundamental factor in Belgium politics, namely profound changes regarding the nature and impact of the ethno-linguistic segmentation (the Flemish versus the French-speaking parts of the population, and on a territorial level Flanders versus Wallonia versus the (bilingual) Brussels region). The escalation of ethno-linguistic conflicts during the 1960s and the 1970s led to a complete transformation of the national party system (Rudd, 1986). One outcome of the escalation of ethno-linguistic conflicts was that each of the three major parties in the country (Christian Democrats,

Conservative Liberals, and Socialists) finally split into two new separate entities, Flemish versus French-speaking. These transformations marked the definitive end of the traditional national party system. From then on there were two types of party systems. Besides a (new) national configuration, party systems at the subnational level developed. The latter fell into two or three categories: a Flemish and a Walloon party system, plus possibly a specific Brussels variant. Another important consequence of course was a considerable increase in the number of political parties. Counting the three smaller 'linguistic/regionalist' parties – the Flemish VU, Walloon RW and Brussels FDF (see Table 3.1) – there was now a total of nine significant actors. What all this amounts to is that the size and power basis of the major parties, on which pillarization politics and the consociational-democracy model in Belgium had rested, were substantially reduced. These parties are no longer a united and unifying force at the level of national politics, and thus they have lost their traditional dominating role.

Then came the 'pacification' of ethno-linguistic conflicts at the end of the 1970s and in the early 1980s, and this finally led to a reform of the state (Huyse, 1982; Zolberg 1978). The constitution has been revised and, in 1980–1, a wide measure of devolution to regional executives responsible to elected assemblies in Flanders and Wallonia was implemented. (The definitive decisions regarding the Brussels region were postponed, as it posed specific problems because of its bilingualism and the statutes concerning the country's capital.) Both of these regional executives have their own ministers, policy-making instruments and public administration apparatus, controlling a large range of economic and social activities. Each region has the right to an indexed proportion of national revenues to finance the initiatives and services for which it is responsible.

Vulnerability of neocorporatist forces

Undoubtedly the dynamics and impact of neocorporatism which is alleged to have become the most prominent and dominating component of Belgian politics from the middle 1970s are to a large extent determined or shaped by the strength and power of the unions. Therefore the more recent changes in the position and role of the unions should be taken into account in a reassessment of the exact nature and potential of a neocorporatist type of politics in Belgium. What has therefore become an increasingly important phenomenon over recent years is a series of specific internal problems hampering the unions, and which so far they have apparently still not managed to solve.

There is the factor of a widening heterogeneity of the unions' members and supporters (Smits, 1983, pp. 192–3). Originally the unions represented mainly the working classes. At present they are defending interests which reflect a much larger range of different professional groups and categories of employees (for example semi- or unskilled labourers, clerical staff, technicians, university graduates, lower/middle-management personnel, and so on). The economic crisis has turned this heterogeneity into a source of internal division and conflict. What started as 'mere' heterogeneity has become a wide spectrum of often totally different (if not simply clashing) wants, demands, claims, sensitivities and expectations.

Moreover the economic crisis has added new elements of fractionalization that could cause serious splits within the unions and undermine their political influence. There are the 'ethno-linguistic' tensions (that is, Flanders versus Wallonia versus Brussels) and the pressure towards increased regional autonomy. The process of regionalization has coincided with the economic crisis. This has inevitably created new and important risks of disagreement and strife between Flemings and Walloons concerning the unions' aims and strategy. Secondly there is the phemomenon that the decline and recession have widened the gap that separates 'rich' and 'poor' economic sectors. The unions, both at the leadership and the grassroots level, have to cope with the confrontation between problem sectors (for example steel, textile, shipbuilding, coal mining) and those that are still experiencing considerable growth (for example banking, insurance, electricity production). A third and somewhat related factor is the distinction, and ultimately the opposition, between those who are working in the private sector and those working in the public sector. One of the characteristics of Belgium's public administration apparatus is that civil servants are in practice guaranteed job-security. The workforce in the private sector receive higher earnings but always has the risk of redundancies. The economic crisis has obviously heightened the political significance of these differences. Another important aspect is no doubt the fact that the economic crisis is generally presented in terms of an over-expansion of the welfare state, of problems of public sector deficits which are the hardest to tackle, and in terms of the restoration and improvement of the country's industrial and commercial resources, as being the only way to true salvation and a new prosperity. This 'good versus bad guys' logic is obviously also something that has contributed to the confrontation between public and private sector unions. A fourth problem is the position and role of the unemployed. In their turn they form another type of separate group within the union movement, representing specific wants, claims and priorities. Over the years it has become all too clear that on many issues – concerning both the impact of and possible solutions to the economic crisis – they do not see eye to eye with those who still have a job. They consider that they are not given enough recognition and sufficient opportunities within the union movement. When it comes to meeting their demands and expectations, the unions' leadership is either completely at a loss or paralysed by strong disagreements. Finally there is the 'militant versus individual member' factor. The militants tend to believe that the unions allow themselves to be too easily manoeuvred into a defensive, moderate and negotiating position.

In their view the unions' leadership prevents them from adopting tougher and more radical action. On the other hand the individual members are disappointed as the unions no longer obtain increased real earnings, it being assumed that this is because the unions are not compromising or pragmatic enough and refuse to negotiate.

Key responses 1981–5

'Special-powers' policies

In 1981 the Belgian government persuaded the newly elected parliament to approve a special-powers resolution which allowed the government to rule by decree, as far as economic policies was concerned. Parliament granted these special powers for a one-year period, which was later extended until the end of 1984.

This is not the first time in Belgium's political history that a government has been granted powers to rule by decree. On several occasions since the First World War parliament has taken a similar decision. Previous special powers acts were promulgated in 1914, 1926, 1932, 1934, 1939, 1945, 1957, 1959, 1961 and 1967. However there are some important differences between these antecedents and the latest example of a government ruling by decree. First of all, the object and the scope of most of the previous special-powers acts were much more limited. Particularly, the postwar variants were mainly aimed at short-range and often only provisional decision-making which would allow the government to implement a relatively small number of new measures, in an attempt to solve a single issue or peculiar problem concerning a very specific and restricted policy sector. Secondly, the previous periods during which the country was ruled by decree have always been brief, rarely exceeding a couple of months. Finally, looking at the latest example of a special-powers act, there is a third element that every observer considers as one of its most important features: never before has a government ruling by decree implemented so rapidly such a welter of major decisions.

The underlying principle of these special powers is very simple. It means that parliament loses its legislative authority, and becomes merely a consultative and supervisory body. The government is practically free to decide and act as the Prime Minister and members of the Cabinet see fit. It is no longer required that laws, regulations, and policy measures should be discussed and adopted by parliament. Of course the government, if it wishes, can still consult parliament but it is under no obligation to do so. Moreover, should the government at some moment or other consider a parliamentary debate appropriate, the assessments, advice or proposals this may lead to will never in any way be binding. And this is also the case with regard to the supervision of, for example, policy-implementation processes or the outcome and effectiveness of the measures that the government has taken: whether parliament approves or not does not really make any difference. Even as a mere supervisory body there is little or nothing parliament can do to sanction the government.

Twice during the 1981–5 legislature, parliament granted powers to rule by decree as far as socio-economic policies were concerned. A first special powers act was promulgated in February 1982 and allowed the government to rule by decree until the end of that year. In early December 1982 the Prime Minister announced that he would request a second special powers term, concerning 'only a limited number of matters and especially problems that were related to reorganising public finances and safeguarding employment'. In June 1983 a new act which allowed rule by decree for another one-year period was approved by parliament.

The government scheduled the policies of austerity and economic recovery linked to both these special powers acts, in three stages (Smits, 1983/1984/1985). Making Belgian enterprises competitive and profitable again was the dominant objective in 1982. During the next year the emphasis was on curbing unemployment. For 1984–5, a reduction of the imbalance in the public finances sector became the first priority.

It is on this basis that between 1981 and 1985 the government's economic rescue plan and far-reaching austerity programme were carried out. In terms of governmental autonomy, room for manoeuvre and the possibility of imposing tough measures and swift action, this type of decision and policy-making has obviously been a considerable success.

The list of reforms that were achieved during these four years is quite impressive. A few examples of the decisions the government announced within a month of taking office will suffice to illustrate this: a devaluation of 8.5 per cent of the Belgian franc; a clear modification of the indexation of wages and social-security benefits; a 12 per cent cut in corporation tax; compulsory wage reduction for workers (5 per cent) and managers (10 per cent) in loss-making industries subsidized by the state; a BF 120 billion decrease in public expenditure. In subsequent years this first set of decisions was supplemented by several more series of decrees. They all reinforced the government's policy of economic restoration.

Reaction of the opposition parties

The relatively weak resistance by the opposition parties has made life considerably easier for the government. After the parliamentary elections in November 1981, which had resulted in the formation of the coalition government of Liberal Conservatives and Christian Democrats (that is the Flemish PVV and CVP plus the Francophone PRL and PSC), there were five opposition parties. Labour was represented by the SP and PS, and there were three smaller 'linguistic regionalist' parties – the Flemish VU, the Walloon RW and the Brussels FDF.

The opposition parties of course accepted neither the government's far-reaching programme of austerity and economic restoration nor its plans to rule by decree. As could be expected, they each voiced firm and vehement protests against the special-powers act, which in their view was a frontal attack on the sacrosanct prerogatives of parliament and thus constituted an unprecedented violation of the country's democratic heritage (in particular the tradition of consensus, compromise and accommodation-oriented politics). However, granting powers to rule by decree requires only a simple majority of votes in parliament, and the opposition protests were therefore little more than a vain rearguard battle.

As far as any alternative economic policies were concerned there were similar symptoms of a paralysis and powerlessness of the opposition parties. This was particularly true in the case of the smaller 'linguistic regionalist' parties. For instance, the socio-economic policy of the Flemish nationalist VU was most vague and ambiguous. The VU claims centre-left affinities but somehow it did not manage to translate this explicitly into a concrete anti-crisis programme or consistent policy priorities. And when one looked more closely it became clear that the views of the VU, although an opposition party, actually corresponded to a large extent with the goals and philosophy of the government's industrial recovery and austerity plans.

Labour found itself in a particularly difficult and awkward position. First of all it had participated in all seven coalition governments between 1977 and 1981. In this sense it shared some of the responsibility for the poor and precarious state of the country's economy. Then there had been the two coalitions – from November 1980 to April 1981 and from April 1981 to December 1981 – based on a Christian Democratic-Socialist alliance. They collapsed because of a fundamental and unbridgable disagreement between Christian Democrats and Socialists concerning economic crisis policies. The reason for this disagreement was that on both occasions the Socialists had categorically rejected the kind of industrial recovery and austerity plans that were at the core of the programme which the new Liberal-Christian Democratic government put forward in December 1981. Their refusal to support this tougher and 'Thatcherite' strategy was clear enough. Unfortunately the Socialists had apparently little to offer, apart from the traditional solutions and remedies, for tackling the economic decline of the country – which, as the disenchanting experience of previous governments during the last five years amply demonstrated, had constantly ended in a miserable fiasco and in which therefore no one really believed any longer. Their slogans invariably referred to 'preventing any dismantlement of the welfare state and in particular of its social security system', 'first priority: fighting unemployment and avoiding further redundancies at any cost', 'no income moderation or de-indexation of wages and salaries as far as the working and lower-middle class groups are concerned', and so on; but they still had not managed to translate all this into a concrete, innovative, realistic, and, above all, credible anti-crisis plan.

Reaction of the unions

Already during its first year in office it had become clear that only on rare occasions would the government be confronted with a united trade-union front (Smits, 1983, pp.195–8). A fundamental lack of harmony between the Christian ACV–CSC (Flemish 'Algemeen Christelijk Vakverbond' and Francophone 'Confédération des Syndicats Chrétiens') and the Socialist ABVV–FGTB (Flemish 'Algemeen Belgisch Vakverbond' and Francophone 'Fédération Générale du Travail de Belgique'), the two largest unions in the country, prevented that kind of united opposition.

A supplementary factor which has naturally played an important role in this respect is the simple fact that a number of representatives of the Christian union movement were members of the government (following the well-honoured custom of 'cooptation' characterising the Belgian model of pillarized and consociational-democratic politics). Moreover, the portfolios that these representatives had been granted covered those areas and sectors which were the object of the government's restoration and austerity programme: Ministry of Social Security, Ministry of Education, Ministry of Employment and Labour, Ministry of Budgetary Affairs.

From the beginning, January-February 1982, when the government launched its special powers policy, the differing positions of the Christian and the Socialist union movement were immediately manifest. The ABVV–FGTB completely rejected the government's socio-economic programme. It decided to organize a general twenty-four hour strike in early February. The ACV–CSC leadership refused to cooperate and decided not to take part in any protest action.

During the autumn of 1982 some kind of reconciliation between the Christian and Socialist unions occurred. This seems to have been the result of the failure of negotiations between the 'social partners' (see below) over a central wage moderation agreement. The ACV–CSC decided, after the breakdown of these negotiations, to stage a series of strikes at the provincial level and to do so in cooperation with the ABVV–FGTB. The Socialist union movement did not immediately declare itself willing to support this move. There was, of course, its resentment towards the ACV–CSC for what had (not) happened earlier on in the year. Another reason for the ABVV–FGTB's hesitations related to different views on what would be the aim and logic of this strike action. The ACV–CSC emphasized that its protest was aimed exclusively against the employers, 'in order to teach them a lesson'. In no way was the ACV–CSC prepared to consider an action against the government; any 'political' strike was completely out of the question. And it was on this point that there was a fundamental disagreement with the Socialist union movement. The ABVV–FGTB wished not only to teach the employers a lesson; its aims and strategy were also overtly 'political', and the Socialist union movement wanted to put pressure on the government too. In the end both unions decided to organize joint actions, at the same time indicating there was no question of a common front. Ultimately the actual strikes reflected the traditional pattern of union protest in Belgium: well supported in Wallonia, sometimes patchy and limited in Flanders; more widespread in the public than in the private sector.

Changing the rules of the game

In 1981–2 besides demanding and obtaining powers to rule by decree, the Prime Minister and his Cabinet, immediately after taking office, also introduced a new hard line and bold style of making and implementing policies. In this respect a closer analysis of the government's new approach to the so-called 'social partners', that is, the unions and the employers' organizations, is instructive (Smits, 1983, pp.193–5).

The logic of the postwar 'social-consultation system' was primarily consensual and compromise-oriented. It had been traditionally based on a fundamental agreement with regard to both the procedures for settling socioeconomic conflicts and the range of problems which could be dealt with through this consultation system. Employers and employees had a large degree of autonomy in their negotiations, and they nearly always succeeded in avoiding situations of acute conflict, by adopting a pragmatic and down-to-earth approach. Gradually the government became a third and important partner in these processes of consultation. The development of a welfare-state type of society implied a more interventionist government. At the same time the public sector expanded and became an increasingly important employer. Then the economic decline set in and it has led to serious crisis symptoms at the level of the social-consultation system. Indeed the government has succeeded in totally altering the logic and mechanisms of the social-consultation system. What was a concertation between three partners has been turned into a consultation, by the government, of the employers' organizations and the unions. No longer merely a third partner, the government has evolved into the actor who defines and decides what the agenda for the discussion will be, and, failing a consensus between the employers' and unions' representatives, imposes the final solution itself.

A good example is provided by the measures based on the second batch of special powers decrees in 1982. These measures were designed to restrain industry's production costs. They included one particularly important item: a change in the existing index-linking mechanisms for wages and salaries. The potential formula which the government presented to the social partners aimed at a 3 per cent reduction in the growth of overall labour costs. The unions (ACV–CSC, ABVV–FGTB, and the Liberal-Conservative oriented ACLVB–CGSLB, 'Algemene Centrale der Liberale Vakbonden' plus 'Centrale Générale des Syndicats Libéraux de Belgique') as well as the employers' peak organization (VBO–FEB, Flemish 'Verbond van Belgische Ondernemingen' plus Francophone 'Fédération des Entreprises de Belgique') rejected all of the government's proposals. Subsequently the government suspended the negotiations and decided to go ahead without the approval of the social partners. The existing system of linking wages and salaries to the retail-price index was abandoned. The normal indexation was replaced by the provision of a fixed amount of limited salary and wage increase (one of the original proposals put forward by the government).

More or less the same scenario repeated itself during the negotiations in the autumn, concerning a new 'interprofessional' agreement. Once more it was the government that defined the agenda. Central items were the incomes policy and a reduction in the working week. However, it was not possible to reach any central agreement on the basis of the government's proposals. Opposition to them did not come initially from the trade unions but mainly from the employers' side. The government then transferred the social-consultation process from the national to the sectorial and later to the company level. In doing so, the government recommended that the negotiations at these levels should be carried out on the basis of its 'national' proposals. In order to apply some pressure on both the employers and workers, the government decided that, in the absence of an agreement, certain sanctions would be imposed on firms (including no extra tax relief for the employers' social security contributions and/or for investments to create additional employment, no permission to change the length of the working week).

Effects of new-style crisis policies: a brief summary

The situation remained much the same for the whole period the government was in office (that is, until December 1985). To a large extent the government's austerity programme and economic restoration strategy, as well as the reactions of other major (socio)political actors to these measures during the three subsequent years, were identical to the 1982 script (Smits, 1984, 1985) and thus reflected (at least, that is how it often seemed) some kind of 'well begun is half done' dynamics. The government persevered, stuck to a tough no-nonsense and 'Thatcherite' type of policy and style of decision-making, and in many respects finally succeeded in achieving its initial objectives. The union front remained profoundly divided; the opposition parties adopted a rather resigned stance and seemed to have accepted the powerless passive bystander role into which they were forced.

Looking back, by the end of its four-year term, the results of the government's ambitious and drastic economic policy efforts appeared, according to most impartial observers, moderately good. A considerable part of the original objectives had been achieved (OECD, 1986; Smits, pp.243–44).

First of all everything indicated that, to a certain extent, the confidence in Belgium's economic potential was restored – amongst both employers and the labour force, as well as the major firms and companies in the country, the banks, the stock exchange, foreign investors and entrepreneurs, and so on. Generally a more optimistic and stimulating climate had been created in terms of public opinion, within the political leadership, within the government and public administration and within business and trade and industry circles. This is an achievement which should not be underestimated, remembering the morose, fatalistic and self-pitying mood that prevailed (and as such had a highly paralysing effect) during the late 1970s. At the same time there was also a whole range of more specific and concrete variables which were definitely pointing in the right direction. For instance, wage moderation went much as hoped for; according to the OECD the government's restrictive measures produced a 6.5 per cent decrease from 1982 to 1984. Inflation had shown a positive trend; the rise in consumer prices eased considerably in 1984–5 and was down to virtually zero by the beginning of 1986. Already in 1984 the growth rate of the GNP had begun to accelerate again (2.2 per cent compared to 0.5 per cent the previous year) and had climbed to the average level for the EEC countries. This coincided with a considerable boost in exports (up 5 per cent). Indeed 1984 seems really to have marked a turning point on the road to economic recovery. From that year on it became clear that corporate profits had begun to rise – and they have continued to do so. In 1984 increase in gross company capital reached 8.7 per cent compared with a 6.8 per cent fall in 1983. Between 1983 and 1984 the difference in the growth rate of investment (at fixed prices) was equally encouraging: an 8 per cent decline versus a 7 per cent increase. Finally there was the remarkable improvement of Belgium's trading position – even though mainly due to wage policies leading to a squeeze on domestic consumption, which in turn reduced imports. A slight current account surplus was achieved in 1985, after a balance the year before.

The recovery of the profitability and competitiveness of Belgium's main business, trade and industry (especially manufacturing and high-technology) sectors was the central axis on which the government had built its economic crisis policies. The higher-level recovery of the national economy as a whole, according to the government's 1981–2 provisions, would naturally flow from this.

Many indicators seem to confirm that this strategy has worked and it cannot be denied that substantial progress was made in several crucially important areas by the end of 1985. On the other hand it is also clear that not all indicators are equally successful. This is undoubtedly true regarding the problems of unemployment (OECD, 1986, pp. 45–46). Although the rise in unemployment had been checked, the level was still slightly above the average for other European countries. Moreover its composition also remained a matter for concern. The period of unemployment for individuals was still exceptionally long compared to the situation elsewhere in the EEC, the proportion of jobless for more than twelve months having stabilized at approximately two-thirds since 1984. At the same time, while the youth (15–24 years) unemployment rate had decreased considerably (to 32.4 per cent) by the end of 1985 compared to what it was two years earlier (36.3 per cent), it remained very high. Within the EEC only the situation in Spain and Italy appeared similar or more unfavourable. One consolation was at least that Belgium's overall rate of unemployment (annual average), no longer the worst in the EEC, had more or less stabilized (13 per cent) over the past two years, and even fell a little (to 12.25 per cent) at the beginning of 1986.

However, it is in the area of public finance that the disequilibria were (and continue to be) the most acute. Indeed, the Treasury borrowing requirement still amounted to 12 per cent of GDP by the end of 1985 and as such was one of the most critical compared to other European countries. A multi-year Budget Savings Plan was launched in March 1984, intended to reorganize the public-finances sector of Belgium's economy and to bring the Treasury borrowing requirement down to 11.4 per cent in 1984, to 10.5 per cent in the following year and to 7 per cent in 1987. But this large-scale operation did not solve the problem and eventually the BSP initiative produced only marginal reductions of the public debt/deficit. The most important obstacle remained the self-sustaining nature of the deficit due to interest payments – for example in 1984 accounting for 9.5 per cent of GNP and 21.5 per cent of current expenditure.

Besides the purely economic effects, the political repercussions of the government's achievements between 1981 and 1985 also deserve mention. There is of course the fact that a government which had to administer such harsh economic measures managed to serve out almost a full four-year parliamentary term, while its predecessors, though they had never dared to impose this kind of tough policy and decisive action, lasted on average for no longer than thirteen months. There is the fact that the power to rule by decree effectively 'protected' the government from any substantial interference or obstruction by parliament. Moreover, the government also succeeded in quelling the protest and resistance to its far-reaching austerity programme from the numerous and powerful trade unions. Last but not least, there is the fact that, after four years of continuously declining real incomes for the majority of the population, the Prime Minister Wilfried Martens and his party of Flemish Christian Democrats, the CVP (which was the major component of the 1981–5 centre–right coalition government) actually won the parliamentary elections in October 1985. The result was that the centre–right majority in parliament increased from

14 to 17 seats (Christian Democrats and Liberals: 115. Opposition: 98) and the outgoing coalition government (headed once again by Mr Martens) returned to office.

One of the bases on which the succeeding CVP–PSC–PVV–PRL coalition government was formed was a pledge that the 1981–5 course of austerity and economic recovery policies would be pursued (and in some respects even extended) with the same relentless vigour. That one had to take this pledge seriously was immediately and clearly demonstrated. After taking office, the government (a) once again asked parliament for powers to rule by decree and (b) intended to use these for the the implementation of a new corrective programme with the aim of reducing the Treasury borrowing requirement. This new corrective programme continued and amplified the 1984 Budget Savings Plan. The major difference with the BSP initiative was a strategy calling for greater efforts in managing public expenditure. For instance, various decisions were announced regarding social welfare which would considerably change the system of benefits. The calculation of unemployment benefits was to be thoroughly reviewed, government intervention as far as employment assistance or early retirement programmes were concerned was considerably reduced, and so on. Furthermore, efforts to curb spending were increased in the secondary education and applied research sectors, as well as in health care provision. A global estimate was that by the end of 1986 social spending by central government could be 10 per cent down. These new austerity plans also meant that transfers to local authorities were cut by BF 16 billion and subsidies to public enterprises by BF 25 billion. To all this should be added a BF 25 billion reduction in central government procurement of goods and services. And finally (undoubtedly a very important and most drastic decision) half the cost of this new batch of public finance corrective measures (in *total* BF 82 billion) was scheduled to be borne by households.

Conclusions

The assumption on which the analysis presented here has been based is that, in order to understand policies of austerity and economic restoration in Belgium, aspects of a primarily political nature are both the most interesting and illuminating. An analysis of the interplay of the postwar evolution of Belgian politics and economic crisis elements is the only way to explain why, in 1981, the Belgian parliament 'abdicated' by voting a special powers act, as well as to understand the decisions which the government has subsequently taken and the policies which it managed to implement.

Since the 1950s the Belgian model of pillarization politics and consociationalism has been increasingly affected by all kinds of processes of change (Huyse, 1985). This ultimately resulted in apparently irreversible 'less democracy for better government' dynamics.

A first important development in this respect is the fact that a constantly increasing number of major problems and issues on the political agenda have traditionally been considered too 'explosive' to be left exclusively to parliament and its established discussion and decision-making mechanisms. These issues and problems could not be solved by mere majority versus minority arithmetic and by the zero-sum victory of the largest camp over its opponents. In such a case the only way out is an attempt to arrange and fix some kind of consensus and compromise, based on a 'give and take' and 'no winners nor losers' rationality, which requires skilful negotiations by a limited group of 'wise men'. It means that any purely ideological debate is banned, and a no-nonsense, business-like and highly pragmatic style of bargaining prevails. With regard to the issues and problems that pass through this circuit of conflict management and political decision-making, parliament merely acknowledges and automatically ratifies the compromises that have been achieved, and it provides the financial backing that will allow their implementation.

A second, and in many respects similar, process of change which has considerably undermined parliament's position and role is directly related to the developments in the sphere of (socio)economic policies. Already in the 1930s it had become customary that parliamentary decision and policy-making with regard to (socio)economic problems and issues would (and should) be preceded by a round of consultations with the unions, the employers' organizations and representatives of other major professional groups (farmers, independents and self-employed, and so on). An important postwar development has been the expansion and increasing institutionalization of this kind of consultation procedure. A whole conglomerate of 'councils', advisory boards, expert committees and concertation bodies was installed. Since the 1960s this consultative conglomerate has acquired increasingly wide-ranging regulatory and legislative powers, and it has become a highly autonomous and very powerful centre of gravity in Belgian politics. The organizations, pressure groups and lobbies that compose this amalgam of consultative institutions were thus transformed from 'social' into major 'political' partners. Together with the government they discuss, plan, programme and decide policy-making regarding economic problems, industrial expansion, health care, social security, and so on. Agreements and compromises which have been negotiated by the government and these 'political' partners are still submitted to parliament but only to be formally approved and made official. Parliament has in this respect no more than a rubber stamp function.

Initially the traumatic erosion of the position and role of parliament has been controlled, exploited by and mainly benefited the political parties. This led to a period of a total partycracy. Then came the 1970s. De-pillarization set in, and at the same time there was both a major escalation and subsequently the 'pacification' of ethno-linguistic conflicts. These developments marked the end of the partycracy period. What happened was the transformation of the partycracy system into a neocorporatist model. However, Belgium's example of a neocorporatist type of parliamentary democracy has one very peculiar feature. Eventually it has resulted in an unparalleled reinforcement of the position and role of the government, which became the dominant force and solid centre of power in Belgian politics. It would probably be even more appropriate to use the terms 'governmentalist' and Cabinet-rule system, instead of neocorporatism, to characterize this new situation.

The next question is of course what precisely has allowed the government to become so powerful and dominating? First of all, a fragmented and intricate policy-making system, such as the one that has emerged in Belgian politics since the 1950s, does not manage to survive or operate effectively on the basis of an automatic stability, spontaneous integration and self-generating balance. It needs hinges and connecting links. These cannot be found at the level of parliament, which is still too weak and powerless. They are no longer provided by a large-scale partycracy. The nature and structure of (neo)corporatism forbids that this kind of *primus inter pares* function would accrue to any of the multiple organizations, pressure groups and lobbies of which it is composed. This leaves only one actor to fill the vacuum: the government. The government guarantees and controls the integration, coordination and stability of the neocorporatist decision and policy-making system. It represents the system's indispensable hinges and connecting-links, thus preventing what would otherwise rapidly degenerate into total chaos and survival-of-the-fittest anarchy.

Within this framework a second factor, which has considerably increased the scope and impact of the government's power, is the debilitating effect on the neocorporatist elements of both the ethno-linguistic cleavage in its new 'regionalized' form and of the economic crisis itself. The escalation (during the 1960s and 1970s) and then the regionalization and devolution type of pacification of ethno-linguistic conflicts have completely transformed the (neo)corporatist system. As has been the case with the political parties, the size and power base of the major lobbies and interest or pressure groups are substantially reduced. The economic crisis has only made matters worse. The unions appear to be particularly affected in this respect. There is, for example, the phenomenon of an increasing heterogeneity within the ranks of the unions' members and supporters, which could become a source of internal division and conflict. At the same time economic crisis problems seem to have added new elements of fractionalization that make the unions more vulnerable and undermines their 'combativeness.'

The end result is what could be called 'neocorporatism on crutches'. This new configuration in Belgian politics means that the intermediary and shock-absorbing levels of both parliament and the parties, which used to be the transit zone between the government and the corporatist front, have to a large extent ceased to function. There is now a constant and very direct and open confrontation which opposes the government and a multitude of major corporatist forces. But this confrontation has not lead the way to the old and unsavoury excesses of a pressure-group democracy. Contrary to what many expected, this confrontation has mainly benefited the government, thus once again enhancing the credibility and acceptability of its hardline, no-nonsense and often merciless new style of decision and policy-making.

Editors' note

Since this chapter was completed there has been a general election in Belgium, caused by the re-emergence of the old linguistic-regionalist quarrel. The outgoing government resigned on October 19th, 1987, and new parliamentary elections were held on December 13th 1987. The period of so-called 'formation negotiations' lasted for approximately six months. The final outcome was a five-party coalition as follows: Flemish and French-speaking Christian democrats, and Flemish and French-speaking socialists, and the Volksunie, i.e. the Flemish 'nationalists'/'regionalists'.

References

Billiet, J. (1984), 'On Belgian pillarization: changing perspectives', *Acta Politica,* 19/1, pp. 117–28.

Dewachter, W. and E. Clijsters (1982), 'Belgium: political stability despite coalition crises' in E. C. Browne and J. C. Dreijmanis (eds), *Government Coalitions in Western Democracies,* New York/London, Longman.

De Winter, L. (1981), 'De partijpolitisering als instrument van de particratie: een overzicht van de ontwikkeling sinds de Tweede Wereldoorlog', *Res Publica*, 23/1, pp. 53–107.

Heisler, M. O. (1974), 'Institutionalizing societal cleavages in a cooptive polity: the growing importance of the output-side in Belgium' in M. O. Heisler (ed.), *Politics in Europe*, New York, McKay.

Huyse, L. (1982), 'België: een wankele natie?' in U. Rosenthal (ed.), *Politieke stelsels: stabiliteit en verandering,* Alphen a/d Rijn, Samsom.

Huyse, L. (1984), 'Pillarization reconsidered', *Acta Politica,* 19/1, pp. 145–59.

Huyse, L. (1985), 'Democratie hoe maakt U het?', *De Nieuwe Maand,* 28/3, pp. 15–21.

Lorwin, V. R. (1966), 'Belgium: religion, class and language in national politics' in R. Dahl (ed.), *Political Oppositions in Western Democracies,* New Haven/London, Yale University Press.

Lorwin, V. R. (1974), 'Belgium: conflict and compromise' in K. McRae (ed.), *Consociational Democracy: political accommodation in segmented societies,* Toronto, McLelland and Stewart.

OECD (December, 1984), 'Belgium–Luxembourg', *OECD Economic Surveys*.

OECD (August, 1986), 'Belgium–Luxembourg', *OECD Economic Surveys*.

Rudd, C. (1986), 'Coalition formation and maintenance in Belgium: a case study of élite behaviour and changing cleavage structure 1965–81' in G. Pridham (ed.), *Coalition Behaviour in Theory and Practice: an inductive model for western Europe*, Cambridge University Press.

Smits, J. (1983), 'Belgian politics in 1982: less democracy for a better economy', *Res Publica*, 25/2–3, pp. 181–217.
Smits, J. (1984), 'Belgian politics in 1983: communitarian struggles despite the economic crisis', *Res Publica*, 26/4, pp. 473–502.
Smits, J. (1985), 'Belgian politics in 1984: the electoral temptation', *Res Publica*, 27/2–3, pp. 229–68.'
Smits, J. (1986), 'Belgian politics in 1985: ''No turning back'' ', *Res Publica* 28/3, pp. 441–74.
Zolberg, A. (1978), 'Splitting the difference: federalization without federalism in Belgium' in M. J. Esman (ed.), *Ethnic Conflict in the Western World*, Ithaca, Cornell University Press.

4 West Germany: from reform policy to crisis-management

EDGAR GRANDE

Main political events

1969	general election formation of Social–Liberal government (SPD/FDP) Federal Chancellor: Willy Brandt (SPD)
1972	general election continuation of Social–Liberal government
1974	resignation of Willy Brandt Helmut Schmidt (SPD) elected Federal Chancellor
1976	general election continuation of Social–Liberal government
1980	formation of Green Party general election continuation of Social–Liberal government
1982	dissolution of Social–Liberal coalition formation of Conservative–Liberal government (CDU/CSU/FDP) Federal Chancellor Helmut Kohl (CDU)
1983	general election continuation of Conservative–Liberal government
1984	strike in metal working industry about 35-hour week
1987	general election continuation of Conservative–Liberal government

Introduction

The economic crisis starting in 1974–5 has been the most serious slump in the development of the West German economy since the Second World War. The economy was stagnating at a time when economic growth was of central importance for the policies of social reform initiated and planned by the governing coalition of Social Democrats (SPD) and Liberals (FDP) after 1969 (Schmidt, 1978). When the number of unemployed – one of the main indicators of economic crisis in West Germany – exceeded one million for the first time in 1975, the ranking of political priorities changed significantly. Instead of social politics (and foreign policy), economic development and the national economic policy moved into the centre of political debates.

At the end of the 1970s West Germany was said to be one of those countries – apart from Japan, Austria and Switzerland – which had dealt with the economic challenges most successfully. The success of the 'West German Model' (Paterson and Smith, 1981; Markovits, 1982) was considered to be mainly a *political* achievement. It was interpreted as being the result of the pragmatic crisis-management of the Social–Liberal government, and of the cooperation of trade unions within this crisis-management. Only a few years later, in the early 1980s, the 'West German Model' had begun to lose its shine. As unemployment increased beyond two million (1983: 2,258,000), the Social–Liberal government broke apart in its attempts to slow down the rapid increase of the national debt by drastic budget cuts. Finally the formation of a Conservative–Liberal government (CDU/CSU/FDP) in autumn 1982 brought the 'West German Model' to its political end.

The following study attempts, in four stages, to analyse the political consequences of the economic crisis and the policy responses to the crisis in West Germany. First the perceptions of economic crisis by political parties as well as the national strategic responses designed to master this crisis will be outlined. Then the political preconditions for the temporary success of West German crisis-management and the political and social costs of the policies of crisis-management will be elaborated for some of those policy fields ranking highest on the political agenda (fiscal, social and environmental policy, industrial relations). Finally the political consequences, with respect to electoral success and unconventional participation, will be analysed.

The political perceptions of economic crisis since 1974–5

In the course of the economic crisis (Table 4.1) the political consensus in economic policy between parties, interest groups and economists, which had been built in the years of the Grand Coalition, deteriorated. As a consequence, not only the perception of the nature and main causes of the crisis has been highly controversial, but so also have the political strategies designed to master this crisis. Two dimensions are relevant for the analysis of political crisis-perception in West Germany: first, with respect to the nature of the crisis, we have to distinguish cyclical and structural explanations; secondly, with respect to the location of the causes of crisis, we have to separate endogenous and exogenous explanations.

Table 4.1 The performance of the West German economy 1970–85

Year	Growth of GDP[1]	Inflation[2]	Unemployment[3]
1970	5.1	3.3	0.7
1971	2.9	5.2	0.8
1972	4.2	5.6	1.1
1973	4.7	7.0	1.2
1974	0.3	7.0	2.5
1975	−1.6	6.0	4.7
1976	5.4	4.3	4.6
1977	3.0	3.7	4.5
1978	2.9	2.7	4.3
1979	4.1	4.1	3.7
1980	1.4	5.5	3.7
1981	0.2	5.9	5.3
1982	−0.6	5.3	7.6
1983	1.2	3.3	9.3
1984	2.6	2.4	9.3
1985	2.6	2.2	9.4

Notes:
1 Year to year percentage changes; at constant prices
2 Year to year percentage changes; all private households
3 Year to year percentage changes
Sources: Deutsche Bundesbank; Sachverständigenrat.

The Social–Liberal government perceived the economic stagnation of 1974–5 as being caused by an international recession. As a result of the intensive integration of the West German economy into the international economy a 'global recession' was said to have fought its way into the domestic economy. In the government's perception this 'imported recession' (Schmidt, 1975, 7/12885 D) could not be overcome but could only be mitigated by domestic means. The government implied that the West German economy was essentially 'healthy'. In contrast the rise of unemployment was at the outset seen as caused by structural problems (for example Bundesregierung, *Jahreswirtschaftsbericht*, 1974, p. 6). Unemployment was interpreted as the result of changes in the international division of labour that have forced reduced employment in some branches of industry (initially textiles, clothing, shoes and leather; later steel and shipbuilding). This sectorally and regionally concentrated structural change was entirely welcomed in the context of the structural modernization of the West German economy. The state's only function was to manage the social effects of these structural changes, so that change could take place without political resistance. A general stimulation of economic demand in order to reduce unemployment was judged as dysfunctional.

The crisis-perception of the Christian–Democratic opposition (CDU and CSU) diverged significantly from those of the government. The CDU/CSU also proceeded on the assumption that the crisis of the West German economy was of a cyclical nature. However, they de-emphasized the importance of changes in the international economy and instead emphasized endogenous factors, especially the failures and consequences of Social–Liberal economic policy as implemented in West Germany in the past. They insisted that the Social–Liberal reform policy had provoked an 'inflation of expectations' among citizens, which led to an inflation (of prices) and to a 'ruinous state of public finance'. Rising unemployment, in their analysis, was not the result of structural changes, but was rather the consequence of the wrong national economic policies and an inappropriate trade union wage policy. On the one hand full-employment guarantees to the trade unions were said to trigger off excessive wage settlements, while on the other hand financial pressures greatly reduced the employers' will to invest.

At the end of the 1970s the structural causes of the economic crisis moved to the centre of debate. By then the Social–Liberal government believed that the crisis not only affected a few branches of industry, but that 'essential parts of the West German economy' (Bundesregierung, *Jahreswirtschaftsbericht,* 1979, p. 17) were being hit by radical changes in the international division of labour. When the economic crisis intensified at the beginning of the 1980s the Social–Liberal government began to realize that the West German economy *as a whole* was in structural crisis.

The Christian–Democrat opposition also perceived the economic crisis of the 1980s as a structural crisis. But the CDU/CSU did not start from the fact that this structural crisis was the result of too much international pressure, but, on the contrary, believed that the dynamic force and flexibility of the West German economy had deteriorated. This 'sclerosis' – and here they adopted their line of reasoning of the 1970s – was seen mainly as the result of Social–Liberal economic and social policy, which was said to restrict the flexibility available to employers and to provoke excessive demands of citizens against the state. In 1981 and 1982 this view coincided increasingly with views within the liberal FDP, whose leader Hans–Dietrich Genscher as early as 1981 called for a change in economic and social policy to break with the predominant 'mentality of expectations'. Hence the collapse of the Social–Liberal coalition in autumn 1982 was preceded by diverging perceptions of economic crisis within the government itself. The perception of crisis prevailing within the Conservative–Liberal coalition was summarized by Chancellor Helmut Kohl in his first declaration of policy:

The international economy at present is in a penetrating structural crisis in large parts of the world. . . But the reference to the situation abroad must not distract the view from our home made problems. The present crisis of the international economy above all is a crisis of the individual national economies as well. The limits of endurance, both of the West German economy and of the working people, first have been tested and then exceeded by far. (Kohl, 1982, 9/7214 C)

Nevertheless by the mid-1980s the talk of economic crisis had almost died down – at least in the governing parties and mass media. However, the new feeling of comfort was only partly the result of an improvement of the West German economy's performance. For example, unemployment especially was as high as ever. This striking paradox of well–being despite obvious economic and social hardships needs further explanation. A closer examination of the growth of unemployment since the early 1970s (Table 4.2) suggests an important qualification: The *rate of change* seems to be a more important determinant of the public perception than the absolute level of unemployment. Thus, the stabilization of unemployment – even at (by West German standards) a very high level – seems to be one of the reasons why unemployment was a minor issue at the general election in January 1987.

Table 4.2 The development of unemployment 1970–85

Year	(a) Total unemployment	(b) Year to year change	(c) Unemployment rate
1970	149 000	–16.8	0.7
1971	185 000	24.1	0.8
1972	246 000	32.9	1.1
1973	273 000	10.9	1.2
1974	582 000	113.1	2.5
1975	1 074 000	84.5	4.7
1976	1 060 000	–1.3	4.6
1977	1 030 000	–2.8	4.5
1978	993 000	–3.5	4.3
1979	876 000	–11.7	3.7
1980	889 000	1.4	3.7
1981	1 272 000	43.0	5.3
1982	1 833 000	44.1	7.6
1983	2 258 000	23.2	9.3
1984	2 266 000	0.4	9.3
1985	2 304 000	1.7	9.4

Source: Sachverständigenrat (cols a, c); author's calculations (col. b).

National strategic responses to the economic crisis

In the main, two major approaches to overcome the economic crisis were developed in the second half of the 1970s: the Social Democratic concept of a 'directive, anticipatory structural policy' (see especially Hauff and Scharpf, 1975) and a market-based programme for economic growth, presented by the Council of Economic Experts (Sachverständigenrat, 1976). Both concepts have only partly guided the practice of Social–Liberal economic policy. This implementation shortfall was the consequence of the predominant distribution of political power. It allowed none of these concepts to mobilize the political majorities necessary to transform the existing institutional framework – one of the main preconditions for the possible success of these concepts in practice. The Social Democratic plans for 'structural policy' (Strukturpolitik) were opposed by business, the Christian–Democrats and even by parts of the governing FDP. The free-enterprise concept suggested by the Council of Economic Experts was rejected by trade unions and by large parts of the SPD. Thus the Social–Liberal government lacked a conclusive strategy to master the problems of slackening growth and structural adjustment.

The economic and social policy of the Social–Liberal government has to be interpreted as an unstable political compromise. The consequence of this constant pressure for political compromise was a shift to a reactive policy style, aiming at coordination with the main actors in economic policy (especially trade unions). Its result, the policies of crisis-management, attempted to optimize policy outcomes *within* the given political and institutional configuration in the face of increasing economic and political strains. Thus the characteristics of the Social–Liberal crisis-management can be summarized in four ways:

- The management of structural change should be, primarily, a function of *business*. This means that a solution to the economic crisis would have to follow economic rather than political principles. The state should facilitate private adjustment efforts in a general way and should intervene only in particular cases (see Bundesregierung, *Jahreswirtschaftsbericht* 1978, pp. 16 ff). In principle the Social–Liberal government argued that structural problems could not be solved by a national counter–cyclical stimulation of economic demand.
- The *state* had two superior functions in this market-led process of adjustment. It had to facilitate structural change by the establishment of an adequate infrastructure and by the promotion of market-based innovation; and it had to ease the social costs resulting from economic adjustment.
- The *trade unions* too had a dual function in economic crisis-management. At a national level they were expected to support the adjustment efforts of business by a moderate wage policy; and at the level of industrial branches and individual enterprises – especially in declining industries – their cooperation should make sure that the necessary reductions of employment could be managed without any collective resistance.

- The *Bundesbank*, legally autonomous from the Federal government, played the leading role in macroeconomic policy after 1974 (Kloten *et al.*, 1985, p. 392; Scharpf, 1987, pp. 253 ff). By a restrictive monetary policy, basically accepted by the Social–Liberal government, the Bundesbank should reduce inflation.

This Social–Liberal crisis-management was burdened with a portentous *dilemma*. The Social–Liberal government accepted that economic change achieved via the market would constantly produce social costs; the state (and the trade unions) would have to absorb these costs without having the chance to intervene directly in the process of structural change. Thus the conditions of success for the Social–Liberal crisis-management would be determined by the (world) market and could not be controlled by the Social–Liberal state (Hoffmann, 1983, p. 131). Therefore the *limits of the Social–Liberal crisis-management* were readily apparent. They were reached as soon as the social costs of structural change had exceeded both the fiscal capacity of the welfare state, and the willingness of the trade unions and their rank and file to make sacrifices. In the second half of the 1970s the Social–Liberal government was able to extend these limits by shifting the costs of structural adjustment on to social outsiders and marginal groups (foreign workers, women, young persons, and so on) (Esser and Fach, 1981). By so doing it was possible to restrict the costs for the members and supporters of the Social Democratic Party and trade unions. The worsening of the economic crisis in 1980–1 finally removed this alternative. Now the 'core groups' of the trade unions too were increasingly hit by the drastic rise in unemployment. At the same time the Social–Liberal government had to adopt a course of fiscal austerity that demanded sacrifices from its social basis as well.

The Conservative–Liberal government has been aiming at a fundamental 'change of policy' ('Wende') in its programme. Its purpose has been a reorientation of economic and social policy and moreover a fundamental change of the spirit and the moral principles of West German society ('geistig-moralische Wende'). The Conservative–Liberal government has adopted central elements of a neoconservative ideology in its programme, especially in the field of economic and social policy. In general, state intervention in the economy should be reduced, the 'Social Market Economy' (Soziale Marktwirtschaft) should be strengthened, and 'a renaissance of entrepreneurship' (Hans-Dietrich Genscher) should be initiated. In summary (for details see Kohl, 1982), the Conservative–Liberal coalition has adopted the following goals: strengthening business profits (mainly by tax reliefs); the stabilization of public budgets; the reorganization of the welfare state by concentrating public social expenditure on the 'truly needy' (Helmut Kohl); and the removal of 'excessive regulation' in order to increase the dynamics and flexibility of the capitalist market. At the end of its first term in office, however, the Conservative–Liberal government has presented a picture of confusion with respect to its own standards of a market-based, non-interventionist economic and social policy. In spite of its neo-liberal economic programme, it has abandoned the interventionist policies of its Social–Liberal predecessors only in a few cases (for example by formulating the Employment Promotion Act). Although some policy outcomes clearly distinguish the Conservative–Liberal coalition from former Social–Liberal policy, its reactive policy style of crisis-management has been the same.

Policy responses to the economic crisis

The policies of crisis-management were not restricted to the narrow field of macroeconomic policy. Its functioning and its limits can be traced particularly in the case of fiscal policy; its main feature however was the *subordination* of the most relevant sectoral policies – such as social policy, research and technology policy, industrial relations, environmental policy and education policy – under the necessities of economic crisis-management. This extension of crisis-management was one of the conditions of success of the 'West German Model' – and of its failure. Since the political stability of the Social–Liberal government was increasingly dependent on its economic success, any intensification of the economic crisis jeopardized the 'model' as a whole.

Fiscal policy and budget deficits

National fiscal policy has been one of the central issues of economic crisis-management, determining to a large degree its social quality and acceptance. After the rapid increase in unemployment and of the public debt during the crisis, fiscal policy was torn between two opposite goals. On the one hand the state was expected (especially by trade unions) to stimulate economic growth by its fiscal policy, thus reducing unemployment; on the other hand the calls for a stabilization of the public budgets were intensified. In detail, we have to distinguish two periods of national counter-cyclical policy (Deutsches Institut, 1982) that stand for different governmental responses to the slumps of 1974–5 and 1980–1. Most significantly, as economic crisis–management developed, budget stabilization was given priority to other functions of the national budget.

In reaction to the crisis of 1974–5, the Federal government relaxed its restrictive course in fiscal policy, which had been pursued since 1973. The goal of fighting inflation was not abandoned, but four special programmes – including a sum of DM 14 billion – were designed especially to eliminate regional and sectoral economic problems and unemployment. These special programmes were complemented by a reform of income tax, which in 1975 caused a reduction of public revenue of the same amount. Thus the state made a significant contribution to stabilizing the national economy – but its fiscal stimulus was too weak to cure unemployment. Nevertheless as early as autumn 1975, the Federal government (as well as the state and local governments) returned to a restrictive course. In its law on the structure of public budgets (Haushaltsstrukturgesetz), the Federal government decided a number of budgetary cuts to improve the structure of the public budgets in the medium term (see Arkenstette *et al.*, 1982, pp. 32–53; Alber,1986); moreover state expenditures almost stagnated. The consequences of this restrictive policy became apparent in 1977 when the rate of growth of GDP was reduced almost by a half compared to the year before. The Social–Liberal government responded to this by a 'dramatic change' (Sachverständigenrat, 1977, p. 19) in its fiscal policy in summer 1977. First it decided a medium-term 'programme for future investment' (Programm für Zukunftsinvestitionen) totalling some DM 20 billion until 1981. Then it enacted changes in numerous tax laws to provide relief to private households and to stimulate investment. The total amount of these tax reductions exceeded even the costs of the 'programme for future investment'; parts of its effects however were compensated by a strong increase in indirect taxes.

When the economic crisis worsened in 1980–1 the Social–Liberal government did not, in contrast to 1974, respond by an expansive fiscal policy. On the contrary, it further depressed the economy by drastic cuts in public expenditure. The political power constellation made the stabilization of public budgets by an increase of receipts (for example tax increases) impossible. In so far as tax increases were considered by the Social–Liberal government, they were not only blocked by the CDU (threatening with its majority in the Bundesrat), but also by the free-market oriented exponents of the governing FDP. As a consquence the West German tax share declined despite growing public debt between 1980 and 1984, from 24.5 per cent (1980) to 23.6 per cent (1984) (Table 4.3). Thus the Social–Liberal government was left with only one possibility: fiscal austerity. The cuts in 1981 and 1982 (especially 'operation '82' and 'operation '83') burdened the private sector in 1982 with DM 14 billion, and in the period to 1985 with DM 21.5 billion annually, which in total is approximately DM 80 billion (Schäfer, 1982). In autumn 1982 the Conservative–Liberal government intensified this policy of fiscal austerity, adding DM 8 billion annually to the fiscal burden on the private sector. Since then it has adhered to its goal of reducing the public deficits drastically (Deutsches Institut, 1983, 1984).

The crucial problem of the economy measures in 1981 and 1982 was the fact that they hit mainly the social and political power bases of the Social Democratic Party and the trade unions: the workers. According to a study done by the trade unions' Institute of Economic and Social Research, 'The incomes of the employees have to provide by far the biggest contribution to the stabilization of the public budgets' (Schäfer, 1982, p.585). Employees

Table 4.3 The deficit of public budgets in West Germany 1970–84

Year	(a) Total public debt[1]	(b) Total debt of Federal government[1]	(c) Public debt as % of GDP	(d) Tax share[2]
1970	125.9	47.3	18.6	22.7
1971	140.4	48.8	18.7	22.8
1972	156.1	55.3	19.0	23.8
1973	167.8	61.4	18.3	24.4
1974	192.4	72.1	19.5	24.3
1975	256.4	108.5	25.0	23.4
1976	296.7	128.4	26.5	23.8
1977	328.5	150.2	27.4	24.9
1978	370.8	177.5	28.8	24.7
1979	413.9	202.6	29.7	24.5
1980	468.6	232.3	31.7	24.5
1981	545.6	273.1	35.4	24.0
1982	614.8	309.1	38.5	23.7
1983	671.7	341.4	40.2	23.7
1984	717.5	367.3	41.1	23.6

1 DM billions
2 Tax receipts of government as a percentage of GNP
Source: Sachverständigenrat (cols a, b, d); author's calculations (col. c).

had to bear more than 90 per cent of the total charge on the private sector between 1982 and 1985. Although the need to stabilize the national budget was almost undisputed between both the parties in government and the trade unions, the quality of economic crisis-management thus changed significantly. The state could no longer afford to mitigate the social costs of economic modernization, but it had to demand sacrifices as well. This was the material reason for the erosion of the political consensus supporting the 'West German Model' (cf. Hoffmann, 1983).

Social policy

Social policy is one of those fields where the shift from an active policy to a reactive one was most pronounced. During its early years in office the Social–Liberal government had expanded social services considerably by introducing new and improving existing programmes. Its assumption that increased social expenditure could be financed by steady and lasting economic growth had already been frustrated by the recession of 1974–5. Since then the costs caused by the crisis have been increasing while public receipts have been falling short of the government's expectations. Unemployment benefits are a striking example: in the early 1970s annual public expenditure on unemployment had been below DM 1 billion; in 1982 and 1983 the Federal Office for Labour (Bundesanstalt für Arbeit) spent DM 20 billion annually on unemployment benefits and short-time work compensations (Bundesbank, 1986, p. 20).

The Social–Liberal government (and its Conservative–Liberal successor) responded to the emerging fiscal crisis of the welfare state by a departure from reform policy, in three stages (Arkenstette *et al.*, 1982; Alber, 1986). In general this departure was characterized by the growing dominance of cost saving at the expense of social security goals. In the early years of economic crisis (1975–7), the Social–Liberal government shifted the main emphasis to 'reforms that cost nothing' (Willy Brandt) and deferred new expensive programmes. Thus a programme for the protection of mothers (Mutterschutzgesetz) in 1979 was the only significant programme to be agreed after 1975 by the Social–Liberal government. At the same time the first attempts to slow down the growth of public expenditure by budget cuts (Haushaltsstrukturgesetz) were made (see above). In the second phase (1977–80) short-term fiscal shortfalls had to be met by a redistribution of resources within the network of different social security systems (pensions, health, unemployment); by increases in contributions; by delays of benefit increases (for example of pensions) to take account of inflation and wage increases; and not last by a growing public deficit. The aim of all these measures was to maintain the existing structure of the welfare state until economic prosperity would finally ease the fiscal burdens.

Because of the worsening of the economic crisis in 1980–1, the limits of this strategy of 'tinkering' became evident. Therefore, in a third step, the government adopted drastic cuts in public expenditure and tried to ease the 'burden of the welfare state' by concentrating social spending on 'the truly needy' (Helmut Kohl). Despite its serious social consequences (see above), the policy of both the Social–Liberal and the Conservative–Liberal government was still mainly reactive. Economy measures did not take place where the inappropriateness or the faulty design of spending programmes was obvious, but where political resistance was expected to be weakest (for example pupils, students, pensioners). Thus it is unlikely that a balance of the social budgets will be achieved in the long term (Bundesbank, 1986, p. 21).

Environmental policy

Environmental protection has become a key topic in West German politics since the beginning of the 1970s. It is now the most important *new* issue on the political agenda. Since mass media coverage of the accelerating death of the forests ('Waldsterben') in the early 1980s, the protection of the environment has ceased to be a concern of only active minorities but has gained wide public attention. According to a survey in 1982, 80 per cent of the population and 93 per cent of the members of the Bundestag considered the conditions of the environment to be 'a problem' (see Müller, 1984, p. 116). Notwithstanding this widespread (indeed mass) concern, environmental policy is a further example of the subordination of sectoral policies to the 'logic' of economic crisis-management.

In the early 1970s environmental protection – apart from social reform – was one of the most relevant fields of an active Social–Liberal domestic policy. Stimulated by international conferences and bureaucratic concerns, the governing parties adopted the issue in their programmes. The general principle of environmental policy was formulated concisely in the FDP's Freiburg programme: 'Environmental protection has priority over the pursuit of profits and individual benefits' (FDP, 1971, p. 455). In a number of Federal laws (on lead in petrol, waste removal, emission reduction, and so on) the government attempted to realize these programmatic goals. Regardless of the economic crisis, the success of this attempt to introduce a rather active policy would have been limited. It was constrained by conceptual deficiencies as well as by institutional restrictions peculiar to West German politics (Müller, 1984; Richardson and Watts, 1985). However it was the oil crisis and the following economic slump that dampened the 'reform euphoria' in environmental protection decisively.

After 1974–5 environmental policy was immediately sacrificed in the interests of economic stability and growth. The established parties (SPD, FDP, CDU, CSU) and interest groups (business organizations, trade unions) aligned in a 'growth cartel' and insulated themselves against the environmentalists' criticism. The political logic that had until then guided environmental policy was reversed by this 'growth cartel': safeguarding employment and the stimulation of private investment was given priority over environmental improvement. Subsequently, environmental legislation was slowed down and new laws (for example on chemicals) fell short of former expectations. Moreover, existing programmes were applied poorly in response to economic interests; both resources and personnel to implement these laws were insufficient. As a consequence, environmental protection was suffering a considerable 'implementation shortfall' (Vollzugsdefizit) (see for example Wey, 1982, pp. 214 ff.).

Nevertheless, under growing pressure from environmentalists and the electoral success of the environmentalist Green Party (Die Grünen), environmental policy debate has been intensified again since the early 1980s without environmental policy becoming more effective. For example, rules governing vehicle emissions, enacted by the Conservative–Liberal government after protracted negotiations, fell significantly short of corresponding regulations in the USA and Japan. The most important institutional innovation was the establishment of a Federal Ministry of the Environment in 1986 – possibly a symbolic measure to pacify public concern after the Chernobyl catastrophy – where some of the formerly fragmented authority in environmental policy was centralized. In reality most environmental damage has been dealt with only temporarily without removing its basic structural causes (Müller, 1984, p.118; Jänicke, 1986, pp. 69–80).

Beginning with the economic crisis of 1974–5, the economic environment of industrial relations has changed markedly. West German trade unions have shared the burden of economic adjustment not only by their moderate wage policy, but also by their cooperation in 'crisis cartels' at plant and sectoral level (Esser, 1982; Esser *et al.*, 1983; Dyson, 1984). By doing this they were one of the main buttresses of the 'West German Model'. However they came increasingly into opposition with the national economic policy, when the costs of economic crisis-management were shifted to the obvious disadvantage of their rank and file in the early 1980s.

In the economic crisis trade unions have significantly reoriented their wage policy, subordinating it to the necessities of economic stabilization (Scharpf, 1987, pp. 248 ff). In contrast to the early 1970s when they fought for wage settlements in double figures, since 1974 the trade unions have attempted only to maintain living standards of their members by seeking increases in line with inflation. In practice, real income could be improved only marginally between 1974 and 1979, and between 1980 and 1985 reductions in real net income were accepted. Wage increases in the public sector have been even lower than in the private sector (Jacobi, 1986, p.222). Nevertheless, trade unions did not strike in support of wage increases, apart from two minor disputes in printing industries (1976) and in ports (1978). Since 1978 the unions have tried to balance their moderation in (quantitative) wage demands per se by qualitative demands (especially for a reduction of working time). Simultaneously their resort to industrial conflict has increased. The unions have adopted a more flexible strategy, for example by the massive threat of token strikes. In 1978 the conflict over the 35-hour week led to an unsuccessful six-week strike in the steel industry. The confrontation over the reduction of working time escalated in the metal working industry in 1984. This biggest industrial dispute in West German history – finally ended by a compromise – lasted for seven weeks and involved 57,000 striking employees, 155,000 who were locked out, and 315,000 who were affected indirectly (Jacobi, 1986, p. 226).

As a consequence of economic crisis-management (and the change of government in 1982), the unions' influence in economic policy-making has been declining remarkably. Their power to achieve their economic policy goals, behind the closed doors of conference rooms, has been weakened; instead they had to write protest letters and to organize demonstrations and mass rallies in order to make themselves heard. This shift in group strategy reflecting the decline of union political power has taken place in several stages. The *formal consultations* between the Federal government, trade unions and business organizations in the 'Concerted Action' (Konzertierte Aktion), initiated in 1967, came to an end when the unions withdrew in 1977. These consultations had already lost their political significance in 1974, when the Bundesbank adopted a restrictive monetary policy to bring down inflation. The 'Concerted Action' was replaced by informal consultations 'Social Dialog') and by sectoral consultations (for example in technology policy). However the growing disagreement between the government and the trade unions, especially about the appropriate way of fighting unemployment, could not be settled at these meetings. Confronted with the Social–Liberal coalition's severe economy measures in the early 1980s, major parts of the trade unions dissociated themselves from the government's restrictive economic policy.

During the Conservative–Liberal coalition the government's relations with the trade unions deteriorated further. On the one hand informal consultations did continue, but they took a largely *symbolic* form. Practical results were not achieved. Moreover in most of these meetings they were not even intended. On the other hand, the confrontation between the unions and the Conservative–Liberal coalition has intensified as a result of the government's support of the employers during the strike in the metal working industry, and of its re-definition of 'state neutrality' in industrial disputes at the disadvantage of the unions (§ 116 Arbeitsförderungsgesetz). This is not to say we have seen a lasting break in the cooperative relation between trade unions, the state and business that has markedly shaped West German post war history. Nevertheless in the course of economic crisis the 'standard operating procedures' in economic policy-making have been changed significantly to the disadvantage of organized labour.

The political consequences of economic crisis-management

In the 1970s Social–Liberal crisis-management was successful not only economically, but also *politically*. The Social–Liberal government was re-elected in 1976 and 1980. Its collapse in 1982 was not at first sight caused by the voters' dissatisfaction but by the FDP's 'treacherous' change of coalition. This political success indicates a high stability of the West German political system in spite of the economic crisis and its social consequences. However this is only partly true. The specific manner in which the economic crisis was managed – not the crisis by itself but the Social–Liberal crisis-management – had two political consequences: on the one hand it increasingly excluded social groups from the political consensus supporting Social–Liberal policy, thus making them 'available' for conservative and 'green-alternative' political arguments; on the other hand the political conflicts within the Social–Liberal coalition intensified – finally leading to the change of government.

Electoral change

The Bundestag election in 1976 (Table 4.4), the first national election following the economic crisis of 1974–5, was striking proof of the high stability of the West German party system (Berger *et al.*, 1977). The established parties (SPD, FDP, CDU, CSU) gained a total share of 99.1 per cent of the votes. Despite mass unemployment and high inflation, the numerous Communist splinter parties remained as unimportant as the neo-Fascist NPD, which had remarkable electoral success in the years immediately following the recession of 1966–7.

Table 4.4 General elections in West Germany 1969–87

	1969	1972	1976	1980	1983	1987
CDU/CSU	46.1	44.9	48.6	44.5	48.8	44.3
SPD	42.7	45.8	42.6	42.9	38.2	37.0
FDP	5.8	8.4	7.9	10.6	7.0	9.1
Greens	—	—	—	1.5	5.6	8.3
Others	5.4	1.0	0.9	0.5	0.5	1.3

Sources: Statistisches Bundesamt.

The worsening of the economic crisis in 1980–1, however, was markedly reflected in both public opinion and voting behaviour in those years (Schmollinger and Stöss, 1984). Between autumn 1981 and autumn 1982 the economic situation was considered by the public to be worse than ever; even worse than in 1974–5. Moreover there was a growing scepticism about the Social–Liberal government's management of the crisis. This shift of public opinion significantly affected the results of the state elections at that time. The Social Democrats suffered considerable losses of votes in the state elections in Berlin (–4.4 per cent), Lower Saxony (–5.7 per cent) and Hamburg (–8.8 per cent). In Berlin the SPD was replaced in government, and in Hamburg (also then an SPD-governed state) the formation of a government was blocked by a stalemate between the major parties (SPD and CDU). Both the Christian–Democrats and the 'Green–Alternative' lists had considerable gains.

In summer 1982 these events came to a head in the political crisis of the Social–Liberal coalition. The results of an opinion poll in August showed the worst assessment ever measured for a Federal government (Berger *et al.*, 1983, p. 564). Finally, in September, the Social–Liberal government collapsed, the final break being a consequence of the conflict over the course of economic and social policy between the Social Democratic Federal Chancellor Helmut Schmidt, and the Liberal Minister of Economic Affairs Otto Count Lambsdorff. The Liberals' withdrawal from the coalition led to the formation of a Conservative–Liberal government in October, headed by the current (1988) Chancellor Helmut Kohl.

The new coalition government faced the electorate on 6 March 1983, for the first time, gaining a clear electoral victory. The CDU failed to gain an absolute majority of votes; but the FDP retained parliamentary representation despite its previous change of the coalition, although suffering heavy losses (−3.6 per cent). Altogether the new coalition had a lead of 12 per cent over the Social Democrats and the Greens. The SPD lost 4.7 per cent of its votes and was reduced to its 1961 position. The SPD's social and political basis was reduced in two ways as a result of Social–Liberal crisis-management: The Social Democrats lost part of the new middle-class voters they had attracted at the beginning of the Social–Liberal government, both to the CDU and (especially young voters) to the Greens; and they lost ground in their traditional domain: the unionized workers. The SPD was not only the object of the frustration of unskilled and semi-skilled workers; it had to suffer the increasing disillusionment of its 'core groups', the skilled workers, as well (Feist *et al.*, 1983).

'New social movements': the rise of unconventional participation

An additional feature of the developing economic crisis was that the consensus on which the Social–Liberal crisis-management had been based, was eroded by the resistance of 'new social movements' (Neue soziale Bewegungen). These new forms of unconventional participation, whose formation dates back to the end of the 1960s, have significantly changed the political culture of West German politics. The pattern of 'civil passiveness', interspersed only with voting in elections, that had characterized the postwar period of 'political Biedermeier', has been replaced to a remarkable extent by the citizens' direct intervention in politics.

During the period of Social–Liberal reform policy until 1974, the formation of citizens' action committees (Bürgerinitiativen) was perfectly complementary to governmental policy. Although 'reform policy' was to be worked out and implemented 'from above', the citizens' activities at the grass roots were functional in two respects. Active citizens were to extend the government's scope for action by providing useful information about local problems and deficiencies; and the pressure of local activities facilitated the legitimization of reform policy against the growing conservative opposition. The parties in government, that is, SPD and especially FDP, as well as the trade unions, adopted the new issues and made them a main point of policy discussion at that time (see above).

The oil crisis and the stagnation of economic growth began to encourage disillusionment with Social–Liberal policy (Roth, 1980b). First the crisis made it increasingly difficult to fund activities in those non-productive sectors where the new social movements were organized. For example, the quality of social services was lowered, user charges were raised, and subsidies to self-help groups were cut. Secondly the specific means of crisis-management intensified drastically the pressures in some other sectors. Public spending programmes for stimulating economic growth (for example by subsidizing large road projects, airports and so on) accelerated the development of local resistance. In particular the construction of nuclear power plants, promoted to reduce dependence on foreign oil, became the focus of the new protest movements. Whyl, Brokdorf, Kalkar, Grohnde, and Gorleben, the sites of some of these plants, were the most spectacular theatres of increasingly radicalized protest. Mass demonstrations and squatting in building sites were the protest's new manifestations.

These conflicts intensified in the second half of the 1970s. The single protest groups, hitherto locally isolated and with a broad range of issues, joined forces in a more homogeneous environmental protest movement. Their protest moved from a concern with *particular* problems towards a more generalized and fundamental criticism of both the Social–Liberal government's policy and, more important, industrial capitalist growth in general (Brand *et al.*, 1983). Three figures may provide a rough estimate of their growing activities. In 1972 it was estimated that 3000 to 4000 citizens' action committees organizing 60,000 to 120,000 members were active. In 1977 the number of activists in environmental groups alone was estimated at 170,000; the total number of active citizens probably exceeded this number by about 30 to 50 per cent (Roth, 1980a, p. 211). In 1981 the Federal Environment Agency (Bundesumweltamt) registered about 5 million citizens that were active in the various environment protection organizations – twice the number of members in the established political parties (Müller, 1984, p. 115).

In the 1980s the disparate ways and levels of action against Social–Liberal (and then Conservative–Liberal) policies have partly been integrated by the foundation of an environmentalist Green Party. Established as a Federal party in January 1980, the Greens have gained representation in eight (out of eleven) state parliaments and city councils and have been represented in the national parliament, the Bundestag, since March 1983.

Conclusion

The economic crisis of 1974–5 was the beginning of a new period of West German post-war history. This new period was characterized neither by far-reaching institutional changes nor by a fundamental shift of political power relations, but mainly by a *change of policy style*. This is not to say that the Social–Liberal reform policy failed only for exogenous reasons. Institutional restrictions on state intervention and the complex political power relations within the federal organization of the West German state had been obstacles to the implementation of an active policy anyway (see for example Scharpf *et al.*, 1976).

Politically the success of Social–Liberal crisis-management in the late 1970s can be explained by two factors: the stable integration of interest groups, especially trade unions, in the process of crisis regulation; and the systematic extension of reactive policy beyond the narrow domain of (macro)economic policy. The result was not a unification of the complex West German policy style (Dyson, 1982, p. 17), but the subordination of the most relevant policy fields (social policy, environmental policy, research and technology policy, and so on) under the necessities of economic crisis-management.

The extension of crisis-management reached its political limits in the early 1980s, when the subsequent costs of economic modernization and structural adjustment could no longer be compensated. The social and political core groups of the Social Democratic Party and the trade unions were then hit by the crisis. Furthermore the new social movements and the Green party – also partly products of the Social–Liberal crisis-management – made it more difficult to pass on the costs of crisis-management to social outsiders and the natural environment.

The breakdown of the Social–Liberal coalition did not mean the end of the policies of crisis-management. The Conservative–Liberal government took office claiming to return – though with neoconservative objectives – to an active policy style. Because of both its internal heterogeneity and external political and institutional restrictions, it has only partly realized its purposes (see Grande, 1987). The few efforts towards an active policy, for example in media or in environmental policy, were insufficient and unplanned. However the Conservative–Liberal government has changed the 'standard operating procedures' of national economic policy-making in one important respect: the influence of trade unions in economic policy has declined significantly. The few meetings between the Federal government and the trade union leadership were by and large symbolic and had no material consequences. Therefore the Conservative–Liberal government's reactive policy style in economic policy – at least on the national level – has tended to be exclusive rather than consultative.

At first sight West Germany has mastered the economic crisis successfully. Inflation virtually disappeared, the annual increase in public debt declined, exports have been beating all records. Unemployment has persisted but has lost much of its political potence. The 'Western German Model' has got new brilliance, and at the end of 1986 foreign observers felt that 'contentment is breaking out in West Germany' (Colchester and Carr, 1986, p. 3). On closer inspection however there is no reason for complacency. The new success has been less the result of national efforts than the (unexpected) consequence of favourable international developments (for example the fall of oil prices and of the US dollar). Structural internal problems have not been solved: there is neither an end in sight to mass unemployment nor an effective removal of the ecological costs of economic modernization; structural reforms of pensions and health services to master the threatening fiscal crisis of the welfare state are still in the state of planning. Moreover, as a consequence of the economic crisis and the subsequent policies of crisis-management, political conflicts have intensified remarkably: the consensus in economic policy between the major parties broke down; unconventional participation in new social movements increased; and cooperation in industrial relations declined in the course of economic crisis-management.

References

Documents and official sources

Bundesregierung, *Jahreswirtschaftsbericht der Bundesregierung.* Bonn, anually.

Sachverständigenrat zur Begutachtung der gesamtwirtschaftlichen Entwicklung (SVR), *Jahresgutachten.* Stuttgart, Kohlhammer, anually.

Secondary sources

Alber, J. (1986), 'Der Wohlfahrtsstaat in der Wirtschaftskrise – Eine Bilanz der Sozialpolitik in der Bundesrepublik seit den frühen siebziger Jahren', *Politische Vierteljahresschrift,* 27 (1), pp. 28–60.

Arkenstette, M. *et al.* (1982), *Sozial–Demontage. Vom Sozialstaat zur konservativen 'Wende'.* Hamburg, VSA.

Berger, M., Gibowski, W., Roth, D. and Schulte, W. (1977), 'Bundestagswahl 1976: Politik und Sozialstruktur', *Zeitschrift für Parlamentsfragen,* 7 (2), pp. 197–231.

Berger, M., Gibowski, W., Roth, D. and Schulte, W. (1983), 'Regierungswechsel und politische Einstellungen. Eine Analyse der Bundestagswahl 1983', *Zeitschrift für Parlamentsfragen,* 14 (4), pp. 556–82.

Brand, K.–W., Büsser, D. and Rucht, D. (1983), *Aufbruch in eine andere Gesellschaft. Neue soziale Bewegungen in der Bundesrepublik.* Frankfurt a.M. and New York, Campus.

Bundesbank (1986), 'Die Belastung mit Sozialabgaben seit Beginn der siebziger Jahre', *Monatsberichte der Deutschen Bundesbank,* 38 (1), pp. 17–25.

Colchester, N. and Carr, J. (1986), 'The right to smile: a survey of West Germany', *Economist,* 301 (7475), 6 December 1986, pp. 1–30.

Deutsches Institut für Wirtschaftsforschung (DIW) (1982), 'Konjunkturelle Effekte der Finanzpolitik 1974 bis 1981', *DIW-Wochenbericht,* 49 (19), pp. 249–58.

Deutsches Institut für Wirtschaftsforschung (DIW) (1983), 'Restriktionspolitik behindert wirtschaftliche Erholung. Zur Entwicklung der öffentlichen Haushalte 1983/84', *DIW-Wochenbericht,* 50 (38), pp. 463–72.

Deutsches Institut für Wirtschaftsforschung (DIW) (1984), 'Defizitabbau behält Vorrang. Zur Entwicklung der öffentlichen Haushalte 1984/85', *DIW-Wochenbericht,* 51 (39), pp. 487–96.

Dyson, K. (1982), 'West Germany: the search for a rationalist consensus', pp. 17–47 in J. Richardson (ed.), *Policy Styles in Western Europe.* London, George Allen & Unwin.

Dyson, K. (1984), 'The politics of corporate crisis in West Germany', *West European Politics,* 7 (1), pp. 24–46.

Esser, J. (1982), *Gewerkschaften in der Krise.* Frankfurt a.M., Suhrkamp.

Esser, J. and Fach, W. (1981), 'Korporatistische Krisenregulierung im "Modell Deutschland" ', pp. 158–79 in U.v. Alemann (ed.), *Neokorporatismus.* Frankfurt and New York, Campus.

Esser, J., Fach, W. and Väth, W. (1983), *Krisenregulierung.* Frankfurt a.M., Suhrkamp.

FDP (1971), 'Die Freiburger Thesen', repr. as pp. 419–58 in R. Kunz, H. Maier and T. Stammen (eds.) (1979), *Programme der politischen Parteien in der Bundesrepublik Deutschland,* 3rd edn. München, C. H. Beck.

Feist, U., Krieger, H. and Uttitz, P. (1983), 'Das Wahlverhalten der Arbeiter bei der Bundestagswahl 1983', *Gewerkschaftliche Monatshefte,* 34 (7), pp. 414–27.

Grande, E. (1987), 'Neoconservatism and conservative–liberal economic policy in West Germany', *European Journal of Political Research,* 15, pp. 281–96.

Hauff, V. and Scharpf, F. W. (1975), *Modernisierung der Volkswirtschaft: Technologiepolitik als Strukturpolitik.* Köln and Frankfurt a.M., EVA.

Hoffmann, J. (1983), 'SPD-Wirtschaftspolitik – am Ende des "Keynesianischen Projekts"?', pp. 116–44 in B. Zeuner (ed.), *Genossen, was nun? Bilanz und Perspektiven sozialdemokratischer Politik.* Hamburg, Konkret Literatur Verlag.

Jacobi, O. (1986), 'Economic development and trade union collective bargaining policy since the middle of the 1970s', pp. 213–35 in O. Jacobi, B. Jessop, H. Kastendiek and M. Regini (eds), *Economic Crisis, Trade Unions and the State.* London, Croom Helm.

Jänicke, M. (1986), *Staatsversagen: Die Ohnmacht der Politik in der Industriegesellschaft.* München and Zürich, Piper.

Kloten, N., Ketterer, K.–H. and Vollmer, R. (1985), 'West Germany's stabilization performance', pp. 353–402 in L. Lindberg and C. S. Maier (eds), *The Politics of Inflation and Economic Stagnation.* Washington DC, Brookings.

Kohl, H. (1982), 'Regierungserklärung vom 13. Oktober 1982', pp. 7213–29 in *Verhandlungen des Deutschen Bundestages, Sten. Berichte,* vol. 112. Bonn.

Markovits, A. (1982), *The Political Economy of West Germany: Modell Deutschland.* New York, Praeger.

Müller, E. (1984), 'Umweltpolitik der sozial–liberalen Koalition', *Zeitschrift für Umweltpolitik,* 7 (2), pp. 115–41.

Paterson, W. and Smith, G. (eds) (1981), *The West German Model.* London, Frank Cass.

Richardson, J. and Watts, N. S. J. (1985), *National Policy Styles and the Environment: Britain and West Germany compared.* Berlin, Wissenschaftszentrum, discussion paper IIUG dp 85–16.

Roth, R. (1980a), 'Das Ende des politischen Biedermeier? Bürgerinitiativen in der Bundesrepublik', pp. 203–35 in V. Brandes, J. Hirsch and R. Roth (eds), *Leben in der Bundesrepublik. Krise des Alltags.* Berlin, Olle & Wolter.

Roth, R. (1980b), 'Notizen zur politischen Geschichte der Bürgerinitiativen in der Bundesrepublik', pp. 74–96 in R. Roth (ed.), *Parlamentarisches Ritual und politische Alternativen.* Frankfurt and New York, Campus.

Schäfer, C. (1982), 'Verteilungs– und Beschäftigungswirkungen von Operation '82, Gemeinschaftsinitiative und Operation '83", *WSI-Mitteilungen,* 35 (10), pp. 579–87.

Scharpf, F. W. (1987), *Sozialdemokratische Krisenpolitik in Westeuropa: Das 'Modell Deutschland' im Vergleich.* Frankfurt and New York, Campus.

Scharpf, F. W., Reissert, B. and Schnabel, F. (1976), *Politikverflechtung: Theorie und Empirie des kooperativen Föderalismus in der Bundesrepublik.* Kronberg, Scriptor.

Schmidt, H. (1975), 'Erklärung der Bundesregierung zur Rezession der Weltwirtschaft und zu binnenwirtschaftlichen Gegenmaßnahmen', pp. 12,885–98 in *Verhandlungen des Deutschen Bundestages, Sten. Berichte,* vol. 94. Bonn.

Schmidt, M. G. (1978), 'Die "Politik der inneren Reformen" in der Bundesrepublik seit 1969', pp. 30–81 in C. Fenner, K. Heyder and J. Strasser (eds), *Unfähig zur Reform? Eine Bilanz der inneren Reformen.* Köln and Frankfurt a.M., EVA.

Schmollinger, H. W. and Stöss, R. (1984), 'Bundestagswahlen und soziale Basis politischer Parteien in der Bundesrepublik (III): Das Scheitern der Sozialliberalen Koalition', *Prokla,* 14 (3), pp. 21–50.

Wey, K.–G. (1982), *Umweltpolitik in Deutschland.* Opladen, Westdeutscher Verlag.

5 Crisis politics in Denmark 1974 – 1987

ERIK DAMGAARD

Important events 1973–87

1973	parliamentary election creates fragmented party system Liberal minority government
1975	parliamentary election Social Democratic minority government legislation settles major labour market conflict
1977	parlimentary election legislation settles major labour market conflict
1978	a 'historic' experiment: Social Democrats and Liberals form coalition government
1979	legislation settles major labour market conflict coalition government breaks down parlimentary election Social Democratic minority government
1981	parliamentary election
1982	Social Democratic government resigns minority coalition government of Conservatives, Liberals, Centre Democrats, and Christian People's Party
1984	parliamentary election caused by the rejection of the government's budget proposal
1985	legislation settles major labour market conflict
1986	government wins referendum on the EC Common Act reform
1987	parliamentary election

Introduction

Towards the end of 1973 Denmark faced very serious economic problems and new political challenges. The economic problems were triggered off by the first oil price increases during the months of October–December. The political difficulties were created by the 'electoral earthquake' of 4 December *and* the need for coping with the new economic problems. Both sets of problems emerged at a time when people and politicians had become used to economic prosperity and political stability. This chapter first describes the perceptions of the economic crisis and the general reactions to it. Then some more specific issues and the way they were handled by different governments are analysed, and finally the overall results of crisis managment are evaluated.

Perceptions of the economic crisis

The period 1958–73 is a unique growth period in Danish economic history. A number of factors contributed to high growth in that particular period, such as the growth of other European economies, liberalization of trade in Europe, increasing international trade and improved terms of trade, and such domestic factors as a growing number of entrants into the labour market (young people, women, foreign workers) and migration from agriculture to urban industries. However, balance-of-payments problems were present as always, and towards the end of the period inflation soared. The period also saw a dramatic growth in the public sector and a concomitant steep rise in the level of taxation. It was generally hoped that Denmark's entry into the EEC in 1973 would help to solve at least the balance-of-payments problem.

December 1973 marked the end of the traditional Danish party system (Damgaard, 1974; cf. Table 5.1 below). Prior to the election of 4 December the Social Democrats were in office (1971–3) relying on the support of the Socialist People's Party for majority formation on important issues. The opposition consisted of former coalition government partners (1968–71): Radical Liberals, Liberals, and Conservatives. All these parties lost heavily at the election, which produced a highly fragmented parliament of 10 parties by the addition of five new parties, most notably the Progress Party and the Centre Democrats. Traditional patterns of government formation were impossible in the new parliament, and to this day no majority government has been formed.

Although the change in party politics occurred at the same time as the first oil price shock, it was not caused by it or even related to it. The sudden realignment was apparently conditioned by a number of long-term changes in the class composition of the electorate, short-term factors such a the rapid increase in taxation, an electoral system without strong barriers against new parties, and the appearance of new and unorthodox party leaders capable of using the persuasive power of television (cf. the interpretation in Pedersen, 1983). Thus a new party system, created towards the end of an economic boom period, had to manage society during the economic recession to come. This turned out to be extremely difficult. In the decade after 1973 five elections were held and five different (minority) governments have tried to cope with the economic problems.

The main problem in Danish economic policy-making was traditionally considered to be the issue of employment versus balance-of-payments. During the 1960s full employment had been achieved at the cost of a balance-of-payments deficit (except for a single year). In the slow growth period to come, unemployment started to increase, and so did the balance-of-payments deficit. To make things worse inflation also increased, and over the years recurring balance-of-payments deficits accumulated to become a major new burden on the Danish economy. Compared to previous experiences these combined developments amounted to an economic crisis. But the crisis was perceived differently by important actors.

Denmark is one of the 'small states in world markets' (to quote Katzenstein, 1985). Because of it smallness, lack of natural resources and open economy the country is heavily influenced by international economic developments that it cannot control but can only adjust to or learn to live with. The crisis of 1974 was orginally considered to be a temporary phenomenon. It required some short-term economic measures and was then assumed, or hoped, to pass away.

The hope turned out to be illusory. The economic problems were not solved by the numerous attempts in the decade to come. The problems were indeed very real, but their solutions were impeded by the lack of élite consensus on the nature of the crisis and the appropriate measures to be taken. The left-wing parties (Communists, Left Socialists, Socialist People's Party) perceived the economic problems as a crisis of the capitalist system of production. Therefore the problems could only be solved through fundamental structural change of society and the international economy. The Social Democrats did not go that far, but found that the growing unemployment, in particular, demonstrated the inherent problems of economic liberalism. Eventually the problems would have to be solved through economic democracy which would make incomes policy and wage restraint feasible and justifiable. The major bourgeois parties, on the other hand, tended to think that the growth of the public sector had got out of control and pointed to the need for increased productivity and international competitiveness of the private sector (Svensson, 1983).

The fragmentation of the party system and the diverging perceptions of the economic problems aggravated the difficulties of crisis management. There was no majority party, no majority coalition, not even an informal working majority of the type that had been quite common in the past (cf. Damgaard,

1969). As the Social Democratic parliamentary spokesman stated in October 1976: 'When we had greater political stability then we have today, the problems were lesser. Now, as the problems have grown, and as new ones have emerged, we have the greatest political disruption in memory' (quoted in Svensson, 1983, p. 297; my translation). Decisions could only be made through cooperation and compromise among a number of parties – in practical terms excluding the parties on the left wing and the (protest) Progress party on the right wing.

General reactions to economic crisis

The politico-economic responses to the post-1974 crisis may be grouped into three sets of factors: budgetary changes, party political reactions, and policy strategies. However it is difficult, or even impossible, to argue that all of these changes were caused solely by the new economic problems. Nevertheless, it seems fruitful to list three sets of developments that characterized the period under study even if their causes may be of a more complex nature.

As mentioned above, public expenditure and the level of taxation increased sharply prior to 1974. The trend continued after 1974 although the reduced economic growth made it much more problematic. In 1973 total taxes amounted to 42.5 per cent of the GNP, in 1985 they had increased to 47 per cent. However, total public expenditure grew at a much faster rate and consequently had to be financed by enormous budget deficits from the late 1970s. The traditional budget surplus gave way to deficit which in 1982 amounted to almost 10 per cent of the GNP (Esping-Andersen, 1985).

Two budgetary developments (in addition to a recurring balance-of-payment deficit) are particularly visible as responses to the post-1974 crisis. The first is related to unemployment which increased from 1 per cent of the labour force in 1973 to almost 11 per cent in 1983. Unemployment support accounted for about 1 per cent of the total public expenditure in 1973 and for 8.5 per cent in 1983. The second is payment of interest on public debt which increased from about 2 per cent of the total expenditure in 1974 to almost 13 per cent in 1983. Taken together these 'new' types of expenditure thus accounted for no less than 21 per cent of all public expenditure in 1983.

The 'political disruption' referred to in the quotation above is illustrated in Table 5.1 which shows the party composition of the Danish *Folketing* since 1971. A number of important observations can be made from the table. First one notes as a sign of political instability that eight elections have been held during the last sixteen years. It should be added that all post-1974 elections – as well as all governments formed and dissolved – were centred on the issue of how to handle the serious economic problems. Secondly, as many as nine to eleven parties have been represented in parliament since 1973. Thirdly, the fates of the various parties have been very different. Thus the Socialist People's Party declined during the 1970s then more than regained its strength during the 1980s. Conversely, the Social Democrats regained strength after the mid-1970s but again lost support in the 1980s. The Radical Liberals and the Liberals never recovered from the defeat in 1973 (except for the Liberal victory in 1975 after a brief period in government). The Conservatives, on the other hand, have managed to increase their support at each election since 1975 (except for the most recent one). The Progress Party started to decline in the late 1970s and became an almost insignificant party after the election of 1984. However it recovered somewhat in 1987.

Table 5.1 Party composition of the Danish parliament (*Folketing*) after elections 1971-87

Number of seats*	Election month and year							
Party	Sept. 1971	Dec. 1973	Jan. 1975	Febr. 1977	Oct. 1979	Dec. 1981	Jan. 1984	Sept. 1987
Common Course	—	—	—	—	—	—	—	4
Communists		6	7	7				
Left Socialists			4	5	6	5	5	
Socialist People's Party	17	11	9	7	11	21	21	27
Social Democrats	70	46	53	65	68	59	56	54
Radical Liberals	27	20	13	6	10	9	10	11
Justice Party		5		6	5			
Centre Democrats	—	14	4	11	6	15	8	9
Christian People's Party		7	9	6	5	4	5	4
Liberals	30	22	42	21	22	20	22	19
Conservatives	31	16	10	15	22	26	42	38
Progress Party	—	28	24	26	20	16	6	9
Total	175	175	175	175	175	175	175	175

Note: *Excluding 4 representatives from Greenland and the Faroe Islands.

The fragmented party system made government formation difficult and majority governments almost impossible. Table 5.2 lists the Danish government parties since the early 1970s. For about a year after the 'electoral earthquake' of 1973 a Liberal government was in power on the basis of only 22 seats. It was followed by a Social Democratic minority government which had to compromise with parties on its right in order to pass legislation. Several years of unstable minority government persuaded the Liberal and Social Democratic leaders to a 'historic' experiment in 1978, namely a coalition government of the two parties. While the government did not quite command a parliamentary majority it was virtually impossible to defeat. However, the coalition lasted only about a year and broke down because of internal disagreement (which had never before happened to a coalition government) about policies to fight the economic crisis. For another three years the Social Democrats ruled from a minority position. Being unable to attract support for its economic policies, the government resigned in 1982. It was followed by a minority coalition of the four Liberal–Conservative parties. The government survived the election of 1984 caused by a rejection of its budget proposal and, albeit with reduced strength, the election of 1987.

Table 5.2 Governing parties in Denmark since 1971

	Party (seats)
September 1971–December 1973	Social Democrats (70)
December 1973–February 1975	Liberals (22)
February 1975–August 1978	Social Democrats (53, 65)
August 1978–October 1979	Coalition of Social Democrats (65) and Liberals (21)
October 1979–September 1982	Social Democrats (68, 59)
September 1982–	Coalition of Conservatives (26, 42, 38) Liberals (20, 22, 19) Centre Democrats (15, 8, 9) Christian People's Party (4, 5, 4)

For a few years after 1974 the governments attempted, without much success, to overcome the possibly temporary economic problems by using various traditional policy instruments. As unemployment continued to rise the Social Democrats in close cooperation with the trade unions developed new programmes to promote employment. The programmes were gradually expanded in the late 1970s and early 1980s to form part of a more comprehensive 'general crisis policy' (Buksti, 1984, p. 235). The Social Democrats had more ambitious plans than those that could be adopted in parliament. In particular they failed to obtain a majority for enacting an economic democracy scheme that would establish wage-earner funds and increase the influence of labour unions. The plans for economic democracy or profit-sharing were intended not only to solve basic economic problems through wage-restraint and increased investment in the private production sector, but also to democratize society and the economy.

In principle all important parties realized a need for incomes policies to reduce costs of production, increase international competitiveness and reduce the balance-of-payments deficit. However, as with the economic democracy issue, the Social Democratic approach differed from that of the Liberal and Conservative parties. According to the Social Democrats, incomes policies should be made through the cooperation and consent of the labour unions (but not necessarily the employers' organizations). The Social

Democrats had about ten such major proposals passed while in office in 1975–82 (Kjaersgaard and Hansen, 1984, pp. 134f). The bourgeois parties, on the other hand, were prepared to impose policies without such cooperation and consent, as indeed they did after coming to office in 1982. Generally their approach was to promote private business activity; and to 'modernize' the public sector within the existing level of expenditures.

Issues and policies

Economic policies

In party political terms the period 1975–82 is one of Social Democratic predominance. Their leader Mr Anker Jorgensen was Prime Minister throughout the period although never in a majority position. Whatever the Social Democrats attempted in order to fight the economic crisis had to be negotiated and agreed with other parties. In proposing policies the Social Democrats also kept their close links with the trade unions, although the relationship was severely strained during the short 'historical' coalition experiment with the Liberals in 1978–9.

The main policies adopted by the Social Democrats included incomes policy, tax increases, devaluations and modest cuts of some public expenditures. On three occasions (1975, 1977, 1979) incomes policies were associated with government intervention to settle major disputes in the labour market, after breakdowns of collective bargaining. In addition, the Social Democrats steadily expanded employment programmes, including a new voluntary retirement scheme and special measures to combat unemployment among young peope. Finally they tried in vain to enlist support for a mandatory profit-sharing scheme in 1979 and 1981.

A new and comprehensive package along similar lines was prepared and discussed with other parties in the summer of 1982 but failed to attract support. Consequently, the Social Democrats realized that their possibilities had been exhausted and left office without calling an election (as they had done without success in December 1981).

In 1982 the economic problems were indeed agonising despite the numerous efforts to cope with them during the preceding eight years. Thus in 1982 unemployment as well as inflation averaged 10 per cent, the interest rate was 20 per cent, the balance-of-payments deficit 4 per cent of the GNP, and the public deficit almost 10 per cent of the GNP. The economic growth rate was 3 per cent after two years of negative growth.

The new Liberal–Conservative minority government (Table 5.2) presented its policy to parliament in October 1982. In its form and content the statement of the Prime Minister Mr Poul Schlüter (Conservative leader) deviated sharply from previous Social Democratic policy statements. The

Social Democratic strategy had called for 'bargained incomes policy', active government measures against unemployment, no major cuts in social welfare programmes or public sector employment, and economic democracy in the form of a mandatory profit-sharing scheme. The Liberal–Conservative approach flatly rejected mandatory economic democracy reforms and 'artificial' job creation programmes. The new governmental parties also rejected devaluation as an instrument of economic policy. Instead their programme contained two key elements: to promote the competitiveness of the private business sector through the reduction of interest rates, inflation and wage increases, and to reduce or limit public spending (*Folketingets forhandlinger,* 1982/83, col. 5–24).

Within a few weeks the new government managed to obtain majority support for its first crisis package (strongly opposed by the Social Democrats and the left-wing parties). The main ingredients of the incomes policy part was a five months wage freeze and suspension of indexation of wages for two and a half years. The suspension was later extended and the indexation has so far not been reintroduced. The main instruments for limiting public expenditure were cuts in social welfare benefits (excluding old age pensions, however), a waiting day for sickness benefits, and increased contributions by employees and employers for unemployment insurance.

The passage of this initial set of bills reflected the Liberal–Conservative government's desire to govern, and if necessary to impose tough decisions without consulting important groups in society. This applied particularly to the labour unions which had negotiated collective agreements with the employers, which now became significantly modified by legislation. Such legislation was unprecedented and could only be adopted through the support of the Radical Liberals and the Progress Party. It was a forceful step, a clear change in policy style facilitated by the resignation of the Social Democratic government and the widespread feeling of economic crisis demanding a tough response.

However, the governing parties also had to change some of their own policy ideas. They wanted to avoid tax increases, not least because past increases were thought to be a major explanation for the electoral success of the Progress Party. They had actively opposed Social Democratic plans for a new tax on pension funds. After the change of government they made a sudden U-turn and passed such legislation in cooperation with the Social Democrats. The government had to resort to tax increases on several other occasions: October 1983, May 1984, April 1985, December 1985, March 1986, October 1986. As a result of these increases the level of taxation reached a historic level of about 51 per cent of the GNP. In addition, payments to mandatory social security and educational schemes were increased, as were user charges for public services. The latter two types of public revenue are not called taxes but – like real expenditure cuts – 'budget improvements' necessary to counteract the permanent pressure for increasing expenditures (*Budgetredegorelse, 1975,* pp. 63–5).

A minority government is always vulnerable. In December 1983 the government's budget was defeated because the Progress Party refused to assume responsibility for it, and because the Social Democrats did not want to step in to save the government – although normally they would vote for the budget (Rasmussen, 1985). The ensuing election turned out to strengthen the bargaining position of the Liberal–Conservative government. The Progress Party lost heavily (and two of its six MPs soon defected from the party), while the governing parties increased their joint share of the seats. With the support of three MPs from the Greenland and the Faroe Islands the government could form a working majority with the Radical Liberals. Soon they reached an agreement about continued incomes policies and efforts to limit public spending. Their most spectacular initiative was legislation settling a major dispute on the labour market along these lines in March 1985, regardless of the views of other parties and protesting unions.

In the main, the economic policy of the government was thus enacted through cooperation with the Radical Liberals. The two main ingredients were imposed incomes policy and limits on public expenditure. While some real cuts were made, the government also had to increase revenue by other 'budget improvements' and by changing its originally stated anti-tax-policy. The latter policy change was facilitated by the gradual weakening of the Progress Party.

A final and important element in the efforts to limit public expenditure was 'decentralization of budgetary problems' to local governments. Prior to 1982 the government and the local government organizations had agreed to keep increases of total local government expenditures within limits gradually to be reduced from one year to the next. This procedure for 'budget-cooperation' (Friisberg, 1984) between the state and local governments was continued after the change of government in 1982 with the purpose of introducing zero-growth in real terms for 1983 and 1984. From 1983 the government, supported by the Radical Liberals, in addition reduced the general state grants to an amount considered sufficient (assuming no change in local tax levels) to finance unchanged activities in the local sector as a whole. In 1985 the government introduced economic sanctions to be applied against individual local governments not keeping expenditure levels for 1986, whereas in the past the ceilings aimed at aggregate local government spending. The overall result of these measures is a centralization of financial policy and a reduction of local government autonomy with respect to the levels of taxing and spending, although the ceilings and sanctions decided for 1987 and 1988 are less severe than those for 1986.

Economic policy, broadly conceived, has been the core area for inter-party competition in Danish politics at least since the Second World War. The new economic problems of the 1970s further emphasized the importance of the economic policy dimension. The Liberal–Conservative government highlighted the economic issue by making it *the* issue for governmental performance and survival. It decided to govern in economic policy matters and, being a minority government, to yield or compromise in numerous other matters (see below). Only in the EC Common Act issue of 1986 did the government not accept a defeat in parliament. It appealed to the people, the majority of whom supported the government view in a referendum.

The rather surprising response of the government to defeat in parliament added a new plebiscitarian element to Danish politics. The referendum is part of Danish constitutional procedures concerning constitutional amendments, change of voting age, and – on certain conditions – with respect to the transfer of sovereignty to international organizations and to bills passed by parliament. It is therefore rather familiar in Danish political history. But the EC Common Act referendum was of a very special nature. Not only was it consultative, it was also used as a means for a defeated government to reverse a majority decision in parliament. It could only be used that way because a parliamentary majority, including the Social Democrats and the Radical Liberals who both voted 'no' to the Common Act, accepted the procedure and made known in advance that they would also accept the verdict of the people.

While the government attached overriding importance to its economic policies it was also committed to a major programme designed to modernize the public sector.

Modernization of the public sector

The initial policy statement of 5 October 1982 contained only a few references to envisaged changes in the scope, structure and function of the public sector. But the 'new government which today presents a new policy to the *Folketing*' (*Folketingets forhandlinger,* 1982/83, col. 5) none the less created expectations of major changes in the mass public. The government immediately launched a deregulation campaign supposed to eliminate or simplify public rules and regulations, and later reported to parliament about the plans and preliminary results (*Folketingets forhandlinger*, 1982/83, cols 10218–30; 1983/84, cols 6962–72). Hundreds of rules were in fact abolished or simplified. There is no reason to question the sincerity of the government, but the whole operation is probably best regarded as an exercise in symbolic politics since ordinary citizens hardly noticed any real changes, despite all the campaign publicity.

The new government also stimulated a debate on privatization. In March 1983 a committee of civil servants was set up to investigate various possibilites for privatization of public tasks. The somewhat cautious report (*Rapport,* 1983), published in December 1983, only had marginal effects and the whole initiative was perhaps an 'ideological crusade' rather than a pursuit of realistic policy alternatives (cf. Kristensen, 1984).

Meanwhile the government had developed and presented a new and more comprehensive programme for modernization of the public sector (*Folketingets forhandlinger*, 1983/84, cols 2380–91, 5998–6050). The programme incorporated the previous attempts at deregulation and privatization, although the latter (and not very popular) term was hardly used anymore, and added some new elements. The overall purpose of modernization is to renew and improve public services within the limits of existing resources. To justify the programme the government argued that since further public sector growth was precluded for economic reasons, new tasks and problems could only be handled by changing priorities within the existing level of expenditure.

An important part of the modernization programme were changes in budgetary procedures some of which had been prepared by a committee set up by the former Social Democratic government (Nielsen, 1984). Numerous reforms of budgetary and planning instruments during the 1960s and 1970s had not been effective in so far as expenditure regularly surpassed planned spending limits (Christensen, 1982). From 1984 on however, ceilings for the total net expenditures have been introduced for each ministry. Thus a minister wanting to spend money on new activities is required to reduce (net) expenditure for other purposes. Such ceilings are potentially very important instruments, but the problem is that they may be ignored by parliamentary majorities with or without governmental approval (Haarder, 1985). Other changes in the procedures aimed at decentralization of budgetary powers and responsibilites within established limits.

The idea of privatization survived and acquired a new label in the modernization programme. The government emphasized the need for 'self-regulatory' and market mechanisms in the allocation of public money to increase the efficiency and flexibility of public institutions and to mitigate the pressure for increase of expenditures.

The modernization programme contained three additional elements: a campaign to improve public services vis-à-vis clients and customers, financial support for acquisition of new information technology, and various measures to improve the qualifications and skills of public leaders and personnel.

Most elements of the modernization programme were not really new in the sense that they had not been proposed or discussed before. The novelty was rather that the government combined a number of different instruments in what appeared to be a general overhaul of the public sector. In a sense the modernization programme was parallel to the economic policy described above, although the effects are less certain and more difficult to measure. Public institutions are not easily changed but at least the government *did* something, and its modernization programme caused the first genuine debate in parliament on the structure, function and development of the public sector since the early 1970s. According to the Minister of Finance, the government will evaluate the effects of the various measures in 1987 (*Folketingets forhandlinger,* 1985, col. 8985).

The symbolic uses of the modernization programme should not be underestimated. The programme signifies a desire to change and renew outdated organizational patterns and procedures, to some extent by drawing on experience from the management of private business companies. However the broad scope of the programme makes it very difficult to identify initiatives or proposals by the government that are *not* part of the great modernization effort one way or another. But that may be part of the trick.

Other issues and change of governmental style

While not insignificant, the modernization efforts were clearly less important to the government than its general economic policy, including the expenditure ceilings. The supreme goal of the government was to help the Danish economy recover after many years of alleged Social Democratic mismanagement. The strategy for achieving this overall purpose involved a quite remarkable change in governmental style compared with traditional norms of parliamentary government. To have its economic policies adopted (through close cooperation with Radical Liberals) the government had to accept a number of defeats in areas that, according to the government, were not vital to its overall performance.

In the past governments, and particularly minority governments, had accepted the need for compromises and in rare cases even defeats in parliament. However the Liberal–Conservative government has accepted defeats to an unprecedented extent in order to stay in power. Only on two occasions did the government not accept a defeat: it called an election when its budget proposal was rejected in December 1983, and it initiated the successful referendum in February 1986 after a parliamentary 'no' to the EC Common Act.

During the first four years of Liberal–Conservative governance (September 1982–September 1986), twenty-eight bills and thirty proposed resolutions were passed against the will of the governing parties. In addition thirty 'motions on the order of business' ending debates on interpellations were carried against the government. Since none of them expressed lack of confidence, the government could stay in office, albeit at a visible price in terms of unwanted policy decisions in many areas. The key player in parliamentary decision-making was the small Radical Liberal Party. It made economic policy decisions with the government and formed what is often referred to as an 'alternative majority' with the Social Democrats and left-wing parties in several other issues.

The alternative majority made rather spectacular decisions in various foreign policy areas, notably security policy. In these matters the alternative majority represents a concern with peace issues, opposition to NATO missiles and the American SDI, support for nuclear-free zones in Europe and the Nordic region, as well as some more traditional anti-NATO sentiments.

The result has been a long series of foreign policy confrontations in which the alternative majority instructed a rather hesitant government to follow the majority guidelines in the conduct of Danish foreign policy. However, the alternative majority was not confined to foreign policy but encompassed several domestic policy areas as well. Thus the alternative majority urged the government to forget about nuclear power as a possibility in Denmark and instead to promote the development of new and permanent energy sources. It also put pressure on the government in environmental matters, it demanded more public spending for cultural purposes, 'progressive' reforms in legal and judicial areas, and so on.

In sum, the government gave top priority to economic policy and decided to accept severe restrictions in other areas, in particular foreign policy, to pursue the overall economic goals. This amounts to a quite unconventional style of parliamentary government in Denmark as does the successful appeal to the people in the EC issue.

The results and lessons of crisis management

The economic problems emerging in the mid-1970s were extremely serious when the Liberal–Conservative government took office in 1982 (see above). How successful have its policy responses been? What did the economic situation look like five years later? What can be learned from the experiences with respect to governance in a small open democracy facing challenges?

New and old types of policy responses

The most conspicuous change in policy style since the mid-1970s is the firm determination with which the Liberal–Conservative government attempted to solve the economic problems. It involved imposed incomes policies and strong efforts to limit state and local government spending despite opposition within and outside parliament. In these respects there were no genuine consultations with important interest groups, or tripartite negotiations of the kind recommended by the Social Democrats. The relative success of this change of policy style was presumably preconditioned by the voluntary resignation of the previous government and by the general feeling that tough measures had to be taken (cf. Eldrup, 1985). In the long run the impositional style may become more problematic.

The government also made some rather well-known responses to economic challenges. In the 1982 policy statement it refused to raise taxes to reduce the public deficit, but soon made a U-turn and raised taxes on several occasions as supplements to 'budget improvements' by other means. The government did not like the ensuing high level of taxation and preferred to talk about a spectacular reduction of the huge public deficit inherited from the Social Democrats. The change in taxation policy was facilitated by the gradual erosion of the support for the anti-tax Progress Party that had previously made tax increases dangerous (Esping-Andersen, 1985). In cooperation with the Social Democrats the government introduced new kinds of taxes on pension funds, business firms and financial institutions, which it is claimed, while increasing the total level of taxation, makes it possible to reduce the taxation of 'households' (*Finansredegørelse 86,* 1985, ch. IX).

The economic policies of the government were associated with a change of political rhetoric. To underscore the predicament of the Danish economy the previous Social Democratic Minister of Finance had used the parable of a 'movement towards the abyss'. The 'new government' with its 'new policy' wanted to restore, redress or reconstruct (*genoprette*) the Danish economy. It also wanted to 'recreate courage and optimism' in business and in the whole population, and 'make it easier to be a Dane'.

Along with a change in rhetoric went a search for new solutions to the problems of the expanded public sector. The first catchwords coined, or perhaps imported from abroad, were 'deregulation' and 'privatization', later to be subsumed by the heterogeneous 'modernization' programme. While parts of the programme may turn out to be important, in particular the new budgetary procedures, most of it is probably of a rather symbolic nature, indicating a sincere willingness to do something new and different while not being able to do very much with respect to reorganization of the public sector.

Finally, the style of governmental policy-making changed markedly in the sense that the government 'abdicated' without resigning in some non-economic areas, notably security policy, while appealing to the people in the EC issue, to get through with its general economic policy. In these ways the government changed informal norms of Danish parliamentary government in order to control the overall economic policy. How successful then were its economic policies?

Economic indicators

According to several economic indicators (*OECD Economic Outlook 38*, 1985; *Finansredegørelse 86,* 1985; Smatryk n. 51, 1986) the Liberal–Conservative govenment has been very successful in fighting the economic crisis. The inflation rate has been reduced to a few per cent, and the interest rate is halved compared to that of 1982. The huge public deficit almost vanished during 1985 and turned into a surplus in 1986. Furthermore, unemployment has been reduced by about 2 per cent to 8 per cent of the (still expanding) labour force. Most remarkable in this respect is that more than 90 per cent of the new jobs were created in the private sector of the economy, thus completely reversing the trend of the previous decades when private sector employment shrunk and public employment grew. The government also managed to minimize, but not to eliminate, the growth of the public expenditure in real terms. This means that the disappearance of the public deficit was caused not by real budget cuts but by increased tax revenue. In fact today the level of taxation is higher than ever (51 per cent of the GNP compared to 45 per cent in 1982). The success story has a darker side, however, namely the balance-of-payments deficit which is also higher than ever (4.6 per cent of the GNP compared to 4.1 in 1982). Thus, while economic improvements are clearly visible, the old issues of unemployment and balance-of-payments are still on the agenda. The former is expected to increase and the latter to improve according to all economic forecasts.

It is difficult, and perhaps impossible, to measure the specific effects of the government's economic policies on these developments compared to those of the changing international economic conditions. Reduced inflation and interest rates are not peculiar to Denmark, and decreasing oil prices from 1983, and particularly from 1985, onwards improved the terms of trade. On the other hand there can be no doubt that the tough incomes policies, the efforts to limit state and local government spending, the stable exchange rate, and tax increases contributed significantly to the overall result. While international economic developments continue to be important, the Liberal–Conservative government has demonstrated the feasibility of independent, and tough, policy adjustments.

The initial drive of the government is losing momentum, however. First, the government's incomes policy may become less feasible and successful in the future. The government effectively controlled salaries in the public sector, but the wage limits imposed in 1985 were not in fact kept in the private sector. This development, as well as problems resulting from decisions to abolish the waiting day for sickness benefits and to shorten the working week by one hour in 1987, made the collective bargainings on the labour market in the spring of 1987 a major challenge to the government. The outcome was a peaceful settlement and substantial pay increases for public employees. The government also realized that its incomes policies were not sufficient to reduce the balance of payments deficit. It therefore launched new and more selective programmes of which the most significant so far is a plan, from 1986, to promote research and development, particularly in high technological areas.

Secondly, public expenditure may become harder to control. As the budget deficit is turned into a surplus, new pressures for increased spending are building up (even though the total public debt is higher than ever.) Public employees in particular do not seem to acknowledge a need for the tight expenditure policy that the govenment wants to continue, and the governing parties lost seats in the election of September 1987.

Democracy and political performance

The new economic and political problems of the mid-1970s amounted to a crisis in the sense that all economic indicators looked gloomy, while the profoundly changed party system was no longer able to sustain stable governments. Although the parliamentary system of government did not break down, and although it was not basically transformed as a result of the new challenges (Svensson, 1983a), it is worthwhile to investigate how well or badly it performed, and how it was affected by the attempts at crisis management. In order to do so, one needs criteria of evaluation that include more than economic indicators. Two dimensions of political performance are appropriate in the present context, namely decisional efficacy and legitimacy.

According to Ekstein (1971, p. 65) decisional efficacy denotes 'the extent to which polities make and carry out proper and relevant decisions in response to political challenges'. Decisional efficacy is hard to operationalize and measure, but Eckstein suggests two general ways of approaching a measurement: budgeting and the allocation of authoritative roles. Budgeting is about the magnitude of resources extracted from society and the reallocation of resources for various purposes, and authoritative role allocation concerns formation and maintenance of governments.

The analysis of Danish developments indeed seems to support the argument on the importance of budgeting and role allocation. At the centre has been economic policy, including the budget, and party competition for governmental office. Has the Danish system performed well or badly with respect to decisional efficacy? The answer depends upon the specific criteria used. Eckstein suggests that decisional efficacy is high to the extent that decisions about budgets and role allocation (a) are taken with promptness and dispatch; (b) involve only a limited amount of élite-dissension; (c) are arrived at by normal deliberative processes.

Promptness and dispatch are not the most proper terms for normal economic or budgetary decision-making in Denmark. Often decision-making has extended over long periods, sometimes no proper decisions could be made, and the budget proposal was even defeated in 1983. On the other hand some decisions were made with promptness and dispatch, including legislation to end major conflicts on the labour market in the 1970s; and in particular several decisions made more recently by the working coalition of the government and the Radical Liberals. The latter decisions are obviously related to the more solid base acquired by the government after the election of 1984. However, that solid base disappeared at the 1987 election, and the pre-1984 pattern of unstable minority government re-emerged.

Élite dissension in economic policy-making has not increased during the economic crisis, but it has become more visible to the general public. This visibility is not least related to the cooperation between the government and the Radical Liberals. An economic two-bloc system appeared to be developing, reminiscent of the pre-1973 period. The outcome is not more élite dissension but a clearer and more visible structure of élite divergencies; that however does not inhibit broadly based compromises in some cases.

In the main, normal deliberative processes were used in economic policy-making. But some important changes of governmental policy style have been noted. The 'alternative majority' and the 'plebiscitarian' element, mentioned above, should not necessarily be evaluated as signs of poor performance. They could also testify to the quite remarkable adaptability of a democratic system of government, the basic features of which are still intact.

The overall decision efficacy was clearly reduced during the 1970s, but then somewhat improved – at least temporarily – in the mid-1980s. The economic performance of an extreme multi-party system produced by a very liberal PR-electoral system presumably has some built-in limits that must be taken into account. This consideration brings us to the question of legitimacy.

Legitimacy refers to the extent that a polity is regarded by its members as worthy of support. There are many possible indicators and they all show that the Danes overwhelmingly support their democratic system of parliamentary government, despite the economic problems, conflicts about the proper size of the public sector and many other issues. The level of electoral turnout and that of many other political activities (Damgaard, 1980; Damgaard and Kristensen, 1982) are high, and there is no support for radically different forms of government. During the first years of economic crisis in the mid-1970s, there was much talk of political distrust, and electoral surveys indicated declining trust and perhaps a decline of legitimacy. These tendencies were soon reversed however, and by the mid-1980s things did not look very different from the pre-crisis period (Andersen, 1986).

In fact even if important economic problems have still not been solved, the Danes appear to be happier with their lives than other people in the European Community. In 1973 the Danes were not very satisfied with 'the way democracy worked', but a few years later only the Germans were consistently reported to be as satisfied as the Danes in that respect (*Eurobarometer*, 1985). As in other countries, the level of aspiration has been reduced in view of the economic problems. People have adjusted expectations and become more 'realistic' (cf. Olsen, 1983, ch. 2). But the Danish welfare state has proved to be robust in times of economic hardship. Privatization ideas do not fit well with the Danish political culture (and after all there is not much to privatize compared to other European countries).

The crisis affected the political parties differently. The predominant Social Democratic party failed in the end to develop a working anti-crisis policy. This presented the Liberal–Conservative parties with an opportunity to test their own approach, which they did with considerable success in cooperation with the Radical Liberals. However their tiny majority disappeared at the 1987 election. The Social Democratic leader

Mr Anker Jorgensen, having lost three elections, decided to step down in September 1987 and was replaced by the former Minister of Labour Mr Svend Auken. Thus the stage was set for a new chapter in Danish politics.

Acknowledgements

The author received valuable comments on an earlier draft from several colleagues, civil servants and politicians. While assuming responsibility for remaining errors of fact and judgment, he wants to thank (in addition to members of the research group) Finn Bruun, Jacob A. Buksti, Jorgen Gronnegard Christensen, Bertel Haarder, Marius Ibsen, Oluf Ingvartsen, Carsten Jarlov, Noel Kent, Ole P. Kristensen, Johan P. Olsen, Erik Rasmussen, Erik Ib Schmidt and Niels Christian Sidenius.

References

Andersen, J. G. (1986), 'Electoral trends in Denmark in the 1980s', *Scandinavian Political Studies,* vol. 9, no. 2, pp. 157–75.

Budgetredegorelse (1985). Copenhagen, Ministry of Finance.

Buksti, J. A. (1984), 'Policy-making and unemployment in Denmark' in Richardson, J. J. and Henning, R. (eds), *Unemployment: policy responses of western democracies* London, Sage, pp. 217–37.

Christensen, J. G. (1982), 'Growth by exception: or the vain attempt to impose resource scarcity on the Danish public sector', *Journal of Public Policy,* vol. 2, pt 2, pp. 117–44.

Damgaard, E. (1969), 'The parliamentary basis of Danish government', *Scandinavian Political Studies,* vol. 4, pp. 30–57.

Damgaard, E. (1974), 'Stability and change in the Danish party system over half a century'. *Scandinavian Political Studies,* vol. 9, pp. 104–25.

Damgaard, E. (ed.) (1980), *Folkets veje i dansk politik.* Copenhagen, Schultz Forlag.

Damgaard, E. and Kristensen, O. P. (1982), 'Party government under pressure' in Anckar, D., Damgard, E. and Valen, H. (eds), *Partier, ideologier, väljare.* Åbo Akademi.

Eckstein, H. (1971), *The Evaluation of Political Performance.* Beverly Hills and London, Sage Publications.

Eldrup, A. (1985), 'Nye instrumenter i udgiftspolitikken', *Samfundsokonomen,* vol. 3, no. 8, pp. 4–7.

Espring-Andersen, G. (1985), 'Governmental responses to budget scarcity: Denmark', *Policy Studies Journal,* vol. 13, no. 3, pp. 534–46.

Euro-barometer, no. 24 (December 1985); no. 25 (June 1986). Brussels, Commission of the European Communities.

Finansredegorelse 86 (1985). Copenhagen, Ministry of Finance.

Friisberg, J. (1984), 'Statens styring af kommunerne: Budgetsamarbejdet' in Mouritzen, P. E. and Jensen, H. T. (eds), *Samspillet mellem staten og kommunerne.* Copenhagen, Jurist-og Okonomforbundets Forlag, 127–145.

Haarder, B. (1985), 'At fa styr pa e offentlige udgifter: En Sisyfosopgave', *Nordisk Administrativt Tiksskrift,* vol. 4, pp. 267–78.

Katzenstein, P. J. (1985), *Small States in World Markets.* Ithaca and London, Cornell University Press.

Kjaersgaard, K. and Hansen, E. D. (1984), *Dansk økonomisk politik.* Copenhagen, Nyt Nordisk Forlag.
Kristensen, O. P. (1984), 'Privatisering: modernisering af den offentlige sektor eller ideologisk korstog?' *Nordisk Administrativt Tidsskrift,* no. 2, pp. 96–117.
Nielsen, P. L. (1984), 'Den statslige budgetreform: Indhold og principper', *Nordisk Administrativt Tidsskrift,* vol. 3, pp. 283–93.
OECD Economic Outlook, 38, December 1985.
Olsen, J. P. (1983), *Organized Democracy.* Oslo, Universitetforlaget.
Pedersen, M. N. (1983), 'The defeat of all parties: the Danish Folketing election 1973', Occasional Paper no. 10. Department of Public Finance and Policy, Odense University.
Rapport (1983), *Rapport afgivet afprivatiseringsudvalget.* Copenhagen, Ministry of Finance.
Rasmussen, E. (1985), 'Finanslovsforkastelse i dansk parlamentarisme: Normer og konsekvenser', *Historie*, Ny raekke 16, 1–1985, pp. 55–118.
Rose, R. (1984), *Understanding Big Government.* London, Sage.
Smatryk no. 51. (1986). Copenhagen, Ministry of Finance.
Svensson, P. (1983), 'Politikerne og krisen', *Økonomi og Politik,* vol. 57, no. 4, pp. 287–300.
Svensson, P. (1983a), 'The crisis of democracy or the democracy of the crisis?' Paper presented at Meeting of the International Society of Political Psychology, Oxford, 10–22 July 1983.

6 The Netherlands and the crisis as a policy challenge: integration or ideological manoeuvres?

J. WIL FOPPEN

The crisis, its background and characteristics

From prosperity to stagnation

The evolution of the economy in the Netherlands since the Second World War can be divided into three phases. Since the initial strong growth in the early 1950s (Fortuyn, 1983, pp. 50-1), and after a period of prosperity (1959–73), several years of reduced growth (1973–9) followed. Eventually this resulted in an economic stagnation after 1979. From 1984 onwards the Dutch economy has recovered slightly. In general one might say that for most industrial countries 1985 was a transition year as far as government policy was concerned (Centraal Planbureau, 1986, p. 62).

Major economic problems are obviously the basic feature of the third phase. On the other hand it is also clear that some of these crisis phenomena originated in each of the two preceding periods. This is more or less evident as far as second phase developments are concerned, but could be a factor which is easily overlooked or underestimated when it comes to an assessment of the apparently happy and carefree 1959–73 period. This period of the Dutch economy has been called 'le miracle hollandaise', an essential element of which was the close cooperation between employers' initiatives and the government (Berge, 1986, p. 37).

At the end of the 1960s and in the early 1970s some highly significant symptoms manifested themselves. There had been a scarcity of labour at the turn of the 1950s and in the 1960s. Inflation, as a consequence of the accumulation of demands for higher wages, increased. Real wages increased faster than labour productivity, which led to reduced profits. During the 1960s unemployment rose due to the closure of mines and the decline of the textile and shipbuilding industry. At the same time there was a developing awareness of the relationship between the high density of industrial activity and pollution of the environment. People started to worry about these and other disadvantages of unrestrained economic expansion, such as the wastage of raw materials and energy.

Fears of the possibility of turmoil and serious disruption of the financial world and international banking, at the end of 1971, had an unfavourable influence on the general economic situation and on the business outlook. The economy was again shaken strongly in 1973–4 following the massive rise in oil prices. This further destabilized the banking and financial systems. Inflation rose and demand in the oil-importing industrialized countries fell dramatically. Five years later a second 'oil crisis' occurred. The resulting limits on production led to a debilitating uncertainty about future supplies of oil and thus to an accumulation of all kinds of speculative strategies on the part of the consumer countries. Many of them devoted most of their (macro)economic policy efforts to enlarging and securing their energy stocks.

When finally a major and severe economic stagnation emerged at the beginning of the 1980s it proved to be a phenomenon of a very complex nature. As far as the Netherlands are concerned, a whole range of different causes is involved. One of the most prominent features of the Dutch variant of the economic crisis is an industrial overcapacity. The mismatch between supply and demand grew considerably in a number of important areas. High structural costs limited profits and this paved the way to labour-saving investments. The consequent loss of employment resulted in a decrease in domestic consumption. On the other hand, the rise in social allowances and benefit payments forced the government to adopt a more cautious, austere policy regarding its other expenditure. For example the government, as a consumer of goods and services produced by the country's business and industrial sectors, began to spend considerably less. This in turn widened the overall gap between supply and demand capacity (Roos, 1985, p. 22).

A less visible (in the beginning) but increasingly more important factor in terms of economic stagnation was the considerable pressure of transfer payments and the large budget deficit in the public sector. The rise in expenditure was caused mainly by the rise in the transfer payments to households (Table 6.1).

The recession had its most dramatic impact on employment, with a massive and continuing number of redundancies. The old scarcity of labour had turned into a new abundance. The depression thus induced a head-on collision, because the Dutch labour system is characterized by a comparatively high degree of centralism, state intervention and public regulation (Doorn, 1983, p. 163).

Table 6.1 The growth of the public sector in the Netherlands 1960–86

% of national income	1960	1970	1980	1983	1986
total public expenditures	38.7	47.8	64.8	70.5	67.1
government expenditures	18.4	21.1	22.7	21.8	19.9
total transfer payments,	20.3	26.7	42.1	48.7	47.2
of which payments to households	11.2	18.5	29.3	32.9	30.5

Source: Miljoenennota 1987 (1986).

Economic development between the 1960s and the 1980s can be characterized by three indicators: economic growth, unemployment and the financial surplus or deficit of the state (Roebroek and van Koten, 1985, p. 294). (See Table 6.2).

Table 6.2 Economic indicators 1970–86

	economic growth	unemployment	budget deficit
1970	5.1	1.7	3.6
1975	−1.1	6.1	5.1
1980	−0.7	7.2	7.1
1983	0.5	17.0	9.5
1986	2.5	15.4	6.9

Source: Centraal Planbureau 1986, pp. 456–9.

Broader repercussions: social security and related perceptions of the crisis

The evolution of the political and societal distribution of influence in the period 1960–86 can be illustrated by examining the social security issue. During the 1970s the position of those organizations and parties wanting to maintain or even expand the existing social security system weakened. Those who favoured an adaptation of the system to 'economic restoration' policies and a reduction in the budget deficit became more influential. This meant that the unions, the Social–Democrats and the small leftish parties were 'defeated' by the employers' organizations, the Christian–Democrats, the Conservative Liberals and the small right-wing parties. In relation to economic development a similar pattern can be identified. Thus initially one sees the growth and dominance of those actors who defended general social provision. The later stage was characterized by the dominance of the proponents of a thoroughly selective social security system.

From the end of the 1970s all major parties emphasized that the social security system was expensive and that reforms were necessary. Notwithstanding ideological diversity and conflict, there was a remarkable consensus on the inevitability of controlling public expenditure. A variety of measures was tested with different results and degrees of success. Others were merely proposed but then disappeared in a time-consuming procedure of seeking advice, studies, reformulations, mobilization of support and comparison of assessments. The central point is, however, that there was general agreement that there was a problem which needed to be solved urgently.

It might be argued that the consensus among political parties went even further. All major parties participated in one or more cabinets during this period and were thus each (co)responsible for the formulation and implementation of an economy programme which integrated the system of social security in a general monetary budget policy (Beus, 1983, pp. 40–1).

Political changes

Depillarization and polarization

For the past two decades the political system in the Netherlands can best be described by the evolution of processes of participation and emancipation. The relation between the political parties has changed accordingly, from one of peaceful co-existence to an 'armoured truce'. Dutch consociationalism gave way to so-called emancipation democracy, with an emphasis on the genuinely specific rights of separate groups and organizations. This process of politicization generated more (and new) expectations, wants and demands, which eventually had to be converted into policy terms. In other words it is a type of change which inevitably placed an extra policy burden on the political system (Schendelen, 1978, p. 51).

The transformation of Dutch politics has taken place at both the élite and mass levels of the system. What occurred initially was a wide-ranging process of depillarization. Depillarization destabilized electoral behaviour and stimulated all kinds of activism. The established élites were therefore threatened and began to fear losing their positions. Especially since 1972–3, they have begun to react more energetically against this threat. In many respects the reactions were characterized by a specific kind of cultural polarization, both personally and positionally profitable for the élites.

Ultimately this cultural polarization paved the way for a 'restorative' trend in the Dutch political system of the 1970s. In part, these changes and transformations have resulted in a restoration of the consociational kind of compromise and accomodationist rules of the game guiding crucial policies and top level decision-making (Schendelen, 1978, p. 52). This traditional rules-of-the-game dimension has been restored, but the fundamental difference from the previous consociationalism model is that at present it is linked with polarization, instead of pillarization. Political leadership finds itself in a position which is unstable, particularly from an electoral point of view, and much more vulnerable than before (Table 6.3).

Table 6.3 Dutch cabinets since the 1970s

July 1971–May 1973	Biesheuvel (PM): Christian–Democrats, Conservative Liberals, Social Democrats
May 1973–Dec. 1977	Den Uyl (PM): Socialists, Christian–Democrats
Dec. 1977–Sept. 1981	van Agt (PM): Christian–Democrats, Conservative Liberals
Sept. 1981–May 1982	van Agt (PM): Christian-Democrats, Socialists and Liberals
May 1982–Nov. 1982	van Agt (PM): Christian–Democrats, Liberals
Nov. 1982–May 1986	Lubbers (PM): Christian–Democrats, Conservative Liberals
May 1986–	Lubbers (PM): Christian–Democrats, Conservative Liberals

Cultural polarization during the 1970s has meant that politicans have been increasingly inclined towards more symbolic outputs. 'Paper' policy outcomes were presented as if they were real and substantial achievements. During the 1980s symbolic politics has been gradually abandoned. The severity of the decisions and measures, which simply had to be imposed, led to a sober, businesslike and no-nonsense approach to policy formulation. At the same time increasingly intense disagreements and an escalation of conflicts between politicians (at a governmental, parliamentary and party leadership level) and established institutionalized pressure groups became inevitable (Schendelen, 1978, pp. 49–50).

From 1980 onwards political élites have tried, by means of propaganda, public relations management and indoctrination, to create a climate of opinion that makes economic recovery via austerity policies acceptable at the expense of the welfare state system. This has created tension between polarization and cooperation, by opposing or allying the various élites of the major parties. In the end, because one cannot rule in the Netherlands without coalition building, most of the élites have had to forsake their polarized attitude and behaviour patterns. The centre of the political system—government and parliament—has become more stable during this period. Detailed agreements between the coalition parties concerning the Cabinet's programme and governmental policies have become more customary. It takes a lot of energy to build a coalition, hold it together and make it work. A considerable decline of parliament's autonomy is part of the price that had and has to be paid for these efforts (Table 6.4).

Table 6.4 Some characteristics of Dutch politics in four phases

1915–65	1965–72	1972–80	1980–7
MASS-LEVEL POLITICAL CULTURE			
pillarized	pluralistic	pluralistic	pluralistic
ATTITUDE TOWARDS ÉLITE			
passive/docile	active/critical	moderate/critical	moderate
ELECTORAL PREFERENCES			
static	dynamic	dynamic	dynamic
ÉLITE LEVEL POLITICAL CULTURE			
consociational	polarizing	conflictuous	conflictuous
ELECTORAL OUTCOMES			
pillarized clusters	fragmentation	concentration	concentration
POSITION OF TOP LEVEL ÉLITE			
strong and stable	acceleration of turnover	high turnover rate	medium turnover rate
FUNCTION OF THE POLITICAL PARTY			
articulation	mobilization	control	control and mobilization
DECISION-MAKING RULES OF THE GAME			
politics of accommodation	critical politics	symbolic politics	sober and businesslike
secrecy	publicity	secrecy	selective publicity
government rules	diffusion of power	informal coalitions	government rules
depolitization	politization	selective politization	professionalized politization

Source: As formulated by Schendelen (1978) for the first three periods; here extended by the author to 1980–7.

Nature and range of policy making

Until the early 1970s government had been rather successful in meeting a constantly increasing flow of wants and demands. Things began to change after 1973 when economic growth and the rise in prosperity came to a standstill. Although claims and expectations did not in any way decline, actual policy performance became more and more restricted.

At the same time economic stagnation revealed and exacerbated a pre-existing but hitherto mainly latent crisis in the governmental system and public administration apparatus. The welfare state type of growth, both in volume and range, of the government's policy efforts had led to an enormous increase in problems of coordination. The accumulation of governmental intervention in all kinds of areas of economic, social and cultural life had a boomerang effect in hard economic times. Moreover, because government was active in almost every sector of society, it became highly visible and easily identifiable as the efficacy and legitimacy of its initiatives and control steadily diminished. The growth of government, together with the decrease of its productivity and credibility, was the essence of the crisis of the welfare state (Hazeu, 1983, p. 71).

This situation was largely determined by the boom and the structural expansion of the public sector—a dynamic which could not be halted. A huge system of regulation and control had been created. This system was preserved not only by its structural nature, but also because of the difficult and cumbersome nature of the legal changes in themselves. Each law generates actors which have an interest in its maintenance—namely administrative agencies, parties and pressure groups. Given a certain stability in the distribution of power, creating a law usually guarantees its endurance.

The expansion of the public sector was achieved at the expense of the private sector and its autonomy. At the same time the growth of the public sector manifested itself not only through the regulatory and legislative monopoly of central government, but also by the expansion of the public administration apparatus. In due course these expansion processes caused their own type of problems—for example an intense departmentalization and far reaching differentiation of functions. Great and complex organizations became far more polycentric than monocentric, with wide-ranging powers and plenty of administrative resources. Alongside these developments political responsibility of different administrative units increased and rapidly growing management problems became even more difficult to handle (Schendelen, 1982, p. 193).

The negative balance sheet of the late 1970s

The poor state of the country's economy acted as a catalyst for the crisis in the political and governmental-administrative system. The system was overloaded because of both its own internal complexity, getting almost totally out of hand, and a relentless rise of the demands being placed upon it. In the meantime it had to initiate and organize a new and far reaching economic recovery programme and administer austerity policies.

Increasingly, the problem of an oversized and dysfunctional public sector was perceived as being a result of structural problems in the decision-making processes. On the other hand there was also the view that, so far, public expenditure had not been reduced because of the fear of losing the next election, because of the resistance of powerful pressure groups, and because of the vulnerability and internal tensions of the governmental coalition.

Government and parliament hesitated and refused to reorganize and limit public sector structures because, it was alleged, its members were afraid of unpopularity. Pressure groups did not cooperate because that would not serve the special interests they were supposed to defend, and would reduce their power and influence. Civil servants would not willingly reduce public expenditure because such cuts might undermine their own position, income, employment and status (Beus and de Wolff, 1984, p. 128).

A final factor should be mentioned in this analysis. The steering capacity of the government has been handicapped by several consequences of its previous welfare state type of interventionist role. Geelhoed (1983) gives some examples of these eventually 'paralysing' interventions of the state in society. For instance, the tendency to refine and regulate procedures as much as possible has been partly a natural outcome of the increased specialization of the government's policies. But this increasing refinement, and the introduction of all kinds of procedural 'buffers', has not necessarily contributed to the effectiveness of governmental performance. On the contrary, the more complicated and determined an intervention is, the larger will be its direct and secondary policy costs. The effectiveness of intervention may then be seriously reduced.

In parallel with this phenomenon, there has been the 'intervention density' factor. All these rules, regulations and procedures produced an associated flood of norms and values, which only experts are able to interpret. The implementation, control and coordination costs have thus become excessive. Moreover, because of overlapping jurisdictions, contradictory interventions are inevitable. Even rules which appear to be ineffective are seldom withdrawn or redefined and adapted, but are generally corrected by a further series of interventions.

Responses to the crisis

The public sector level

As far as public reactions to the crisis post-1980 are concerned, one should not underestimate the fatalistic attitude and traumatizing sense of decline adopted by a large majority of citizens. Unemployment grew, national income per head decreased, as did the average spending power of wages and the transfer incomes of those not working. Moreover, the general public had become dissatisfied with the quality of welfare policies – no doubt one of the negative effects of the inefficiency of public administration. As a consequence, public support for the basic components of the welfare state system – such as the financing of social security – declined somewhat. 'Sense of decline' signals were also increasingly articulated by the political establishment itself – some analysts believing that the citizens' sense of decline had been primarily a reaction to the politicians' signals, rather than the other way round.

In the early 1980s when, at long last, the government reduced its expenditure, it obviously marked an important turning point. Parliament did cooperate and sanctioned these tight and 'sober' budgetary policies. Pressure groups in their turn agreed to control the costs of each of the areas and sectors they represented and supervised. All kinds of societal organizations, for example in the public health sector, have participated in supporting and achieving austerity measures, although there have been differing views on the *pace* and *volume* of these cutbacks. In effect there was no alternative. After hesitation at the end of the 1970s it had become essential to economize in the 1980s. Those who remained sceptical or reluctant were considered to be poor politicians, evading and postponing problems. (Beus and de Wolff, 1984).

By then the government was aware of and openly acknowledged the fact that the bureaucracy was too large, that there were too many regulations making life unnecessarily complicated and restrictive for the private sector, and that available resources were not used efficiently. Much analysis and research have been put into reforms and improvements. In the Netherlands these initiatives have been labelled 'the big operations'. There are six of them: the reconsideration of governmental tasks; deregulation; privatization; the 'minus 2 per cent operation'; decentralization and the reorganization of the central administrative system. The reconsideration process is considered the basic and most crucial operation. Deregulation and privatization originate from it. Together 'the big operations' are supposed to contribute to the three main objectives of the two cabinets headed by Lubbers:

(a) reduction of the budget deficit and size of the public sector
(b) strengthening of the private sector
(c) redistribution of labour.

Each of the 'big operations' has multiple goals. The reconsideration process aims for more efficiency and effectiveness of existing programmes, a more effective resource allocation process, and a lower level of public provision. Privatization aims at budget savings, slimming down the administration apparatus, and a reinforcement of the private sector. Deregulation has to lead to more transparency of the relations between government and society, to streamlined, simplified and reduced regulations, and to greater effectiveness and representation.

The 'minus 2 per cent operation' is designed to reduce public expenditure by reducing both the cost and the number of civil servants. Decentralization has three objectives: improving the relation between central and subnational governments; offering new opportunities for democracy at a lower level; and forcing central government to operate more effectively. The reorganization of central administration is designed to improve the structure and functioning of the administration itself, to improve policy coordination, and to increase the transparency and flexibility of administrative organizations. A later goal was the reduction of the number of civil servants through increased efficiency, 'less and better' (Tjeenk Willink, 1986, pp. 182–3).

These six operations are supposed to produce early results, although there is a risk of their being purely rhetorical. Although they aim at fundamental changes, this does not necessarily mean that these changes will really take place. In the event, only marginal changes may have occurred. In that case it has been more a 'big mouth' than a 'big operation' (Nispen, 1986, p. 14).

In terms of measures to streamline public administration, it might be thought that deregulation is a fairly simple and straightforward type of reform. That has not been the case. On the contrary it has turned out to be a very complicated process. As a consequence of deregulation all kinds of interests, pressure groups and societal organizations experience a change in their interrelationships and in their relationship to government. Existing regulations formalize and strengthen the influence and authority of some actors at the expense of others. Deregulation of course weakens the position of vested interests, and they will naturally try to prevent that. Moreover, an existing set of regulations is not just a specific model of law and rule setting; it is also the institutionalization of a whole range of basic sociological components (Doorn, 1982). Deregulation has therefore become an aspect of a fundamental social change through which, for example, the economic sector regains most of its former central and dominating position, with or without an employer-oriented system of 'regulation'.

Finally there is the frequent phenomenon of rules which have not been entirely abolished but have been replaced by alternative ones (or by other control instruments), and the emergence of policy succession dynamics (see Hogwood and Peters, 1983). For example, financial incentives are examples of different instruments which do not mean fewer rules, but more reregulation. Reregulation is designed to improve and adapt and is intended to improve existing regulations. One possibility is that the existing rules and regulations should not be abandoned, but rather the regulatory agencies themselves. 'Regulatory reform' has become a more acceptable label than deregulation.

In terms of reductions in social security expenditure there was only a moderate reduction prior to 1983. The government appeared to search for a package of measures, a policy mix, that would create the minimum of discomfort and suffering, although it is now clear that, of those eligible for social welfare payments, those who were not supported by any interest or pressure group and had relatively little electoral power were the first victims of the budget cuts. On the other hand, workers in the private sector had to face hardly any income losses. A general and equitable distribution of the effects of the government's austerity measures across all income groups had not been achieved (Beus, 1983). The reduced importance, as far as social security is concerned, of the advisory work of the Social and Economic Council (SER), the most important corporatist consultative body of the government on socio-economic matters, illustrates some more general trends in Dutch politics. A very clear development has been the disintegration of the compromise that constituted the basis of the welfare state, following the increased automony achieved by successive governments as they reformed social security provisions (Roebroek and van Koten, 1985, p. 299). This change in the distribution of power has meant a loss of influence for those who favour the welfare state, and a strengthening of the position of the 'austerity-minded' and 'recovery-oriented' reformers.

Another significant development in this respect is that, to the disadvantage of the unions, the labour system has become increasingly a matter for which the government is primarily concerned. Government has even displaced the unions in their traditional role of opposing employers. Growing unemployment reduced the power of the unions and made government the central actor in the labour market. The main reason for this change are the costs of unemployment which had to be met by the government – hence the unprecedented and intensive concern of the Ministry of Social Affairs with labour market dynamics. So far, however, the ministry's approach has focused more on the 'non-active' groups than on the working and employed groups within the population. Central government has therefore emphasized the creation of employment and lowering the welfare state costs rather than concentrating on the needs of those in work. This approach has caused conflicts with the unions (Doorn, 1983, pp. 164–65).

More generally, the partial success of the government's retrenchment operations in the public sector is mainly due to the adoption of new internal procedures, affecting the relationships between the ministries. For example, the Ministry of Finance has tried to improve the budget-allocation process. First the annual discussions in the February and March Cabinet meetings are to produce multi-year budgets with non-negotiable retrenchment clauses for each ministry. Ministry of Finance proposals are to suggest specific economies rather than the old system of proportional cuts which often lacked realistic political priorities. All ministers can now see a clear picture of the budgetary position of other policy areas. Once the Cabinet has agreed on an allocation of the 'retrenchment tasks', this decision sets a fixed framework for the subsequent general budgetary drafting. When ministers cannot suggest any feasible alternative to the retrenchment scheme that is submitted, the initial proposal put forward by the Ministry of Finance becomes Cabinet policy. The underlying assumption is that, given an initial proposal, each minister will do his utmost to find alternatives that are acceptable and easier to sell to the ministry's clientele. If he is successful in this attempt the end result can only benefit the Cabinet's general strategy.

Symbolics and political leadership

51lhonjIt is hardly surprising that, in terms of the transformation and improvement
of the public sector's machinery and processes, there have also been numerous 'utopian' reorganization proposals: another structure for the central government and administrative system; introduction of fiscal rules, a

reform of several Cabinet procedures and so on. One of the factors complicating the crisis considerably was that many of these proposals could best be characterized as exaggerated in their claims and serving only a symbolic purpose. Other similar examples were a flight into purely formalistic approaches to problems, and development of parliamentary activism, with more motions, questions, amendments and so on, accompanied by a different debating style and an increased concern with public relations. This has been the case especially on such issues as emancipation, science policy, safety, minorities and the so-called 'broad societal discussion' on nuclear energy (Hazeu, 1983). Many politicians seemed satisfied by tackling problems in theory without achieving any concrete results. As Edelman suggested much earlier, these are tactics which systematically prevent public awareness that the outcomes of formal procedures are largely symbolic or marginal in character (1977, p. 124).

On many occasions it appeared that this kind of behaviour was not in any way meant to be effective but was intended only to keep voters, pressure groups and the media at bay, and to occupy the opposing parties. Meanwhile, the actual power of MPs and their influence over legislation has merely decreased (Franssen, 1982; Hazeu, 1983). Political leadership responses to the crisis have thus been especially problematic in terms of such measures as mobilization, justification and solving dilemmas. Some observers have even wondered whether politics could survive when public provision stagnates or recedes (Wolff, 1984, p. 152). In this sense, the change of political debate, from representation to the integration of specific interests, led almost inevitably to symbolic policies. Of course not all policies were symbolic. The purpose of this development was not only to continue the illusion for politicians that there still is something 'to give away', but primarily to maintain that idea vis-à-vis their voters. In addition verbalist tactics have delayed adaptation to new circumstances and have disguised the politicians' embarrassment as not yet having an adequate response to the change situation.

Responses to the crisis have not unexpectedly often resulted in dilemmas. Governments and government agencies at different levels have grown very dependent on central instructions and regulations from the Cabinet. The Cabinet itself often depends on directions from the political centre, that is, from the parties in power and their leadership. When that centre does not rule effectively – as was the case during the cabinets lead by van Agt between 1977 and 1982 – then the governmental and administrative system will eventually maintain the status quo, even when circumstances change dramatically. Almost no political party in that period felt moved to initiate a public discussion of any difficult and unattractive alternatives.

The directives emanating from van Agt's first cabinet were often characterized by signs of 'court politics'. In the 1980s however, the same Dutch politicians who opened cleavages between themselves and business during the 1970s have been busy mending relationships. Because of the continuous economic recession, they began to favour trade and industry as a kind of 'offering' from the political centre (Schendelen, 1982, p. 195).

Finally, the phenomenon of political 'entrepreneurship' has been a notable but underestimated response to the crisis. One of the bases for political entrepreneurship has been the coalition agreement of the Christian Democratic–Conservative–Liberal Cabinets of Lubbers since 1982. That agreement was formulated through close cooperation between the Cabinet and the coalition parties in parliament. This had not been done before. Most of the really economizing measures of the government's austerity policy are related to the mobilizing influence of that agreement. The agreement has shaped and steered the operation of central administration, the attitudes of pressure groups such as the employers' organizations and unions, and even public opinion. After the Lubbers Cabinet took office, minor interventions gradually became major transformations of the governmental bureaucracy and public administration machinery, for example the application of profit principles, privatization and contracting out, the delegation of authority and responsibility, dropping certain tasks, and reduction of civil servants' wages (Beus and de Wolff, 1984, p. 128).

The continuation of the Lubbers Cabinet after successful elections in 1986 illustrates that politicians can not only survive, but can even strengthen their position in periods of cutbacks.

The economy and the private sector

Undoubtedly one of the most remarkable features of the government's new type of economic recovery and austerity policies in the Netherlands was the introduction of a more or less alternative Keynesian strategy after 1973. The characteristics were a combination of general and indirect steering using fiscal and monetary instruments, with selective and direct interventions, through structure-oriented measures stimulating the labour market by means of an employment policy and control of the rise of wages and prices. *Ad hoc* policies were replaced by a middle term perspective – more than hitherto – based on planning and research, and needed the cooperation of the major interest organizations and pressure groups. This strategy was essentially monetary and as such was different from traditional Keynesian principles with regard to influencing and steering market mechanisms.

The post-1973 approach of the Dutch government became increasingly directed towards control of the money supply, which was supposed to be central to the working of the economy. This was definitely a crucial turning point in the evolving relations between the state and the market. On the other hand, there are some clear indications that changes in the role of the state in economic processes have also been partly ideological. What actually happened was a withdrawal of the state from some sectors of the economy and more intervention of the government in others. Bearing in mind the government's plans and options, particularly from the early 1980s (that is, a reduction of the budget deficit at the expense of the country's welfare state system and a regeneration of the competitiveness and viability of business sectors), this was probably an inevitable outcome.

To understand the strategic choices made by the government in the last decade, a typology of state intervention has been developed. It focuses on form and intensity as two basic dimensions of state intervention that will determine the sort of crisis management through which the government hopes to realize its policies. An 'indicative intensity' means that the government does not interfere with the executive role and decision-making power of societal groups. It uses mostly indirect tactics such as influencing public opinion, appeals to a sense of responsibility and moderation of the groups and organizations concerned. When the intensity is more 'imperative' government curtails the power and authority of groups and organizations by law or other legal means. Discontent and resistance from these groups and organizations is then more likely because of the restrictions imposed upon them.

The different forms that state intervention can take relate to the inclusion or exclusion of interest organizations and pressure groups in public policy-making and implementation processes. Theoretically there are two distinct forms that are optimal from the politician's and the government's viewpoint. The first option is authoritarian and as such gives absolute priority to decision-making by parliament, excluding any direct and overt contact with interest organizations or pressure groups. Cooperation is the second form and implies the realization of policy strategies by means of discussion and consultation with most of the groups and organizations involved (Table 6.5). This typology of state intervention (similar to the concept of policy style) helps to classify and explain the characteristic way in which the Dutch government has intervened in social and economic processes and has dealt with political issues over the last fifteen years.

Table 6.5 State intervention

intensity	form	
	authoritarian	*cooperative*
imperative	tight centralism	restricted neo-corporatism
indicative	relaxed centralism	voluntary neo-corporatism

Source: Based on the scheme of Keman *et al*. (1985).

In the Netherlands since the late 1970s and early 1980s there has been a shift in policy style from concertation to an activist alternative, with several new aspects of regulation. In the area of, for example, higher education policy, one can see that government not only regulates but also imposes a market model on universities and medical schools. The decades of economic prosperity and social emancipation were marked by more or less unrestrained neo-corporatism as the dominant policy style in the Netherlands. Since the crisis this has been replaced, and a democratic centralist approach has become increasingly important (Table 6.6). During the economic crisis, instead of societal demands and wants, it was the government or its executive branches that were the driving force behind decision-making. The dominant role of government, especially in the field of monetary and financial matters, is not based on any thorough political analysis or substantial (re)appraisal of priorities, but is the outcome of purely technical administrative policy evaluation (Wolff, 1984, p. 202). Basic assessments, fundamental priorities and crucial choices are implicit. Because of all kinds of zero-sum constraints, nobody is really keen on initiating a public discussion that would go into these elements with the risk of producing equally unattractive and unpopular alternatives, compared to the present option.

Table 6.6 State intervention in the Netherlands 1972–87

	strategy	form	perception of economic problems
1972	traditional Keynesian	voluntary neo-corporatism	low
1974–6	expanding Keynesian	restricted neo-corporatism	moderate
1978	monetarist	relaxed centralism	high
1980	monetarist	relaxed centralism	high/moderate
1982	monetarist/ Keynesian	tight centralism	high
since 1984	monetarist	tight centralism	high

Source: The typology of Braun and Keman (1984) for 1972–8; supplemented by the author from 1980.

This has led to highly frustrating developments in some areas, for example in labour relations. Policy concerning labour relations, particularly with regard to wages, has shifted from corporatism to neo-capitalism. It has lost its high level of stability and peaceful cooperation and has been replaced by more or less conflictual negotiations. At the same time however, the essential willingness of the unions to cooperate with the state under governments with a varying political composition and different ideological profiles, did not disappear (Akkermans and Nobelen, 1983, p. 185). Nevertheless, the lack of both interest and a cooperative stance on the part of the government has continued and has led to an accumulation of labour-related conflicts.

All the considerations that have been presented here prelude a correlation between the size and severity of the economic crisis, the choice of a specific governmental strategy and the form of the state's intervention. Neo-corporatism is a perfect example in this respect. It presupposes the willingness of all political actors to participate in an exchange of interests. This implies the possibility of withdrawal from that exchange process. The exchange potential as such, however, is affected by more factors than the willingness of political and societal actors alone. There are structural links between politics and the economy, as our discussion of the fiscal crisis of the state shows, but there is also an ideological relationship between politics and the economy. In addition, the overloaded political agenda – caused by the rising expectations of citizens, polarization, the vicissitudes of electoral fortune, the coordination problems with the public sector, the immobilizing effects of too much regulation – had a considerable impact on the form and intensity of state intervention as well as on the outcomes of different decisions and measures.

Concluding comments

It is important to note that so far the situation (directly connected to the crisis) within the public-administration and governmental apparatus has not *really* been changed. The economic situation has evolved as outlined, but no *substantial* transformations have been achieved either in the structure or functioning of the public sector. Last but not least, within the sphere of politics, the dominant actors have continued to be preoccupied with their own position and its stability.

The foregoing analysis of reactions to the post-1973 crisis in the Netherlands has focused, among other things, on the economic policy efforts of successive governments. Table 6.6 gives an overview of the perception of economic problems and of the strategy and form of policy reactions. It has been argued that the different governments during the 1970s and early 1980s, irrespective of their ideological-political profile, have invariably opted for a possibly mistaken economic theory or perspective. The Lubbers Cabinet (1982–6) wanted an end to the crisis and adopted a monetarist austerity-oriented policy, although the state of the economy, according to Schouten (1986), actually by then required a Keynesian approach. On the other hand, in an earlier period of economic expansion and prosperity, until the mid-1970s, the very thing the country would have needed but which the government did not opt for was precisely the opposite course. The errors of Den Uyl's Cabinet (1973–7) and its excesses, namely believing in the effects of tight and decisive interventionism, were lessons which unfortunately the Lubbers Cabinet (1982–6) frequently neglected. Because of a non-interference and 'laissez-faire' strategy, the 1982–6 Cabinet failed to use its influence at the time and in a way which might have been useful and positive for more integrative policy and decision-making.

This implies a criticism of the centre-right cabinets of van Agt (1977–81) and Lubbers (1982–6 and since 1986). During the van Agt II Cabinet (1982), which lasted less than a year, the major protagonists in the government had stuck to objectives and instruments which they considered to be the most important from their own political perspective. The overall policy objective of solving the unemployment problem could not therefore be achieved. The Minister of Finance was a Christian–Democrat and keen on reducing the budget deficit. The Social Democrats were mainly interested in the so-called job creation plan of their own Minister of Social Affairs and Employment. The Liberals wanted to restore business investments, which was strongly advocated by their leader, the Minister of Economic Affairs.

As Prime Minister of the succeeding Cabinet, Lubbers initially developed a more integrative (macro)economic approach based on three tracks: balancing the budget, redressing the position of Dutch trade and industry and tackling unemployment problems (Seumeren, 1986). The operationalization of this approach, however, by the two Lubbers cabinets has left management and control of economic developments almost completely in the hands of the private sector. The dominating position of the employers, resulting from this, has led to a neglect of the workers' and unions' wants, demands and interests.

The failure of the van Agt II government was due to the lack of integration of its three major objectives, which was a direct consequence of the political differences and varying interpretations of the economic situation. The lack of 'integrated' achievements of the Lubbers cabinets on the other hand has been caused by the absence of almost any *external* coordination of its three-track policy by the unions and the employers. The priority given to budgetary measures in favour of a free enterprise and against a welfare state type of economy has shifted recent policy responses to the crisis away from integration towards a more right-wing direction.

References

Akkermans, T. and P. W. M. Nobelen (eds) (1983), *Corporatisme en verzorgingsstaat*. Leiden Antwerpen, Stenfert Kroese.

Berge, H. van den (1986), 'De relatie tussen de politiek en het bedrijfsleven in Nederland'. Rotterdam, vakgroep Politicologie.

Beus, J. W. de (1983), 'De contractie van sociale zekerheid als politiek strijdpunt', *Beleid en Maatschappij*, 1–2, pp. 39–51.

Beus, J. W. de and L. J. de Wolff (1984), 'Bezuiniging als aanpassingspraktijk', *Beleid en Maatschappij*, 5, pp. 125–29.

Braun, D. and J. E. Keman (1984), 'Developments in the regulative character of state intervention: towards a new form of crisis management'. Paper for the ECPR workshops in Salzburg, 13–18 April.

Centraal Planbureau (1986), *Centraal Economisch Plan*. Den Haag.

Doorn, J. A. A. van (1982), 'Maatschappelijke krachten achter regulering', *Beleid en Maatschappij*, 8, pp. 182–9.

Doorn, J. A. A. van (1983), 'Herverdeling van arbeid als hervorming van het arbeidsbestel', *Beleid en Maatschappij*, 6, pp. 158–65.

Edelman, M. (1977), *Political Language: words that succeed and policies that fail*. New York, Academic Press.

Fortuyn, W. S. (1983), *Kerncijfers 1945–1983 van de sociaal-economische ontwikkeling in Nederland*. Deventer, Kluwer.

Franssen, H. M. (1981), *Tweede Kamer en Binnenlandse Zaken*. Assen, van Gorcum.

Geelhoed, L. A. (1983), *De interveniërende staat – aanzet voor een instrumentenleer*. Den Haag, Staatsuitgeverij.

Hazeu, C. A. (1983), 'Van smalle marges naar malle charges', *Beleid en Maatschappij*, 3 pp. 65–75.

Hogwood, B. and B. Guy Peters (1983), *Policy Dynamics*. Brighton, Wheatsheaf.

Keman, H., J. Wolderdorp and D. Braun (1985), *Het neokorporatisme als nieuwe politieke strategie*. Amsterdam, CT-press.

Miljoenenennota 1984, Den Haag, Staatsuitgeverij.

Miljoenenennota 1987 (1986), *Vergaderjaar 1986–1987* (19700). 's Gravenhage, Tweede Kamer der Staten-Generaal.

Nispen, F. K. M. van (1986), 'De grote operaties' in F. K. M. van Nispen and D. P. Noordhoek (eds), *De grote operaties*. Deventer, Kluwer.

Roebroek, J. and B. van Koten (1985), 'Sociaal-economische raad en sociale zekerheid', *Beleid en Maatschappij*, 11, pp. 293–300.

Roos, W. A. A. M. de (1985), *Bevrijdende economie – over welvaart, arbeid en consumptie*. Assen/Maastricht, Van Gorcum.

Schendelen, M. P. C. M. van (1978), 'Verzuiling en restauratie in de Nederlandse politiek', *Beleid en Maatschappij*, 2, pp. 42–54.

Schendelen, M. P. C. M. van (1982), 'Politieke achtergronden van deregulering', *Beleid en Maatschappij*, 8, pp. 190–202.

Schouten, D. B. J. (1986), *Het wankele evenwicht in de economie*. Leiden/Antwerpen, Stenfert Kroese.

Seumeren, H. van (1986), 'Kabinetten falen door kortzichtigheid', *De Volkskrant*, 22 maart.

Tjeenk Willink, H. D., 'Samenhang grote operaties' in F. K. M. van Nispen and D. P. Noordhoek (eds) (1986), *De grote operaties* (Deventer, Kluwer), pp. 175–88.

Wolff, L. J. de (1984), 'De grenzen van de bezuinigingspolitiek', *Beleid en Maatschappij*, 5, pp. 152–6.

Wolff, L. J. de (1984), 'Overheid en maatschappelijke organisaties: van corporatisme naar étatisme' in J. W. de Beus and J. A. A. van Doorn (eds), *De Interventiestaat* (Meppel, Boom), pp. 199–226.

7 France and the economic crisis 1974–1987

VOLKMAR LAUBER

Important events 1970–88

1969 de Gaulle resigns; Pompidou elected President
1972 Shift to conservatism of Pompidou and government; union of the left; common programme signed
1973 majority of the right in National Assembly elections
1974 Pompidou dies; Giscard elected President against Mitterand
1976 Giscard dismisses Prime Minister Chirac; replaces him with Barre; Chirac starts rebuilding Gaullist party
1977 union of the left breaks apart over update of common programme
1978 right wins National Assembly elections
1981 Mitterrand elected President against Giscard; in subsequent National Assembly elections Socialists obtain majority of seats; still include Communists in government
1984 Communist ministers resign from government; Prime Minister Mauroy replaced by Fabius; Le Pen's National Front registers first successes at local level
1986 right wins National Assembly elections
1988 Mitterrand reelected President against Chirac; in subsequent National Assembly elections Socialists emerge as strongest party and form government.

Introduction

By the end of the Second World War France's previous long-term economic and demographic decline gave rise, over the next two to three decades, to a powerful response in politics, administration, and the economy (Hoffmann,

1963). Expansion and national grandeur became central preoccupations; much of de Gaulle's legitimacy (in terms of constitutional change and practical policy) is explained by this setting. Success was obviously facilitated by the long postwar boom, which in France as in many other countries lasted until the mid-1970s. The Gaullists strongly identified state-guided expansion, modernization and the new political institutions of the Fifth Republic with the goal of remaking France as a strong nation, one of the world's leading powers. Their legitimacy was first shaken when an austerity plan, applied fairly rigidly in the mid-1960s, led to (or at least amplified) the explosion of May 1968. In retrospect it appears that the wage settlement negotiated in 1968 actually stimulated economic growth; the economic break came in 1974.

After de Gaulle's withdrawal from politics in 1969 President Pompidou continued an actively interventionist, expansive policy. There was a new reason for this. The left, after a long period of absence and internal division, finally managed to reorganize in the early 1970s (foundation of the new Socialist Party in 1970; Communist–Socialist alliance in 1972). Now it could start mounting serious challenges to the Gaullist-Centrist camp in power since 1958, beginning with the parliamentary elections of 1973, the presidential elections of 1974, the parliamentary elections of 1978 and finally (and successfully) the presidential elections of 1981; followed by a huge success of the Socialist Party at the parliamentary elections a few weeks later.

During the build-up of this challenge, the left created expectations which it could not fulfil when it came to power, partly because those expectations were unrealistic to begin with, partly because they had become so as a result of the economic crisis which the left hesitated to acknowledge – since it wanted to place the blame on capitalism and the policy of the right. It seemed, however, that the crisis advanced inexorably under all regimes and policies, with only brief deviations from the long-term course. Thus unemployment grew from a half million in 1974 to one million at the end of 1975; after a brief stabilization it resumed its growth and had reached about two million by the time the Socialists came to power. After a second stabilization which lasted almost two years it increased by another half a million. Clearly the most powerful influences on unemployment, investment, inflation, and so on, came from the economic environment, in particular the two oil shocks (for economic statistics see Table 7.1). The crises greatly dampened industrial investment which until 1974 had grown fairly rapidly and regularly; they increased inflation and (particularly under the Socialists) led to important increases in the foreign debt (OECD, 1985). All governments suffered from this adverse situation, including the Socialists who lost support despite a quite remarkable economic policy performance from 1983 on. As a result the achievement of one of Mitterand's long-standing political goals – to make the Socialists the first party of

France at the expense of the Communists – resulted in a pyrrhic victory when in 1986 the near-collapse of the Communist Party was not balanced by the acquisition of new support from the Centre. In the circumstances, the right returned to power. The Socialists – though now the strongest party – did not even have a credible ally.

Thus the economic crisis started in France in an environment of political competition after a decade and a half of clear Gaullist dominance. Both sides experimented with different prescriptions for economic improvement. The left claimed that it could greatly improve economic performance by a break with an increasingly sterile liberal capitalism that was unable to secure economic expansion and social progress. The last ten years have seen, at first, the increasing acceptance of this claim by the electorate, facilitated by the fact that the liberal policy of Giscard-Barre did not seem to lead to success; then after the left had been in power for two or three years an ideological reorientation on both sides of the political spectrum accompanied by an important change in the political mood of the country.

Summing up, one can distinguish three areas of response to the crisis. First the area of defining the problem and of conducting day to day policy (an area marked by frequent reversals often inspired by very practical problems); secondly the area of political structures, where in the French context changes can be observed mainly in the relations between the government and the major interest groups, such as employers or trade unions; and thirdly the area of political orthodoxy and ideology, where an effort was made to redefine the world (above all the political-economic world) in new ideological terms.

Problem definitions and policy responses

The analysis of the problem varied among the four major political parties, and also over time; there were very clear learning effects. The following description will stress the approach of the leading party in power: the Centrists (Giscardiens) from 1974–81, with a brief interlude in 1975–6; the Socialists from 1981–6; and the neo-Gaullists from 1986 onwards

The Giscard presidency

During Giscard's period of office there were three distinct phases of economic policy. Already in the early 1970s Giscard criticized the policy of rapid economic growth because it imposed on French society growing and hardly tolerable strains. This critique was more on a philosophical level and led to an argument in favour of 'gentle growth'. But it was in keeping with this approach that in 1974 Giscard defined the economic problem confronting French society as being primarily inflation, caused in part by excessive investment and excessive consumption, particularly given the rapid increase in the prices of oil and other raw materials. He reacted with a tax on investment and a policy of deflation. The effect of these measures largely surpassed the expectations of their authors: given the dismal international background (Giscard expected an early economic upturn rather than a recession spreading worldwide) investments collapsed, industrial production and business profits fell, bankruptcies doubled and unemployment soared. Despite all that, wage increases remained high, probably because of the narrow electoral victory of 1974 combined with the trauma of 1968. In fact, the government made an effort to ease the effects of the recession by asking employers not to dismiss redundant workers and by making dismissals subject to administrative approval. Faced with these problems, in mid 1975 Giscard reversed course upon the insistence of his Prime Minister Jacques Chirac, a Gaullist leader who had helped him into the saddle, but also an early critic of 'gentle growth'. The analysis underlying governmental policy was now turned upside down: inflation was traced to the paralysis of the country's productive resources (unemployment, idle capacities) while consumption continued unabated. The remedy was seen in an energetic policy of deficit spending to stimulate economic growth. In fact profitability resumed and unemployment and business bankruptcies fell; but inflation increased and the balance of payments deficit very nearly exploded (see Table 7.1). Within a year reflation was doomed, Chirac sacked, and a new Prime Minister (Raymond Barre) appointed whose economic policy remained steady over the next five years.

Barre proclaimed that the central problem was inflation. France was living beyond her means; hence the heavy balance of payments deficit. The remedy was not to maniputlate the business cycle, but to improve the performance of French firms and of economic actors generally. This could be done by reducing input costs (essentially wages and to a lesser extent taxes and social welfare charges) to make French products more competitive, and by shifting the distribution of the value added in favour of business profits. Stronger business firms and higher profits would mean more and better investments, which in turn would also bring unemployment down to 'acceptable' levels.

This policy implied a stronger reliance on market forces and (in the French context) a partial withdrawal of the state from economic life. Barre wanted to shift responsibility to private entrepreneurs: they should draw their motivation from healthy profits and profit opportunities rather than from job subsidies, investment premiums, capital transfers, reflations, an artificially low exchange rate or similar contrivances of economic policy, all of which would only produce greenhouse plants that would not survive the first frost of international competition. This was accompanied by repeated warnings that the government would not bail out firms whose managers were too 'soft' on the wage front. French wages, Barre tirelessly repeated, were at unrealistically high levels and simply had to come down. The only thing that government could do for business was to stabilize taxes and social welfare

Table 7.1 France: key economic statistics 1973–87

	1973	1974	1975	1976	1977	1978	1979	1980	1981	1982	1983	1984	1985	1986	1987
Real GDP growth %	5.4	3.1	−0.3	4.2	3.2	3.4	3.2	1.6	1.2	2.5	0.7	1.4	1.7	2.1	1.9
Variation in consumer price index %	7.3	13.7	11.8	9.6	9.4	9.1	10.8	13.6	13.4	11.8	9.6	7.4	5.7	2.5	3.0
Standardized unemployment rates %	2.6	2.8	4.0	4.4	4.9	5.2	5.9	6.3	7.3	8.1	8.3	9.7	10.2	10.5	10.6
Surplus on current transactions as % of GDP	−0.2	−2.3	0.0	−1.5	−0.7	0.6	0.0	−1.4	−1.4	−3.0	−1.7	−0.8	−0.8		
Total outlays of government as % of GDP	38.5	39.7	43.5	44.0	44.2	45.2	45.5	46.4	49.1	51.1	52.0	52.7	52.4		
Net lending of government as % of GDP	0.9	0.6	−2.2	−0.5	−0.8	−1.9	−0.7	0.2	−1.8	−2.7	−3.1	−2.9	−2.6	−2.7	−2.0

Source: OECD (1986), *Historical Statistics*; (1986), *Economic Outlook*, no. 40; (1987), *France*.

payments, consistent with its general withdrawal from the economic sphere.

This liberal free-market rhetoric was unusual for France, even for a Conservative government. The only time when economic liberalism really thrived in France was under King Louis-Philippe of Orleans (1830–48). It was never really important after 1944. However, Barre's rhetoric of wage sacrifices and the free market contrasted with a much more moderate practice. Unlike Margaret Thatcher, the French Prime Minister expressly wanted to avoid strong shocks to his country; in his view a liberal policy (and one of austerity as well) could only be successful if it was gradual. And while he rejected reflation as an artificial stimulation of demand, he admitted the necessity of some Keynesian deficit spending, due to the temporary imbalance in French demography, which was causing a rapid growth of the labour force. His government also presided over the rescue in 1979, by quasi-nationalization, of the two biggest French steel companies (Usinor and Sacilor, nearly a duopoly). In addition subsidies were still given fairly indiscriminately to much of French industry, although some progress was made towards greater selectivity in favour of promising firms (for example Estrin and Holmes in 1983).

It is hard to claim that Barre's policy was a striking economic success. Wage increases came down slowly compared to other OECD countries during this period; taxes and welfare contributions continued to rise (mostly due to growing unemployment); business profitability showed some improvement but investments continued to decline and the penetration of the French market increased; exports actually declined in volume (*Le Monde,* 10 March 1981). Inflation stayed at high levels, close to 10 per cent before the second oil shock, and nearly 14 per cent in 1981; the balance of payments showed some mild improvements at first but deteriorated again dramatically after the second oil shock (Table 7.1). In political terms Barre was subjected to intense criticism, not only by the left but also by his own allies, the neo-Gaullists under Chirac. Until early 1981 Chirac criticized governmental economic policy for its passive stance – for standing by as unemployment grew, economic growth rates declined and French industry decayed. In the National Assembly Barre repeatedly resorted to forcing the Gaullists to either support him or openly vote against him (which they could hardly do despite their rancour); the constitution of the Fifth Republic provides for this possibility. Ironically in early 1981 Chirac changed his economic analysis and discovered ultra-liberalism; in due course this was to change the whole range of public opinion in France. But the immediate winners of the 1981 election were – resoundingly – the French Socialists.

Mitterrand and the socialist majority 1981–6

In the common programme of 1972, the left had argued – despite the high growth rates still prevailing at the time – that capitalist waste and mismanagement stunted French growth potential and that taking over the key industrial sectors and the banks, taxing business profits and luxury consumption more heavily while at the same time reflating the economy would permit a large-scale redistribution through increased wages and welfare expenditure. This position was refined somewhat in the second half of the 1970s, probably as a response to the failure of the reflationary policy of Chirac. The left, particularly the Socialists (there was another split with the Communists in 1977), now viewed recession and unemployment not just as the result of an insufficient demand that left national resources (labour and invested capital) unused and idle, but also of a parasitical capitalism that drained those funds which should have gone into industrial renewal. They discovered – this analysis ran under the heading 'industrial socialism' – that France was backward in relation to the leading capitalist powers of the United States, Japan and the Federal Republic of Germany because she had failed to develop large modern and oligopolistic corporations that could lead technological innovation, appropriate the rent resulting from such leadership, and impose their will on the world market.

The remedy flowing from this analysis was to set up oligopolies that could dominate a whole production line or *filière* from raw materials to the finished product, rather than to promote an industrial structure specializing only in selected areas and having terms and conditions set by multinationals. Examples of such production lines are steel, chemicals, aerospace, information technology, biotechnology. In the Socialist analysis the right was unable to bring about the necessary change because private capital was too weak and the capitalists too concerned with the short-term maximization of profits, which were still insufficient – and in addition were largely diverted into real estate rather than reinvested in industry; nor could Conservative government provide the necessary leadership to decisively promote the industrial sector. Only socialism could offer an answer by nationalizing the leading candidates for successful oligopoly, plus the entire banking sector, thus providing the funds required for a massive build-up of investments that would yield returns, not immediately but over the medium term. Hence the importance of nationalizing the banks, which were judged to be insufficiently entrepreneurial. Such a policy would endow France with powerful industrial structures which in due course would concentrate innovation, employment and profits in France, allow a return to a higher growth rate without running into the dilemma of balance of payments deficits, and permit a generous redistribution that would finally reconcile the French working class with industrial society (Boublil, 1977).

When the Socialists came to power they proceeded according to this analysis, though their timetable was set more by political than economic considerations. A reflation (more moderate than in 1975) followed the elections of 1981; the nationalization law came a few months later (February 1982). It was unclear from the beginning how the anticipated beneficial effects of the nationalizations could possilby arrive in time to save the reflation from its usual fate, that is, the import surge. However, the government and most international experts (OECD, IMF) expected an early international economic upturn that would have eased the problem. When that upturn did not materialize, the results of reflation were not as catastrophic as the right had predicted but sufficiently negative to lead to important reversals by 1982, and particularly by March 1983.

Reflation had much the same effect as in 1975: rapidly increasing balance of payments deficits, increasing foreign debt, devaluations of the franc (compounded by the seemingly inexorable rise of the dollar), and no end to these problems in sight. In 1982 the first austerity measures were taken; before they were reinforced in 1983 Mitterand briefly considered a more autonomous, more nationalistic economic policy that would have allowed higher growth rates, but rejected it in the end as unrealistic. Wages and prices were first frozen in 1982, then eased only very gradually and for the most part kept under a tight lid. Inflation was brought down successfully: from 14 per cent in 1981 to 3.4 per cent in March 1986. This would have been a fantastic success for any conservative stabilization policy in the postwar French context. However it could hardly appeal to a leftist electorate; and with each tightening of austerity popular support for the left (which had promised a different approach) declined markedly.

In the area of industrial policy the reversal was similarly pronounced. Most of the nationalized firms were in deep financial trouble, without any early prospect of profits. They needed large capital transfers just to stay afloat; this handicapped the anticipated build-up of investments. After pumping large sums into these firms, the government finally decided (in 1983–4) that they had to revert to profitability quickly, thus mandating the kind of market behaviour which its earlier policy had tried to transcend. Some public sector firms even sold subsidiaries to private owners for needed cash, in rather quiet operations of doubtful legality. This 'creeping denationalization' was never legalized, the government being afraid of submitting the necessary law to the National Assembly for fear of strong opposition from Socialist ranks.

By 1984 the key terms of industrial policy were 'restructuring' and 'enterprise'. Restructuring meant the belated adjustment to realistic production levels (market shares), especially for large firms; it amounted to significant cuts in the labour force at a time when unemployment was rising again after a brief period of stabilization achieved by the Socialists' stopgap measures. Depite an outcry from union organizations, a dramatic strike wave in the steel industry and heavy criticism from the Communists, the government stood firm on this line and passed a few measures only to alleviate the shock (retraining programmes and the like). 'Enterprise' meant a return to market incentives, efforts to increase business profitability (which meanwhile had reached a new low), efforts to improve the lot of private entrepreneurs, and efforts to promote new risk capital for business. An important step was the reform of the capital market, which produced a tremendous stock boom, reinforced by the effect of the nationalizations (the expropriated owners looking for opportunities to reinvest – but then similar booms developed in other countries, though mostly in those headed by conservative governments). Again this policy was a clear success in terms of traditional financial orthodoxy; precisely for that reason it did little to impress leftist voters who viewed it as a betrayal (Lauber, 1985, 1987) or even businessmen who thought the right could do better yet. Indeed the right, which had been unable or unwilling to conduct an effective stabilization policy during the preceding decade, now promised a liberal businessman's paradise.

The right after 1986

The right also learned from the unpopularity of Barre's austerity course. For years neo-Gaullist leader Chirac had criticized Barre's passive stance in the face of rising unemployment. But by 1981 he made an ideological U-turn, shifting from conservative interventionism to agressive liberalism in the style of Thatcher and Reagan. This was confirmed during the years in opposition, and again after coming to power in 1986. The right benefited from the fact that the Socialists had carried out much of the unpleasant task of stabilization and had removed austerity from the area of political controversy.

The main 'new' idea on the right which developed during the opposition years was to severely cut back the state's role in economic life (Lauber, 1986, 1988). State interventionism was to be cut out root and branch and public sector firms reprivatized, even those nationalized under de Gaulle himself immediately after the Second World War. Regulations inhibiting economic freedom were to be repealed, above all the one requiring administrative approval of dismissals introduced by Chirac's goverment in 1975, but also price controls, exchange controls, and so on. Taxes were to be cut, state and social welfare expenditures restricted and the budget deficit reduced, with the shortfall resulting from the tax cut financed by the proceeds from reprivatization (another case of 'selling the family silver'?). Much of this programme appears in fact as symbolic politics: a detailed study by a leading economic research organization showed that the economic effect of many measures was likely to be marginal. (Avouyi-Dovi *et al.*, 1986).

The programme must also be viewed in terms of the electoral calendar: the presidential election of 1988 being generally viewed as decisive, Chirac had to prepare the ground for that. Since there was little time (and not an overwhelming mandate) to get much else done by that date, symbolic issues could be used to give the impression of activism. In any case Chirac succeeded in shifting the ground of controversy considerably to the right, much further than it had ever been since the Second World War, in an effort that replicated developments in many other West European countries. By Autumn 1987 many points of the programme had been translated into law. The first reprivatizations were highly successful, and the biggest part of the programme was scheduled to be completed before the 1988 presidential elections. The proceeds from the reprivatizations plus additional revenues from business and sales taxes (both due to lower oil prices which increased both company profits and private consumption) did in fact permit the simultaneous lowering of taxes and a reduction of the budget deficit. However this was achieved at the expense of some of the financial discipline introduced by the Socialists in 1983; it is doubtful that this relaxation can extend beyond 1988.

Despite this success in terms of public finances, the economic situation remained morose. Rising unemployment could be hidden temporarily by social welfare measures which clearly could not go on for very long; the increase in consumer spending, the decline in international competitiveness of French industry and the slow increase in industrial production led to a marked deterioration of the balance of payments in 1987, with even worse to come in 1988. France was thus in a poor position to face oil price increases in the future.

Governability and structural change

As pressures on governments grow in a crisis, a search for greater efficiency usually sets in. Often this leads to the grant of greater authority to the executive, and generally to expanded state control over economy, society and their main actors. In the 1980s however a reverse phenomenon appeared: reducing the role of the state was now presented as the new instrument for increasing economic efficiency. The left had taken the first steps in this direction, beginning in 1983. The right committed itself to going much further and began to do so in 1986. This enterprise will undoubtedly take many years if it is to be carried out.

Before this controversy there was remarkable continuity. Its origin probably resided in the constitution of the Fifth Republic, adopted in 1958–62. This constitution gives the executive considerable powers to govern efficiently without having to worry unduly about parliamentary or even public opinion, at least until the next election – that was its major purpose. Even a government that in critical matters (such as austerity policy) does not command majority support in the National Assembly can still survive as long as it has at least half-hearted allies who, while being critical, do not want to go as far as to bring it down. It was thanks to this provision of the French constitution (Art. 49) that Barre managed to survive repeated crises. The Prime Minister can also secure from parliament the right to legislate by decree in urgent social and economic areas, within the framework of a general authorizing law; this provision was used repeatedly by left and right. But the decrees need to be signed by the President of the Republic, a clause that became important when Mitterrand refused to sign several such decrees in 1986, forcing the right to pass detailed legislation in the National Assembly. Because of its strong autonomy from parliament, the government also has effective control over the civil service. The biggest controversy concerning the latter during the crisis years was whether the number of civil servants should be increased to absorb unemployment (thus the left at first) or reduced to cut state expenditure (so the right after going into opposition). Also in this context it is worth mentioning that the Socialists had few problems trying to assert their political (party) control over the civil service (Stevens, 1985).

A serious crisis was widely expected if President and government should reflect opposing majorities. In 1986 this occurred for the first time in the history of the Fifth Republic. It resulted in a net loss of power for the President but did not reduce him to a purely symbolic figure. It did not lead to a political crisis either but seemed to introduce what in American constitutional language would be called a check on powers of the government, something that in two years did not cause major problems. In one area though, the political-administrative system was reformed, and the reform was at least helped by the crisis: the regionalization that started in 1981. It appears, however, that this was not done to transfer governability problems to the periphery. After de Gaulle had stumbled during a decentralization referendum in 1969, the subject was not touched again for many years, though *de facto* central bureaucracy control over local and regional authorities diminished. In the 1970s the left became strong at the level of those authorities and asked for a transfer of real power so as to be able to deal with the economic crisis. Conventional wisdom holds that in France such desires wane as soon as the group holding them secures control of the national government. In 1981 things were different: the left very quickly carried out the first reform steps and continued along this line even after the right, having improved its own standing in local and regional elections, clamoured for a share of power of its own. Regionalization thus appears hardly as a matter of passing on the hot potato of dealing with the crisis and its consequences (Mény, 1985): more appropriately, it appears as a departure from the Crozier model of French society in which problems are regularly kicked upstairs to the central bureaucracy so that direct dealings among opponents can be avoided.

Probably the biggest structural change occurred in the relations with the major interest groups, though here too developments were hardly dramatic. One governmental strategy in hard times could be to reduce the ability of the interest groups to exert pressure. From this perspective one might have expected from Giscard and his Prime Ministers (especially Barre) an attempt to weaken the trade unions. However this was not the case; the shock of 1968 was still too close, and the outcome of the 1974 elections too close for the government to risk a head-on conflict with the unions, even though union membership was already weak (below 20 per cent of the labour force) and kept declining after 1976, along with militancy (Lauber, 1983). Only the employers tried increasingly to bypass the unions and deprive them of their functions, by instituting a new system of labour relations (Pouchin, 1980; Bonis, 1981). As to governmental relations with employers, there were some conflicts over Giscard's early and soon abandoned reform projects and over his determination to make the employers carry part of the burden of the economic crisis (making dismissals more difficult by requiring administrative approval; setting up an unemployment scheme financed to an important degree by employer contributions). However, the employers' organization (the CNPF) soon returned to identifying closely with the government.

The Socialists tried to change this situation somewhat, but only half-heartedly and in any case without much impact (at least in the intended direction). A key fact in this context was the absence of any massive wave of labour mobilization after the left's victory: in 1936 (Popular Front) or in May 1968 it had been those mobilizations which had prepared the ground for a 'historic compromise' between business, labour and government, with the union organizations negotiating on behalf of the workers rather than as their mandated representatives. Because of the lack of such mobilization no new compromise was hammered out in 1981, and on many important questions the unions were not even consulted. This was of course complicated by the fact that there are three 'major' trade unions strongly competing with each other, plus a few others. So unions had little influence on nationalizations, the reduction of working hours with maintenance of full wages (one union, the CFDT, had already gone out on a limb to explain to its members the need to accept sacrifices on this account, out of solidarity with the unemployed), the wage and price freeze, and industrial restructuring.

In the 1970s the French Socialists had declared how proud they were not to be mere social democrats. Once in government, and unlike many social democratic parties, they did not produce plans to give unions a significant voice in policy-making at the national level (Wilson, 1985; Eisenhammer, 1985; Goldey, 1985). It must be kept in mind that the unions could be expected to be difficult partners in power, especially with the largest union more or less controlled by a Communist Party unable to settle on a clear course. Only on deregulation were the unions consulted, or rather the matter was left to agreement between the unions and the CNPF – an agreement which did not materialize. This was despite the fact that the CNPF had promised as part of the deal the creation of nearly 500,000 new jobs as long as these were exempted from certain labour regulations such as the one requiring administrative approval for dismissals.

On one level, however, the Socialists did try to strengthen the unions – namely, plant level, through the Auroux laws assuring them representation and consultation rights in management. The reform only brought French labour relations a little more in line with conditions prevailing in other western capitalist countries; even so it raised the fury of many employers who voiced their worst fears. In this case however the dust settled, and by 1986 the right had accepted most of the Auroux laws (Ross, 1986).

The Socialists attempted a real coup only in one area (where in fact it backfired). This was when they tried to restrict the employers' organization (the Conseil National du Patronat Français or CNPF) by making use of a crisis that shook that body, in order to make it less determined and less capable of opposing leftist ideas and programmes. The CNPF originated from, and was long dominated by, the French steelmasters. But with the decline, near-bankruptcy and quasi-nationalization of that industry in the second half of the 1970s, the steelmasters' hegemony faded. Instead of big industrialists, it was now provincial businessmen coming from smaller firms who decided the CNPF leadership elections in late 1981; these were followed by an intense battle at the top of the organization between old and new forces. The nationalizations further weakened the big firms sector, and the government at one point threatened to pull the nationalized companies (important to the organization because of their membership contributions) out of the CNPF altogether. In the end they stayed but hardly as champions of private enterprise. In addition the Socialists created competition for the CNPF by recognizing a breakaway organization of small business, the SNPMI. Soon however this particular game got out of hand. SNPMI tried to take advantage of the anti-governmental mood among many small businessmen by espousing a politics of radical protest and taking to the streets. The CNPF in turn had to follow suit to some degree in order to demonstrate to its members that is was still the best defender of business interests after all, while at the same time remaining 'moderate' and at least prepared to negotiate. Having first secured the hostility of the CNPF by seriously threatening its existence, or at least its position, the government now needed that very same organization to get the demonstrators off the streets again. The result was a CNPF stonger and more independent than before, due to the intervening mobilization of its formerly fairly quiescent membership (Berger, 1985; Goldey, 1985) and also due to the new competition (after the U-turn on 'enterprise') between government and opposition about who would do more for private business. Now the CNPF was no longer restrained by the close relationship with government that had once prevailed under rightist rule and could formulate a far-reaching programme of liberalization, tax reduction and deregulation that proposed to undo much of the legislation passed earlier by rightist governments.

When the right prepared for its return to government before 1986 it found a situation of changed power relations among the major groups: a stronger and more independent CNPF, trade unions further weakened by loss of membership and demoralization (Noblecourt 1985a). It considered taking advantage of this situation by challenging the 'monopoly' position of the 'representative' unions (those officially recognized as such by decree and who, on the basis of this recognition, can run for elections to certain bodies without any further proof that they are indeed representative of their electorate) (Noblecourt, 1985b). Such a challenge would most likely present an important setback to unions already plagued by decline in almost every area over the past ten years. But the weakness of the unions has its own dangers. This was demonstrated by the railway strike at the end of 1986. The movement started as a wildcat strike, and it proved difficult to organize negotiations. As a result the strike dragged on and caused considerable damage.

With reprivatization, the right has taken decisive steps to restructure economic power in France. The share issues of the former public sector companies will increase the value of the stock traded at the Paris stock exchange by more than 30 per cent; the number of small shareholders will be multiplied. Perhaps more important, about a quarter of the stock of each of these companies was sold to a 'hard core' of major enterprises in banking, insurance, industry, and so on (*Conjoncture,* 1987). These investors are supposed to provide the reprivatized firms with stability of control and with consistent strategies. In any case they will represent a business oligarchy with considerable power on the basis of relatively little capital – and perhaps with no special managerial competence in the area of their new acquisitions.

The 1980s also witnessed a new phenomenon in the area of governability: the emergence on two occasions of massive protest movements against ideologically motivated reforms in the educational sector. In the spring of 1984 a leftist school reform plan had to be shelved in the face of some of the largest mass demonstrations in French history – which seemed to originate with genuine opposition to the specific reform plans rather than from general opposition to the government. In late 1986 student protests against a university reform bill found a similar echo and forced retreat upon a government that strove to make a show of strong and unwavering leadership and authority. This added a new dimension to French politics. The new *ad hoc* movements were hardly organized as such; this meant strength as well as weakness, since it made it impossible to anticipate their reactions or to deal with them in the way usual with interest groups. The implications of this development are as yet difficult to predict.

Adjustments in ideology, structure and institutions

The economic crisis had a learning effect on all major actors, partly as a result of intense political competition. Confronted with rising unemployment in 1975 Chirac applied a Keynesian policy of reflation, which under the conditions of the first oil crisis led to a rapid deterioration of the balance of payments. Under these pressures, and after Chirac's replacement, the right, now under Barre, shifted to a policy of financial conservatism and tried to disentangle the state from the economy. Unemployment continued to rise and French industry showed little dynamism. Meanwhile the left learned that Keynesian reflations harbour dangers of their own. As a result it built up its critique of French capitalism, which it now judged as too timorous, and stressed that only nationalizations, resulting in more dynamic large industries, could secure full employment, a rising standard of living and better redistribution in the long run. But the Socialist government could not wait long enough to see whether its policy of building up the new public sector industries would bear fruit. The experiment had to be cut short and the Socialists, not without great internal strains, converted to a liberal policy of encouraging private enterprise, although within a framework of social welfare regulations, to ease the impact of such liberalization. This policy shift was probably also meant to secure electoral support from the centre; in any case it failed to do that, partly because, in the meantime, the right had shifted its own stance. But there was also another element: while at first the Socialists tried to maintain that their policy reversals did not mean the abandonment of Socialist principles, but only their temporary suspension and postponement, it soon became obvious that the change was bound to be more long-lasting. The fact was that the top Socialist leaders had isolated the one faction (around Michel Rocard) that might have been able to fit these changes into an alternative vision of socialism, combined with their own defensive posture to deprive the Socialist Party of legitimacy in terms of the norms and expectations it had laid down earlier. This was keenly felt (and resented) on the part of those who had voted Socialist in 1981 and who might have been prepared to accept a shift in policy as long as it could be justified by some coherent set of principles. In any case the Socialist Party emerged as economically 'responsible' and financially orthodox – an image that most of its leaders, and particularly Mitterrand, had strongly resisted in the 1970s.

Perhaps due to the fact that it was in opposition, the right found it easier to carry out a similar shift. After 1981 it was relieved of the burden of advocating an unpopular policy of austerity; after the Socialist's U-turn that policy could be taken for granted. Looking for a more popular alternative, the right discovered ultra-liberalism as the new panacea for the economic crisis: a new liberalism including denationalization, deregulation, tax reduction and so on. These were all policies that the Socialists had also tried or practised, although with a bad conscience, being unable to legitimate their own reversals by some principle that could credibly be referred to as Socialist. By contrast such programmes and actions fit in well with the ideological universe of the right – and also with the mood of the country from 1983 on.

A time of crisis might be expected to mobilize radical centrifugal political forces in a polity. The 'radicalization' of the right is undoubtedly part of such a development. It is surprising, however, that this phenomenon does not extend to the left. The Communist Party failed to adjust to the new economic (and perhaps cultural) realities and also to come up with a clear political line regarding its relationship with the Socialists in party and government. Because of this, it was reduced from a strong organization able to count on 20 per cent and more of the electorate, to a position of near-marginality (around 10 per cent) in which it could hardly mobilize working class people, even through its own trade union organization. Mitterrand's strategy of keeping the Communists from breaking away was also successful; when they did, it was too late to assert an identity which they had already surrendered on the occasion of earlier Socialist U-turns (Serge July, 1986). On the extreme right by contrast, Le Pen's National Front, with its racist ideology and its violent stance against immigrants, achieved considerable success, almost pulling level with the Communist vote in 1986. While the established parties of the right rarely cooperated with the National Front at the level of national politics, many of its leaders joined Le Pen's rhetoric in order to stem the further loss of voters. This shift became important for the law and order stance of the right but less so for its economic policy and programme (Lauber, 1986, 1988). By late 1987 Le Pen appeared rather isolated politically.

In the sphere of group relations, the picture that emerges is one of groups becoming less closely linked to the political parties or camps for which they have a 'natural' affinity. That this would be true for the CNPF is plausible enough: first because of the strains resulting from Giscard's early reform plans, but mostly because of the organization's fight for survival in its battle against the Socialist government, a battle to which the parties of the right, given their political weakness at the time, could not make a significant contribution. Returning to strength because of a mobilization of businessmen at the grassroots level, the CNPF could strengthen its position vis-à-vis the rightist parties as well.

More surprising is the case of the unions. Giscard and Barre spared them, mostly out of political weakness. From the leftist government one might have expected an attempt to incorporate them into the national policy-making structures, whether formally or informally. But no such attempts were made, perhaps because the Socialist leaders actually feared political competition from unions (Goldey, 1985). In 1986, as after the 1978 elections, the unions assumed a less political, more interest-group oriented stance to prepare themselves for dealing with a government of the right. Given the continuing decline in membership and having already conceded severe austerity to its own camp (that is, to the Socialist government), they are bound to remain vulnerable and to see their position weakened further under the rightist government that came into office in 1986. However a revival of militancy at the shop floor cannot be entirely ruled out; weak unions may mean more wildcat strikes.

Thus the lasting and indeed intensifying economic crisis produced important changes in the policy and ideology of the major political actors. These learning effects were motivated partly by the search for greater success in the area of economic policy, partly by the search for greater electoral support. In the case of the left this led to increased realism after 1983. The case of the right is more complicated; its passage into opposition produced a loss of realism and an emphasis on symbolic politics that were still prevalent in 1986. In any case the economy provided few occasions for triumph. Unemployment rose more or less steadily from the outset of the crisis, with the two reflations of 1975 and 1981 (and a similar phenomenon in 1986) figuring as temporary holding operations that produced a serious deterioration in the balance of payments. On inflation, success came to the Socialists after 1983. The inflation rate fell to 3.6 per cent early in 1986 after hovering around 10 per cent in the second half of the 1970s and almost reaching 14 per cent in 1981. (The Socialists did not have to cope with another oil crisis, and indeed benefited from falling prices for oil and other raw materials; but they did practise a tougher incomes policy than the right.) Investment emerged from stagnation twice, first in 1978–79 and then again in 1984–5. Thus economic indicators certainly yielded to policy changes, but deteriorations occurred suddenly; improvements were achieved more slowly. In the face of these important ideology and policy changes, it seems remarkable how few proposals for institutional and in particular constitutional change were discussed in French political circles during this time. This is all the more surprising if one considers Mitterrand's long-term opposition to the Fifth Republic constitution as 'usurpationist' in character, and his promise to 'return power to the people' if elected. The absence of such a discussion may be one of de Gaulle's belated political triumphs. It indicates that at least with regard to the institutional framework, the French political system may have settled on stable terrain. Given the earlier widespread expectations of an inevitable constitutional crisis in the event of the President and the parliamentary majority (and thus the government) coming from opposite political camps, the cohabitation that lasted from 1986 to 1988 was remarkably smooth even though it probably opened a new chapter of constitutional development.

References

Avouyi-Dovi, S., Gubian, A., and Sterdyniak, H. (1986), 'Vers un moindre poids de l'Etat? Une évaluation chiffrée des projets de l'opposition', *Observations et diagnostics économiques,* no. 14 (January 1986), pp. 5–58.

Berger, S. (1985), 'The Socialists and the patronat: the dilemma of coexistence in a mixed economy' in Machin, H. and Wright, V., *Economic Policy and Policy-Making under the Mitterrand Presidency 1981–1984* (London, Frances Pinter), pp. 225–44.

Bonis, J. (1981), 'Nouveaux modes d'action managériales et syndicats', *Economie et humanisme* (May-June 1981), pp. 31–9.
Boublil, A. (1977), *Le socialisme industriel.* Paris, Presses universitaires de France.
Conjoncture (July 1987), monthly economic bulletin of the Paribas bank.
Eisenhammer, J. S. (1985), comment on F. Wilson contribution in Machin and Wright (eds), *Mitterrand Presidency,* pp. 279–83.
Goldey, D. (1985), comment on S. Berger contribution in Machin and Wright (eds), *Mitterrand Presidency,* pp. 244–54.
Hoffmann, S. *et al.* (1963), *In Search of France.* New York, Harper and Row. Contributions by S. Hoffmann and C. P. Kindleberger.
July, Serge (1986), 'Sur l'impopularité de François Mitterrand', Sofres, *Opinion publique* (Paris, Gallimard), pp. 11–21.
Lauber, V. (1983), *The Political Economy of France.* New York, Praeger.
Lauber, V. (1985), 'Reinventing French socialism: economic policy, ideology, political strategy', *Parliamentary Affairs,* 38:2 (Spring 1985), pp. 152–62.
Lauber, V. (1986), 'France after March 1986: macroeconomic policy forecast', *French Politics and Society,* no. 13 (March 1986), pp. 7–10.
Lauber, V. (1987), 'The economic policy of the French socialists' in P. McCarthy (ed.), *The French Socialists in Power.* Westpoint, Greenwood.
Lauber, V. (1988), 'The French right from 1944 to 1986' in B. Girvin (ed.), *The Transformation of Contemporary Conservatism.* London, Sage.
Lettre and *Revue de l'Observatoire Français des Conjonctures économiques.*
Mény, Y. (1985), 'Local authorities and economic policy', comment by M. Keating in Machin and Wright (eds), *Mitterrand Presidency,* pp. 187–204.
Noblecourt, M. (1985a), *Le Monde,* 12 July 1985.
Noblecourt, M. (1985b), *Le Monde,* 7 November 1985 and 2 January 1986, shows a decline of union membership from about 20% in 1975 to about 15% in 1985.
OECD, yearly reports on France. Paris.
OECD (1986), *Historical statistics 1960–1984.* Paris.
Pouchin (1980), 'Syndicalisme en crise', *Le Monde,* 6 and 7 March 1980.
Ross, George (1986), 'La politique sociale', *French Politics and Society,* no. 13 (March 1986), pp. 10–14.
Stevens, A. (1985), ''L'Alternance' and the Higher Civil Service' in Cerny, P. G. and Schain, M. (eds), *Socialism, the State and Public Policy in France* (London, Frances Pinter), pp. 143–65.
Wilson, F. (1985), 'Trade unions and economic policy' in Machin and Wright, *Mitterrand Presidency,* pp. 255–78.

8 Political change and economic crisis in Spain 1974–1987

JOAN SUBIRATS

Main political events

1973	ETA assassinates Admiral Carrero Blanco, President of the government, considered the most likely successor to Franco.
1975	General Franco dies; Juan Carlos I crowned King of Spain
1976	'Political Reform Bill' approved by public referendum and transition to democracy is formally begun
1977	first democratic elections held; UCD, a moderate party wins the elections with a relative majority and Adolfo Suarez is elected President of the government
1978	new Spanish Constitution approved by public referendum
1979	general elections; UCD wins with a relative majority; Adolfo Suarez continues President of the government; first democratic local elections held
1980	elections in the Basque country and Catalonia
1981	Suarez resigns; there is an unsuccessful attempt at a military coup
1982	general elections; PSOE triumphs with an absolute majority; Felipe Gonzalez is elected President of the government
1983	local and regional elections
1986	Spain enters the EEC
	public referendum held to determine whether Spain will remain in NATO; general elections; another victory with an absolute majority for PSOE; Felipe Gonzalez starts a second term as President of the government

Introduction

Spain has seen some difficult times, both political and economic, from the mid-1970s until the present day. In fact the various governments which have been in power since the first democratic elections of June 1977 have had to operate in an extremely unfavourable climate both within the country and abroad.

A peaceful and gradual transition from a dictatorship to a democracy obviously poses problems: a legal situation that is as treacherous as quicksand, the stubborn resistance of the old establishment versus the people who want to rise to the challenge of making democracy a reality and of structuring a new state that will respect regional autonomy. Still, this did not necessarily have to coincide with the century's second most serious economic crisis. It is a cruel coincidence (Boyer, 1986) that the two occasions (1931 and 1976) Spain has had a chance to forge a system of civil liberties have coincided with extremely difficult outside conditions. This prevented Spain from enjoying a period of economic well-being such as the Italian, French and German republics enjoyed when they restablished their democracies and consolidated their welfare states after the Second World War. The fact that Spain has none the less managed to shape a solid democracy and reduce social tension to European limits clearly demonstrates that good sense has prevailed throughout the entire process.

This chapter attempts to give a general survey of the relationships between politics and economics during these years, with particular emphasis on the way the various governments have approached the economic crisis and the impact of the crisis on the political sphere.

The economic crisis in Spain

The Spanish economy is naturally affected by the same elements that constitute the world economic crisis. However, these elements affect Spain more intensely than other countries in the same geographic area, proving that Spain's economy is more vulnerable. Furthermore the economic crisis in Spain is aggravated by certain elements that are peculiar to this country. In fact it is perfectly acceptable (Lagares, 1982; Sevilla, 1985; Ministerio de Economía y Hacienda, 1985) to label the Spanish crisis as 'differential'.

A more intense crisis

In the Spanish economy 1964 to 1975 were boom years. Then production fell, as it did in all OECD countries, but the fall was greater in Spain. As shown in Table 8.1, this fall was reflected not only in the decline in growth of the GDP, but particularly in the galloping pace of inflation and the tremendous increase in unemployment.

Table 8.1 Economic data: Spain and OECD 1960–86

	1960–73		1974–83		1984–6	
	Spain	OECD	Spain	OECD	Spain	OECD
Growth of GDP %	7.2	5.0	1.6	2.3	1.9	3.4
Inflation %	6.7	3.9	16.8	9.2	9.0	6.0
Unemployment %	2.7	3.4	18.1	9.0	21.8	8.3

Source: *Statistiques retrospectives OECD 1960–1982; Perspectives Economiques de l'OCDE*, December 1984; *Anuario El Pais*, 1986. Author's calculations.

A more vulnerable economy

Several things seem to support the idea that the Spanish economy is more vulnerable than most to the factors which caused the general economic crisis. First we must remember that the economic crisis was triggered by the hike in oil prices in the 1970s. Spain is highly dependent on oil for its energy requirements and is consequently extremely sensitive to any fluctuations or changes in the price of oil. Spain's domestic production covers only 33 per cent of the country's energy needs, while the other OECD countries supply an average of 60 per cent of their own energy.

We are well aware that economic crisis has caused great concern about increased production costs. When a country has a labour-intensive production system, this is another sign of vulnerability. Spain's production system continues to be more labour-intensive than most, although there has been a slight improvement in this situation in the past two or three years (Lagares, 1982; Malo de Molina, 1984).

Furthermore there is an excess of interventionism which made it difficult to improve the efficiency of the Spanish production system. This interventionism was responsible for the low wages in Spain: in 1973 gross wages were 48.5 per cent of the EEC average (Malo de Molina, 1984). The employment policy was so rigid that it was difficult for employers to adapt to economic fluctuations. As a result, when the crisis developed Spanish industry was overstaffed and this made it difficult to adapt the necessary new technologies. In short, when the crisis broke the Spanish economy was extremely vulnerable: the country was highly dependent on imports of raw materials for energy and was thus particularly sensitive to fluctuating oil prices; the industrial structure was dominated by smokestack industries and was therefore more sensitive to the phenomenon of technological 'displacement'; production was excessively labour-intensive and thus more sensitive to wage increases. Interventionism was rampant, the economy far from efficient and certainly not very able to adapt to the far-reaching changes resulting from new market conditions.

What 'differentiates' the Spanish economic crisis?

The onset of the international economic crisis coincided with the death of an authoritarian, highly interventionalist regime in Spain and the later transition to a democratic system with all sectors and forces of society competing to achieve their individual goals. This difference is the key to the peculiar way in which the economic crisis has developed in Spain. Between 1973 and 1979, when the new Constitution was approved, the country's main priority was a political one: how to restructure the Spanish political system along the lines of other western European countries. The alternatives appeared to be reform or rupture, and the economic crisis, and its attendant consequences, tended more to be the stuff of political and social debates than major problems requiring solution. The very need to make a peaceful and non-traumatic political transition led to compromises which are difficult to explain today, when attempts are at last being made to find solutions to the country's economic problems.

During the years of transition, issues such as the legalization of all political parties, the recognition of autonomous territories, amnesty, and the drafting of a new Constitution which would summarize and symbolize the dawn of a new political system in Spain, took precedence over inflation, unemployment, the public deficit, industrial restructuring or the need for technological innovation. In fact the major triumph of those years was the successful transition to democracy, but it is this very transition that differentiates the Spanish crisis and delayed the country's response to this crisis, causing it to become more complex and serious as time passed.

The repercussions of this 'differential' element on the labour market were considerable, particularly in terms of wages. Between 1970 and 1982 labour costs increased by 190 per cent. Between 1973 and 1979 the annual increase in wages (as a whole) was 361 per cent in Spain compared with 169 per cent in the rest of the OECD. During this same period labour costs increased 40 per cent faster than production costs (Malo de Maltona, 1984). Obviously these sizeable increases in wage costs were bound to have an adverse effect on Spain's competitiveness. While it may be true that higher inflation caused wages to soar more in Spain than elsewhere, the basic reason for the wage increases is that those years were marked by a tremendous increase in labour militancy. The number of working hours lost through strikes was four times greater in 1976 than in 1975, while the number of striking workers rose from one million to 3.6 million. This period of tension and unrest had its peaks and troughs, but lasted until 1980 (Ludevid, 1982). In short, the struggle for democracy also awakened the Spanish labour movement, whose agitation caused an increase in wage costs per unit product far greater than that of the OECD countries as a whole and which was a 'reflection and expression of the shift in the distribution of power' (Sevilla, 1985). But the working class alone was by no means to blame for aggravating Spain's economic crisis. At least in the beginning, the Spanish business community displayed a tendency to 'passively adapt' to the crisis (Sevilla, 1985). When production rose due to increased wage costs, employers simply raised their prices, thus theoretically maintaining their rate of profit. But no matter who is to blame the fact remains that increased labour costs, which were most certainly caused by the 'differential' element (the transition to democracy), served to further aggravate the Spanish economic crisis (Malo de Malina, 1985); (Perez Diaz, 1986).

The transition to democracy also caused the business community to view the future with increasing uncertainty, and this may partly explain the sharp decline in investment. This theory appears to be born out by the data: investment reached its lowest ebb in the years when uncertainty was greatest: 1975 and the death of Franco; 1977 and 1979 and the general elections; 1981 and the attempted military coup (Lagares, 1982). In conditions of uncertainty, businessmen fear for their future investment profits and prefer to make investments that either reduce manpower needs (Zabalza, 1985) or increase productivity. Investors may well find either state bonds or investing abroad more attractive (Donges, 1984). We realize that this reluctance to invest is not due solely to fear of possible political instability, but there is no doubt that, at least until 1982, the political situation was one of the most immediate concerns of any potential investor, more so than the experts suspected at the time (Martinez Mendez, 1982; Marzal, 1985).

When reviewing the consequences of this 'differential' element of Spain's economic crisis, we must also consider the sizeable increase in public spending by the post-Franco democratic governments, which increased subsidies and social welfare as part of a policy of redistribution of wealth. At the time of the democratic transition, the quality of public services in Spain was far inferior to that of other western European countries. Political claims triggered social conflict and, as numerous civic organizations and movements (labour unions, neighbourhood associations, users of public utilities) were legalized, there was a 'blast wave' that led the State to increase social benefits. This in turn caused such a great and rapid increase in public spending that it cannot be compared with any other European country in terms of its rate of growth. The percentage of the GNP consumed by public spending increased from 18.75 per cent in 1960 to 24.7 per cent in 1975 and reached 39.6 per cent in 1985. Nevertheless the average social benefits provided in Spain still lag far behind those of other western European countries, and Spain can hardly be qualified as a consolidated welfare state (Castells, 1986).

Attitudes and general reactions to the Spanish economic crisis

Since 1973 Spain's political structures have undergone radical changes. The country has changed from a dictatorship where political parties were outlawed, to a democratic state steered by a Socialist government with an absolute majority. From a centralized state, hostile to regional differences, it has become a state that recognized regional autonomy and accepts official bilingualism in Catalonia, the Basque country and Galicia. Spain has weathered several attempted military coups and is engaged in a pitched battle against terrorism.[1]

Once internationally isolated except for the US military bases located on Spanish soil, Spain is now a member of both the EEC and NATO. During the last ten years there have been three national referendas, four general elections and two local and regional elections. Some of the political parties have been shaken to their very roots. UCD actually disappeared from the scene, only six months after controlling the nation's government and a considerable share of municipal powers. Other parties have also registered noteworthy changes (Barnes, MacDonough and Lopez Pina, 1986) (see Table 8.2). The political situation has seriously conditioned any strategy of response to the economic crisis and has given rise to a diversity of attitudes towards the situation, and a variety of attempts to tackle the crisis.

1973–7

During the first phase (1973–7) the government was politically insecure and either chose to ignore the economic crisis or adapted a 'wait and see' policy (Lagares, 1982). There were many reasons for this. Spain was genuinely unaware of the true magnitude of the crisis. Furthermore there were no reliable sources of information about the possible effects of the crisis on an economy like Spain's, which at that time was characterized by considerable state interventionalism and a high degree of protectionism. In addition Spain had deliberately chosen to play a subordinate role in international decision-making, and this caused the country to wait submissively and see what measures other countries might take to combat the crisis. Above all, this period was so difficult politcally that it would have been almost presumptuous for any government to make decisions or devise medium or long-term programmes for dealing with the crisis. As a result governments chose to gamble that the crisis was a temporary phenomenon, which explains why measures enacted in Spain in 1974, 1975 and 1976 have little or no relationship to those adopted in the rest of Europe. Spain paid dearly for this attitude: foreign trade reserves evaporated, and on the domestic scene inflation rose to almost 25 per cent in 1977. A 'wait and see' policy seemed to be the only approach to a situation where management of the economy was secondary to the political transition, and where state interventionalism made it difficult to 'receive' messages signalling the extent of the crisis.

1977–9

During the next period (1977–9) the policy seemed to be 'politics first'. Until the new Spanish Constitution came into effect, Spanish political leaders

Table 8.2 Electoral results and party composition in Spain 1977–86

	Legislative election (month and year)											
	June 1977			March 1979			October 1982			June 1986		
Party	votes*	%	seats	votes	%	seats	votes	%	seats	votes	%	seats
Centre (UCD)	6309	34.7	165	6228	34.3	168	1494	7.1	12	—	—	—
Socialists (PSOE)	5240	29.2	118	5469	30.0	121	10127	48.4	202	8887	44.0	184
Communists (PCE)	1655	9.2	20	1911	10.5	23	865	4.1	4	930	4.6	7
Conservatives (AP)	1503	8.3	16	1067	5.8	9	5478	26.2	106	5245	26.0	105
Democ. Centre (CDS)	—	—	—	—	—	—	604	2.9	2	1862	9.2	19
Nat. Basques	304	1.6	8	275	1.5	7	395	1.8	8	308	1.5	6
Nat. Catalans	666	2.8	13	483	2.6	8	772	3.7	12	1012	5.0	18
Others	—	14.2	10	—	15.3	14	—	5.7	4	—	10.7	13
TOTAL		100	350		100	350		100	350		100	350

Note: *number of votes in thousands.

in general seemed to take this approach to the economic crisis. As Suarez, then President, said on 10 September 1976 in a televised message, when presenting the Political Reform Bill

> let's not fool ourselves. In other times the economic measures agreed upon by the Cabinet would have been enough to drastically change the course of the economy, but now they have not been as effective as we might have hoped and this is due to the impact of politics in our economy. So long as the country is haunted by unknown quantities in politics the economy cannot be reactivated or stabilized. (ABC, 11 September 1976)

The quote accurately reflects the stance, not only of the government but also of all the political parties which, once legally recognized, would participate first in the elections of 15 June 1977 and later in the drafting of the new Constitution.

The 'Moncloa Pacts' are the best example of the consensus policy which characterized this period. The 'Moncloa Pacts' were signed by all the political parties represented in parliament, as well as by the UCD government. They combined economic measures (income and employment policies and social security reform) with political actions which could not be delayed until the Constitution was approved (freedom of expression, right of assembly, reform of the penal code and the system of military justice). The pacts managed to reduce inflation by setting a ceiling on wage increases and bringing the balance of payments into line by devaluing the peseta. The remaining measures covered by them were never really implemented, because the government did not have sufficient power in parliament, or sufficient internal cohesion to enforce them. However they did manage to keep the economic problems, which had accumulated since 1973, from distorting the social situation to such an extent that it would have been impossible to achieve the priority goal: a Constitution based on consensus. 'The economic policy 'pacted' in October 1977 enabled the political parties involved to gain the time necessary to draft the Constitution' (Fuentes Quintana, 1983). But the very political situation, the very priority given to political issues, prevented the pacts from going beyond these essential measures designed to get the economy back on a more even keel.

1979–82

The 1979–82 period was further aggravated by several new factors. The second energy crisis struck: the state of the Spanish balance of payments worsened and unemployment spiralled. Furthermore, the diagnosis of the crisis and its possible solutions caused a rift between the government and the opposition, ending the period of consensus. Internal strife within the governing party worsened and this affected the government's approach to the economy. Within the government, 'which in the past several years has become a hodgepodge of different factions' (*El País*, 1982), every ministry operated in isolation and this made an efficient general approach impossible. The ministries incurred expenditure that was difficult to meet and acted without the guidance of any kind of well thought out general plan for combating the crisis.

This is just another example of how UCD's internal strife and political weakness lessened its ability to deal with the crisis (Subirats, 1986). This inability translated into yet another postponement of the moment when drastic measures would have to be enacted in order to combat Spain's crisis. In short, politics continued to play a major role in Spain's approach to the economic crisis.

It was at this time that unemployment began to soar, toppling inflation from its position as the number one public concern. In 1979 the unemployment rate accounted for 10 per cent of the active population. Just prior to the 1982 general elections, unemployment registered 16 per cent. This policy echoed that of previous governments which simply 'muddled through' or 'passively adjusted' to the crisis. It seemed as though the status quo would be maintained and this caused delays, high social costs and made the Spanish economy more dependent than ever (Segura, 1983).

1982–6

Starting with the Socialist (PSOE) victory in October 1982, there was a marked changed in the approach as the new government began taking advantage of its absolute majority in parliament. One of the many strategies that can be adopted in an attempt to combat the economic crisis is that of making radical structural changes a condition for solving existing problems. The Spanish Socialists definitely tend to favour this approach. They presented 'change' as the magic word which expressed the the need for a radical restructuring of the whole of Spanish society. The 'change' was also understood to be the best proof that Spanish institutions were democratically effective and capable of supporting political change. The Socialist change gave the country a government that was far more capable of solving the country's serious economic problems than its indecisive predecessors. The 'change' promised that the public sector and state investment would be the principle means for reviving the Spanish economy and generating employment. Unemployment had become the country's leading problem and the Socialists promised to create 800,000 new jobs.

The Socialist government enjoyed tremendous electoral and parliamentary support, and was not as conditioned by political concerns as its predecessors had been. Taking advantage of this situation, the Socialists chose to apply an economic policy which can be labelled as the 'Schmidt law' (after Germany's former Social Democratic chancellor): 'today's business profits are tomorrow's investments and tomorrow's investments are the next day's new jobs' (Fuentes Quintana, 1985). This stance differs substantially from the

Socialist's electoral promises: it implies that emphasis will be on fighting inflation by keeping wages down, by deregulating the labour market and so on, that is, by removing all impediments to the growth of business profits, leaving the creation of new jobs as a fruit of business recovery.

The reason for this apparent change of heart may be found in the resounding failure of the French Socialists' economic policies; it may be due to the desire to give the business community and the world powers an impression of cautious action, well within the guidelines set by the OECD, in order to quell possible fears about the first Socialist government in Spain for almost fifty years; or it may be due to the fact that different people drafted the programme from those who direct the government's economic policy.

So, once in power, the Socialists' promised 'change' turned into a new strategy of 'modernization'. The objectives of this modernization were: 'to make democracy more firmly rooted, to reform the State, break with the centuries-old tradition of corporatism, make up for lost ground in industry, science and technology and put an end to our international isolation' (Benegas, PSOE, *El País,* 21 July 1985). The economic problems caused by the crisis, and Spain's delayed reaction to it, now took a back seat to a general 'modernization' strategy. This strategy was to cause 'additional short-term costs and unwanted, but unavoidable, effects which would cause, and have in fact caused, inevitable discontent', but 'PSOE was obliged to opt for a basic clean-up of our national economy in order to settle a number of issues, among them the pressing problem of unemployment, by creating jobs without increasing the public deficit' (resolutions of the 30th PSOE Congress, December 1984). In other words the strategy of 'change' was traded in for a new strategy of 'modernization' which changed, or more accurately postponed, the priorities, but which continued to link solving economic problems with overcoming delays and inefficient processes, which were branded as 'centuries old'.

1986

The general elections of June 1986 were a new proof that the public solidly approved the performance of the Socialist government. Despite the fact that they lost some votes in relation to 1982, the Socialists still have an absolute majority in parliament, and though the referendum on NATO membership placed them in a difficult position, they emerged from it relatively unscathed.

Since the elections, there has been almost perfect continuity. Only three Cabinet ministers have been replaced and almost no changes have been made in other key posts in the administration. Furthermore, there have been no appreciable changes either in the approach to economic policy or in the basic team of policymakers. Nevertheless relations between the Socialist government and the labour organizations have become increasingly strained. This is particularly true of the government's relations with the Socialist union (UGT). In fact things have reached such a point that some of the top ranking union officials, who are also Socialist MPs, voted against the 1987 budget proposals.

In the 1987 local and regional elections, PSOE lost more than one million votes in comparison with the general elections of 1986, and relinquished control of some provincial capitals and regional governments. Still, the Socialists retain the majority of city councils and regional governments and there appears to be no viable alternative to socialism as yet. The sizeable loss of votes led the government and the Socialist Party to admit that they need to 'adopt a style a government that is more open to dialogue' (*El Pais*, 22 June 1987).

Issues and policies

As our analysis has shown, the key issues in Spain varied according to the government in power. Up to 1982 the main issue was the political transition and the subsequent consolidation of democracy. From then on, the Socialists have been working towards the 'economic transition': guiding Spain into decision-making and productivity centres of the western world and trying to bring the country's economic variables in line with those of the rest of the developed world.

Different governments have used different means to achieve their purposes. In some cases agreements were reached through dialogue and consensus. The wage policy was set either by means of trilateral pacts (1981, 1984) or simply through agreements between business and labour (1980, 1983). In other cases the government chose to take a firm stand, arbitrarily imposing measures, such as industrial reconstruction, which were only 'negotiated' after the decision. On some occasions they have used Spain's faulty statistical bases in an attempt to manipulate the definition of some of the country's problems (the employment level, price and productivity increases). On other occasions the government has chosen to ignore certain issues in order not to aggravate the economic situation. Prime examples of this are the shadow economy and the failure of some businesses to pay their social security charges. Generally, one of the arguments most frequently used by the Socialists is that theirs is the 'only possible' economic policy or at least the one that will guarantee bigger and better modernization of the country, despite the 'sacrifices' that this will involve, particularly from the working class (PSOE declaration, 1 May 1985, *El País*).

Unemployment, the labour market and the shadow economy

The almost 3 million people registered as unemployed are currently one of the government's main concerns. While the unemployment rate was around 10 per cent in 1979 it had leaped to 16 per cent by 1982. Since then unemployment has been one of the major subjects of economic and political discussion in Spain. The various governments have applied policies that tended to promote indirect job creation measures, convinced that direct measures would only aggravate the situation in the public sector by increasing its deficit. Thus tax reductions were given in exchange for creating new jobs, employment contracts for young people or people over forty-five were subsidized, and special privileges were given to the geographic areas hardest hit by unemployment. Special lines of credit were established to help create new businesses. In certain areas the public administration offers temporary (community) employment. Other measures have reduced the number of working hours, increased the years of compulsory education and lowered the retirement age.

The Socialist government has also attempted to analyse the impact of Spain's shadow economy, in order to get an accurate idea of the real extent of unemployment, and is using this as an argument in favour of deregulating the labour market. According to a recent survey[2] unemployment in Spain should really be considered as 15.9 per cent instead of the official 22 per cent. However, the survey recognizes that a large number of people employed in the shadow economy are employed only sporadically and in marginal types of job. The survey also concludes that in the shadow economy, which is of great importance in a number of different productive sectors (agriculture 30 per cent, construction 18 per cent, the garment industry 43 per cent, the shoe industry 38 per cent, and so on), the educational level and professional skills are lower, there are more unskilled labourers and more people working in their own homes and at lower wages (*El País,* 16 October 1986).

When the Socialists came to power in 1982 they soon changed one of the planks in their election platform: the promise to create 800,000 new jobs. Instead they have tried to stimulate employment by encouraging business operations. According to business representatives, as well as experts from OECD and IMF, this will mean eliminating, or at least considerably reducing, the tremendously rigid regulations on the the labour market. Although they guarantee a level of labour stability, higher even than that of Japan, these regulations have also helped create a shadow economy which keeps a large number of workers employed in precarious conditions at wage levels far below those established in the tripartite pacts. The Socialist government has attempted to make the labour market more flexible by eliminating existing restrictions on temporary hiring (which increased by 244 per cent in 1985 alone), but they have done nothing to change the system whereby any employee dismissed must be paid an indemnity. Business leaders contend that this makes it impossible to adapt the labour market more closely to productive needs. Business and labour are diametrically opposed in their attitudes to this and the Socialist government has been obliged to walk a tightrope between the two.

Industrial policy and public corporations

Industrial 'reconversion' has been one of the chief goals of recent years, although it was only in 1979 that the first steps in this direction were taken.

The political problems inherent in the transition, and the very weakness of the centrist governments (UCD), caused Spain to lag far behind other European countries in tackling this problem. Industrial 'reconversion' or transformation was basically triggered by excess production of specific products for which there was a very limited demand. 'Reconversion' meant eliminating jobs and setting wage ceilings, as well as modernizing the structure of production. The sectors most affected by 'reconversion' are home appliances, metalworking, shipbuilding and the textile and shoe industries (see the sector by sector survey in the *Financial Times*, 20 January, 1986). Attempts to reduce the number of employees in these industries met with tremendous resistance, and the situation was very strained when the PSOE government took power after having announced that industry would be reconverted come what may. The current reindustrialization policy has taken the shape of ZUR (Urgent Reindustrialization Zones). Regional and local governments have bargained hard and have applied constant pressure in order to have their particular areas included in the scheduled ZUR.

Regarding public companies, their situation is rather different in Spain. The volume of public companies and their contribution to the GNP is considerably lower than is the case in other European countries. Here, the public company was originally an offshoot of the government and soon became a refuge for people the government wanted to reward in some way, or a haven for retired politicians. UCD was scarcely in a position to institute a reform in this sector, when the very structure of the party itself encouraged this tendency.

In their 1982 electoral platform, the Socialists viewed public companies as capable of creating new jobs and encouraging recovery. But in practice they have chosen a very different policy: returning some publicly-owned business to private hands, as in the case of the automobile companies which have been sold to Volkswagen and General Motors. The latest declarations made by high-ranking Socialists in the public sector appear to herald a new drive to return public companies to private ownership, particularly in sectors not officially considered 'vital' (the food and textile industries, for example).

Reforming the social the security system

Economic difficulties and the increase in social benefits provided by the state logically provoked the problems of public deficit which we described earlier. In this context, one of the unsolved problems of recent years is how to reform the social security system, whose current structures date back to 1972–4 (just before the effects of the economic crisis first began to be felt). During the years in which UCD governed Spain, the problem was clearly identified (social security reform was one of the clauses contained in the Moncloa Pacts) but UCD's lack of strength and internal cohesion made it powerless to alter the situation. By 1981 the attitudes of the various parties involved were quite clear: business wanted their contributions reduced to the EEC level and wanted steps to eventually place the social welfare system in private hands. Labour wanted more, and more rationally distributed, benefits. The government, fully aware that the social security system was operating on a serious deficit which could only get worse, was unable to do anything until some consensus could be reached. This appeared utterly impossible. However, the Socialist government accepted the challenge of reforming the system and issued a decree-law which reduced promised payment to future pensioners and made it more difficult to even qualify. This arbitrary move triggered sharper protests from both business and labour. The former criticized the move as timid, while the latter considered it yet another act of aggression by a Socialist government that had betrayed its own electoral programme. The protests ultimately led to a general strike (the only one during the Socialists' term in power) which was called by the Communist labour organization and backed by a broad segment of the population. The government later backed down on its initial stand, and instead submitted a bill to parliament, where the proposed measures were negotiated and ultimately took on a less drastic form.

Technological policy, foreign investment and trade protectionism

The Spanish technological deficit (the difference between expenditure and income for royalties and sale of capital goods) has grown constantly in the past few years. The situation has worsened of late due to the difficulties in the South American market, traditional purchasers of Spanish technology and capital goods. But the most important cause of this technological deficit is the small amount allocated to research and development by business firms and the state. Furthermore, half of the research effort is made by public agencies totally unrelated to the productive system, which means that it is difficult to make any subsequent industrial use of research findings. In an attempt to make technological transfer possible, particularly in the fields of production know-how rather than in those of innovation and development, the Socialist government has made it easier for foreign capital to enter Spain.

There has been an impressive increase in foreign investment in recent years. The prospective entry of Spain into the EEC, and the major business expectations offered by the Spanish stock market, spurred this increase, which reached its peak when the Socialists took power. Foreign investment in Spain rose from 80.3 billion pesetas in 1979 to 182.8 billion in 1982, and reached 280 billion in 1985 and 266.9 billion by September 1986 (*Anuario El País,* 1985, 1986). Foreign investment has been steadily encouraged through government promises of further deregulation of foreign investment and offers of a great number of advantages and tax reliefs.

In contrast, the foreign trade sector of the Spanish economy has suffered such a chronic trade deficit that a surplus has been registered only sixteen times in the past 150 years (essentially during the years of the two world wars). The reason for this is a perennial shortage of energy products, technological dependence on other countries, and a rigid agricultural sector. There has always been a great temptation to apply a protectionist policy and both business and labour exert pressure in this direction in order to maintain industries which are in decline. But within the next seven years (1993) Spain's tariff barriers with EEC countries will be completely dismantled and the current Spanish custom duties for third countries will be replaced by the EECs common external tariff.

EEC membership and the NATO referendum

Entry into the EEC put an end to one of Spain's most important items of unfinished business. The country has long had problems in integrating with the rest of the world. We do not need to go back to the Inquisition to find the reason: the enforced isolation of the Franco years suffices. Thus the great majority of Spaniards viewed EEC membership as the end of long struggle, and as a recognition that Spain is no longer different – at least not politically. The Socialist government worked tirelessly to achieve EEC membership before the end of their first legislature and managed to acquire it on 1 January 1986. This made it somewhat easier for the government subsequently to keep a troublesome electoral promise made in 1982, and hold a referendum on continued NATO membership (Kourliansky, 1986).

Spain joined NATO at the end of 1981. UCD, even then in its death throes, took advantage of its last months in power, and of the attempted military coup of February 1981, to make Spain a NATO country. Prior to 1982 the Socialists had generally been anti-Atlantist but once in power, they began to change their attitudes towards NATO, gradually shifting to the opinion that NATO was Spain's only alternative, and that EEC membership was inextricably linked to staying in the Alliance. During an extremely tense campaign President Gonzalez and other PSOE leaders pressed hard for the pro-NATO vote, and the world's first referendum on a military alliance was won by the Socialist government (with spectacular results in the parts of the country where unemployment is highest: Andalucia and the surroundings of big cities) (Gooch, 1986; Vallés, Pallarés and Canals, 1986).

EEC membership has dealt the Spanish economy a hard blow, particularly because it affects the level of industrial competitiveness. The first few months only aggravated the trade deficit: Spanish exports have increased more than imports only to Ireland and Greece. In the first ten months of 1986 purchases from other EEC countries increased by more almost 30 per cent while exports increased by only 6 per cent. This was more or less expected and is not a particularly serious matter because Spain has abundant reserves of foreign currency. The first year of EEC membership is generally considered to have been a positive experience and the Spanish economy has managed successfully to absorb the first impact of membership.

The results of crisis management

The fact that the economic crisis and democracy arrived in Spain simulataneously means that spectacular changes have taken place in the past fifteen years. From a highly centralized country with no political liberties, that was outside the mainstream of European organizations but had an economic system that was developing fast, with full employment and a highly protectionist outlook, Spain has become a new democracy with seventeen regional governments, EEC membership and an economic situation characterized by almost three million unemployed, and a tremendous increase in trade and financial dealings.

Economic indicators

Two serious problems have plagued the Spanish economy in recent years. From 1975 to 1979 and then 1982, inflation was the main concern of the various centrist governments. From 1982 on the main problem has been unemployment. Other major issues, such as the public deficit, the technological deficit, a lopsided balance of payments and industrial 'reconversion', all pale beside the problem of unemployment.

It can be said generally that during the years of UCD rule (1977–1982), economic problems were of secondary importance,and inflation was only kept to an endurable (but high) level thanks to pacts with business and labour which kept wage increases below the increases in consumer prices.

The Socialist government, which first came to power in 1982 and was returned to office in 1986 with a large majority, has given absolute priority to solving the country's economic problems. The results so far have been encouraging and this is acknowledged (albeit with reservations) by OECD and IMF in their annual reports. The difference in Spain's inflation rates and those of the other European members of the OECD has been reduced; the Spanish trade balance and foreign currency reserves have registered a definite improvement; the technological level of the country is higher (largely thanks to heavy foreign investment) . . . industrial 'reconversion' has been approached with determination, and the level of business profit has increased every year since 1982 (*Le Monde,* 1987). According to OECD's final report for 1987, the Spanish economy is in good shape and growth for 1988 may well be higher than in the rest of the industrialized countries.

The major unsolved problems continue to be unemployment and the public deficit. Temporary hiring measures have made it relatively easy to create new jobs. But even with the savings caused by the drop in oil prices, the public deficit has not improved. From 1975–78 the public deficit accounted for 0.78 per cent of the GNP. It rose to 4.09 per cent for the period 1979–85 and no appreciable reduction has been noted from one year to the next. Now (at the end of 1987), the public deficit has *decreased* notably (by over 20 per cent) due to the tremendous increase in the amount of income and

VAT taxes colleded. However, the decrease has been offset to a certain extent by the regional governments' increased spending and indebtedness. Nevertheless, the general climate has improved considerably in the past few years. A recent survey[3] revealed that after a decade of pessimism about Spain's economy, the public has begun to feel increasingly that both national and individual family economies are improving.

The political situation and the process of decision-making

After Franco's death, Spain's prime necessity was to make the transition to democracy. At that time UCD was the most suitable party for steering the country peacefully and gradually through the transition. Made up of reform-minded politicians from the Franco regime, as well as members of the moderate opposition, UCD's heterogeneity enabled it to avoid conflicts and accept opinions that would otherwise have made the transition extremely difficult. Unfortunately this very heterogeneity also meant that the party was torn by inner conflicts that eventually caused its disintegration (Sanmiguel, 1981).

A look at the legislative process during this period reveals a consistent lack of cohesion. Every minister searched within 'his' parliamentary group for 'his' spokesman to defend a particular bill. General discussions between the government and UCD's parliamentary group were deliberately avoided in order to keep latent differences of opinion from coming to the surface. Only when the differences were so great that the viability of the bill was threatened, would an arduous process of negotiation begin between the government and its own MPs (this was the case with the University Reform Bill, the Divorce Bill and even the 1981 Budget). Furthermore, the fact that UCD did not have an absolute majority in parliament meant that the government was continually obliged to negotiate and pact with other parliamentary groups (Subirats, 1986). This put a further strain on the party as the different factions accused each other of being weak or making too many concessions to either the right or the left. The opposition pressured the government, criticizing its lack of consistency and its irresolute policy, and made it increasingly difficult for Suarez or Calvo Sotelo (the two UCD Presidents), harassed by intra-party problems and under constant attack from the opposition, to continue leading the country.

PSOE has a long history in Spain. When it emerged again in the 1970s it was with a group of young leaders and a modern platform which resembled the doctrines preached by Europe's modern and powerful Social Democrats. Following a marked upsurge in growth during the transition years, there was a period when the party was torn by controversy over whether or not is was Marxist in nature. This led to a confrontation between the 'critical' faction and the party leaders, headed by Felipe Gonzalez and Alfonso Guerra. Following Gonzalez's dramatic resignation at the 28th Congress in May 1979, and his clamorous re-election in September of the same year, the 'critical' faction of the party was left weakened, while the Gonzalez-Guerra team was firmly entrenched in terms of organizational and political strategies. PSOEs success in the 1979 municipal elections, the impressive public image of Felipe Gonzalez and the Socialist alternative, and the debate following the Socialist motion to censure the Suarez government, all presaged the 10 million votes cast in 1982 for PSOE and its much-touted 'change'.

Furthermore, the Socialists have an absolute majority in both houses of parliament, govern in twelve of the country's seventeen autonomous regions and all leading cities of Spain.

The mechanisms of decision-making are as different as the political situation. While UCD was split into many different factions, PSOE is a highly centralized party, where the Secretary and Vice Secretary-General are the outstanding figures. These offices are held by Felipe Gonzalez and Alfonso Guerra, who also happen to be President and Vice-President of the government. Since none of their Cabinet ministers is simultaneously a member to the party's Executive Committee, this makes the position of Gonzalez and Guerra even stronger.

Analysis of the government's relations with parliament and the Socialist MPs also reflects this centralization of decision-making. Every single bill drafted by the government is jointly discussed by the minister or ministers responsible and those Socialist MPs who are specialists in the particular subject of the bill. These meetings result in agreement about which amendments are to be proposed. In the event of disagreement, the opinion of the President or Vice-President is decisive. The relationship between the PSOE government and its parliamentary group is echoed throughout the legislative process, disciplining the parliamentary group and assuring its loyalty, but also disciplining the government as well because it can no longer arbitrarily designate spokesmen or present amendments, as was the case during the UCD era.

All the foregoing serves to point out the government's leading role in political relations and the great extent to which decision-making is centralized in the President and Vice-President of the government. (In June 1986 this centralization was further reinforced when it was decided that Alfonso Guerra would preside over the Commission of Sub-Secretaries – from each ministry – which meets prior to any meeting of the Council of Ministers. This decision robs the council itself of some of its power and gives the Vice-President tighter control over the entire decision-making process). The party, the government and the parliament all converge and intersect in this team of leaders who, incidentally, have a close personal relationship (Lopez Garrido, 1985).

Political results of crisis management

Achieving and consolidating democracy has been Spain's principal accomplishment in recent years. This has involved developing a broad range of political freedoms, developing a state made up of autonomous regions, and has given the country a degree of tolerance and individual liberty unprecedented in its history. Spanish society has adapted to the new scale of values with surprising speed, quickly 'forgetting' the years of dictatorship. The tenth anniversary of Franco's death passed with almost general indifference, except for some discussions among politicians as to what their exact position or role had been in those years. Spain's entry into the EEC brought these years of transition to a logical and much desired close.

The *El País* survey (see note 3) confirms the general impression that the Spanish population tends to regard the country's political situation favourably. Now that the difficult years of 1980–2 are past, Spanish society has gradually become accustomed to the new democratic values which can now be said to be firmly entrenched in the country.

PSOE capitalized on their years as militant anti-Franco politicians, adapting to the conditions of the transition better than any other political party, and replacing their former top-ranking officials with men and women who were scarcely marked by the past, although as a consequence they had little experience in government.

The transition period was conditioned by the fact that the apparatus of the Franco state remained almost intact, and by the impact of two simultaneous crises: the international crisis brought about by the transformation of the productive system and the advent of technological innovation, and the strictly Spanish crisis brought about by the demise of the Franco Model of economic growth. During this period, PSOE not only became the leading opposition party, but also the only alternative to UCD.

PSOE rapidly took its place in the government, first on a local level and shortly afterwards at the head of the nation's government. As the leaders of the country, PSOE had to undertake tasks that had long been postponed. Even without exercising full control over the apparatus of the state, PSOE was obliged to modernize the productive sector, reform the state, and promote decentralization of a historically centralist state. All this was expected of a party that was traditionally Marxist, anti-monarchist, anti-military and Jacobin. Under these conditions, PSOE changed rapidly and began channelling all its political and ideological convictions into reform, which it presented under the general heading of 'modernization'. But in practice the party has constantly been faced with the dilemma of either reforming the state or of adapting it.

All of this continues to take place within a social framework where political parties and labour organizations are extremely weak, with among the lowest number of militants in Europe. The constant crises in the political parties to both the left and right of PSOE have made the Socialists seem to be simultaneously moderate, right, centrist and leftist (Solé Tura, 1986).

The dangers of a situation like this are evident, and Felipe Gonzalez has pointed them out publicly. There is a danger that PSOE will create an oligarchic situation where relations between the party and the administration are excessively close (as has long been the case in Mexico). The very relationship between the state and society seems to be taking on a style that appeared to have been surpassed: there is a marked absence of political debate, and society is overwilling to delegate power to the country's administrators. Spanish civil society continues to be weak in comparison to the state, which it regards as interventionalist and paternalistic. In fact the most recently detected changes of attitude reveal that society tends to maintain, and even increase, its rate of dependency upon the State.

The last elections demonstrated that the public has confidence in the Socialist administration, despite the serious economic and political problems that still remain to be solved. As has been pointed out (Schmidt, 1983) there is no particular reason why PSOE's success at the polls need necessarily be synonymous with a high rate of successful political solutions. As was suggested earlier, PSOE occupies a very special position in the Spanish political system, and its highly personalized and centralized methods of decision-making – its very eocnomic policy – guarantee that it will continue to dominate the scene for a some time to come.[4] It does not seem likely that Conservatives (in constant crisis and lacking a strong leader) or the left (which was incapable of capitalizing on the almost 7 million votes cast against continued NATO membership) can offer a viable alternative to PSOE within the near future.

Notes

1 If we consider the period between 1976 and 1986, the deaths attributable to ETA have been 479; of these 117 were police officers; 143 from the Guardia Civil; 47 officers of the armed forces; and 172 civilians.

2 *Condiciones de vida y de trabajo en Espana.* The surveys of 63,120 people conducted in November 1985 revealed a large number with some sort of temporary, non-continous occupation which prevents them being officially considered employed. Madrid, Centro de Investigaciones Sociologicas, 1986.

3 The survey carried out by the newspaper *El País* in December 1986 attempted to measure the outlook of Spanish citizens on the threshold of the new year. *El País,* 4 January 1987.

4 In an interview the president of *Banco de Vizcaya,* one of the biggest private banks in Spain, said: 'Any alternative to PSOE must consider that this party has taken its economic platform. I don't believe that any conservative government would have had a different economic policy. . . I think that PSOEs economic policy is an acceptable policy for business, although there are some disagreements' (*El País,* 1 February 1987).

References

Barnes, MacDonough and Lopez Pina (1986), 'Volatile parties and stable voters in Spain', *Government and Opposition,* vol. 21, no. 1, pp. 56–75.

Boyer, M. (1986), 'La politica economica espanola durante los ultimos diez anos', *El País,* 4 May.

Camiller, Patrick (1986), 'Spanish socialism in the Atlantic order', *New Left Review,* (March–April), pp. 5–36.
Castells, A. (1986), 'L'esquerra i la reaccio conservadora', *L'Opinio Socialista,* no. 2, pp. 17–44.
Donges, J. B. (1984), 'La insuficiencia de la productividad en la economia espanola' in *Espana, un presente para el futuro,* (Barcelona, Planeta), pp. 97–123.
Fuentes Quintana, E. (1983), 'La prioridad politica de la economia espanola' *Recesion. Naturaleza y opciones, Pensamiento Iberoamericano,* no. 3, pp. 118–27.
Fuentes Quintana, E. (1985), 'La ley de Schmidt', *El Correo Catalan,* 2 February.
Gooch, A. (1986), 'A surrealistic referendum: Spain and Nato', *Government and Opposition,* vol. 21, no. 3, pp. 300–16.
Kourliansky, J. J. (1986), 'L'Espagne entre Eureka et Disneyland', *Politique Aujourd'hui* (May–June), pp. 133–6.
Lagares, M. J. (1982), *Deficit Publico y Crisis Economica.* Madrid, Instituto de Estudios Fiscales.
Lopez Garrido, D. (1985), 'Gobierno y Parlamento: dos modelos de relaciones internas (UCD–PSOE)' in *El Gobierno en la Constitucion Espanola,* Diputacion de Barcelona, pp. 231–44.
Ludevid, M. (1982), 'Las relaciones laborales en la Espana de la transicion', Paper from the *Southern European Fellowship Conference,* Ford Foundation, Castelgandolfo (mimeo).
Malo de Molina, J. L. (1984), 'Distorsion y ajustes del mercado de trabajo espanol', *Los Ajustes de la Economia Espanola, Papeles de Economia Espanola,* no. 21, pp. 214–35.
Malo de Molina, J. L. (1985), 'Coherencia del sistema de relaciones industriales y eficiencia del mercado de trabajo', *Empresarios, Sindicatos y marco institucional. Papeles de Economia Espanola,* no. 22, pp. 244–64.
Martinez Mendez, P. (1982), *El Proceso de ajuste de la Economia Espanola 1973–1980,* Servicio de Estudios del Banco de Espana.
Marzal, A. (1985), 'Actitudes empresariales y actitudes de los empresarios' in *Papeles de Economia,* no. 22. pp. 62–83.
Ministerio de Economia y Hacienda (1985), *Programa Economico a medio plazo 1984–1987.* Madrid, Secretaria General de Economia y Planificacion.
Le Monde (1987), *Bilan Economique et Social 1986. Contre-chocs.* Le Monde. Dossiers et Documents.
Perez Diaz, V. (1986), 'Politica economica e patti sociali durante la transizione', *Stato e Mercato,* no. 16, pp. 57–92.
Sanmiguel, L. G. (1981), 'The ideology of UCD', *European Journal of Political Research,* no. 9, pp. 23–37.
Schmidt, M. G. (1983), 'The welfare state and the economic periods of economic crisis: a comparative study of 23 OECD countries', *Policy Sciences,* no. 1, pp. 1–19.
Segura, J. (1983), 'Crisis y estrategias alternativas: el caso espanol' in *Recesion: Naturaleza y opciones* pp. 93–113.
Sevilla, J. V. (1985), *Economia Politica de la crisis espanola.* Barcelona, Critica.
Sole Tura, J. (1986), 'Una reflexion para toda la izquierda', *El País,* 31 October.
Subirats, J. (1986), 'An approach to the legislative production of the Spanish parliament (1979–1982)', *European Journal of Political Research,* no. 14, pp. 321–38.
Vallés, Pallarés and Canals (1986), 'El Referèndum del 12 de marzo de 1986 sobre la permanencia de Espana en la OTAN y sus consecuencias para el sistema politico', *Revista de Estudios Politicos,* no. 52, pp. 183–215. English version, *Electoral Studies,* 'The referendum of 12 March 1986 on Spain's remaining in NATO', vol. 5, no. 3, (December 1986), pp. 305–11.
Zabalza, A. (1985), 'Desindustrialitzacio i politica industrial: el cas catala' in *Desindustrialitzacio a Catalunya. Causes i Propostes de Futur* (Barcelona, Col. legi d'Economistes), pp. 99–112.

9 Austria: a crisis resolved or a crisis postponed?

PETER GERLICH and WOLFGANG C. MÜLLER

Important events 1970–87

1970	parliamentary election: Social Democratic minority government formed by Kreisky
1971	parliamentary election: majority for the Social Democrats under Kreisky
1975	parliamentary election: third term for Kreisky and the Social Democrats
1978	use of nuclear power rejected by first Austrian referendum
1979	parliamentary election: fourth term for Kreisky and the Social Democrats
1980	General Hospital scandal made public
1983	parliamentary election: Social Democrats lose majority Kreisky resigns as Federal Chancellor Coalition government of Social Democrats and Freedom Party formed
1985	construction of a new hydroelectric power plant near Vienna is prevented by large demonstration
1986	Kurt Waldheim elected as Federal President rank and file revolt inside the Freedom Party Social Democrats cancel coalition earthquake general election
1987	coalition government of Social Democrats and the Austrian People's Party led by Vranitzky

Introduction

Many observers of Austrian politics have been struck by the contrast which the republic's history provides. While Austria could not successfully solve its economic and political problems during the interwar years it did so with much more success after 1945 (Steiner, 1972). In general this is attributed to grand coalition government as well as to the corporatist arrangements of the so-called *Sozialpartnerschaft*. While the increasingly precarious cooperation between parties was discontinued in 1966 when the bourgeois Austrian People's Party (ÖVP) formed a one party government, effective interest group cooperation continues today. In 1970 the Conservatives were replaced by the Social–Democrats (SPÖ) under Kreisky, who rather successfully presided over a one party government until 1983. Then he resigned after losing his absolute majority. A somewhat luckless small coalition between SPÖ and the small third party, the FPÖ, was formed which broke up in 1986. In many ways this year brought upheavals in Austrian politics, including an 'earthquake' general election and a rather dramatic decline in the country's international reputation, particularly in connection with the election of Kurt Waldheim as Federal President. Since the beginning of 1987 a new grand coalition government has been formed by SPÖ and ÖVP, which, however, has to work within a framework rather different from the old type of grand coalition.

Like other European countries, in the early 1970s Austria was confronted first with economic and later, at least by its own standards, also with political difficulties. The following sections describe how these crises have been perceived, and how they have been dealt with generally. Some information is also provided about specific issues and policies, particularly in the field of economic policy. Finally the Austrian experiences are summed up and evaluated.

Perceptions of the crisis

The oil crisis of 1973 caused a shock even in Austria. But awareness of the full impact of this and the subsequent economic difficulties grew only slowly and in stages. For a long time it was hoped that Austria would be spared the fate of other countries and somehow would not be affected. The 1973 concerns were soon followed by a sense of relief as 1974 turned out to be a good year economically. At the time, politicians and their advisers believed that Austria could once again, as in the recent past, escape the negative international cycle.

However, when in 1975 economic conditions deteriorated rapidly (Table 9.1) and business analysts again had to lower their forecasts (Lehner, 1982, p. 26), politicians interpreted this as an indication that the downward movement had belatedly reached Austria after all. It was thought, however, that Austria could 'dive through' this international cycle by a policy of deficit spending.

In mid-1977 the Austrian government changed its interpretation of the situation in view of the continuing high levels of unemployment outside the country. Instead of viewing it as merely cyclical, politicians now recognized the crisis as a structural one.[1] Therefore macroeconomic demand management was to be replaced or at least accompanied by structural reform policies.

In both phases the government believed that it had the means to successfully influence the economic development of Austria and to guide the country through the deep international recession. Nevertheless, at the beginning of the 1980s, with the second oil price shock, with the effects of the US policy of high interest rates and with its own increasing budgetary problems, the Austrian government also began to lower its aspirations. The situation now was defined as one of a continuing structural crisis of global dimensions, which had been worsened by inadequate policy responses of the major western countries. Nevertheless, the Austrian strategy remained to keep on course as far as possible, while recognizing the need for structural change within Austria.

The coalition government consisting of SPÖ and FPÖ, which replaced the SPÖ government in 1983, abandoned some of the promises made during the first phase of the crisis. But while stating that everything was 'very complicated' and that one would have to 'realize that not everything can be achieved by politics'[2] the government did not try to establish a policy pattern substantially different from the previous one.

When in 1986 it became obvious that *political* success could thus not be maintained, the SPÖ changed both its Chancellor and its analysis of the situation. While the previous interpretation of the crisis included the strategic option of a specific 'Austrian way' economically different from the mainstream of western countries, this was now implicitly rejected. The crisis was perceived as really affecting the country, so that Austria too now had to face the full impact of harsh realities. Instead of muddling through, an active forward-oriented policy was proposed, which broke with some of the principles previously accepted. This analysis of the required economic policy strategy, although it was already announced under the SPÖ-FPÖ coalition, also constitutes the economic policy consensus of the new grand coalition (see below).

As regards the non-economic dimension of the present crisis, the new types of demand upon the political system, as well as the increased demands for participation which steadily grew in intensity during the period under review, constitute a new axis of politics cutting across old cleavages. Materialism versus post-materialism appears to confront the traditional continuum of left and right (Müller, 1984). From the perspective of Austrian

Table 9.1 Austria: key economic statistics 1973–87

	1973	1974	1975	1976	1977	1978	1979	1980	1981	1982	1983	1984	1985	1986	1987
Real GDP growth %	4.9	3.9	−0.4	4.6	4.4	0.5	4.7	3.0	−0.1	1.2	2.1	2.0	2.7	2.6	1.0
Variation in consumer prices index %	7.6	9.5	8.4	7.3	5.5	3.6	3.7	6.4	6.8	5.4	3.3	5.6	3.2	1.7	2.0
Unemployment rates %	1.1	1.4	1.7	1.8	1.6	2.1	2.1	1.9	2.5	3.5	4.1	3.8	4.8	5.2	5.9
Surplus on current transactions as % of GDP	−0.3	−1.0	−0.1	−2.3	−3.6	−0.7	−1.0	−2.7	−2.0	1.1	0.6	−0.8			
Total outlays of government as % of GDP	41.3	41.9	46.1	46.9	46.8	49.7	48.9	48.9	50.3	50.6	50.7	50.0			
Net lending of government as % of GDP	1.3	1.3	−2.5	−3.7	−2.4	−2.8	−2.4	−1.7	−1.8	−3.2	−4.1	−2.7	−2.1	−2.6	−3.3

Source: OECD (1986), *Historical Statistics*; (1986), Austria.

career politicians, these new ideas and movements appear to question their monopoly of policy-making and political competence. Even more relevant are the possible effects of these new movements on the process of majority-building. The introduction of the new axis of politics implies, in effect, that for either of the two big parties the possibility of achieving majorities has seemed more problematic since the early 1980s. In general it could be claimed that the ability to achieve a majority at all is now decided on this new axis, while the question of parliamentary majorities itself is being decided on the traditional left-right axis.

General reactions to the crisis

The budget

As far as the economic aspects of the contemporary crisis are concerned, its consequences were most clearly felt and expressed in the area of budgetary policy. In this respect 1975 turned out to be a black year. Initially the government reacted as in other years of recession and resorted to deficit spending. The deficit however was larger than ever before, amounting to 5.7 per cent of the GDP. Predictions at the end of 1975 suggested a growth rate of GDP 1.5 per cent for 1976, minimal by the standards of the 1970s. Thus, unlike in the past when deficit spending was limited to short periods, another year was planned with an expansive budgetary policy and a deficit of 5 per cent of the GDP. This was later actually further increased to 6.1 per cent, although in 1976 economic developments turned out to be rather satisfactory both in Austria (growth of 4.6 per cent) and internationally (OECD-Europe: growth of 4.7 per cent). Deficit spending was continued in 1977 to counteract the danger of a 'premature stabilzation' and again in 1978, because of the worsening economic situation (Nowotny, 1985, p. 74; Butschek, 1985, p. 156). The deficit then amounted to 5.3 per cent (1977) and 6.1 per cent (1978) of the GDP.

The period 1979–81, in contrast, was characterized by attempts to stabilize the budget. Newly acquired debts of the federal government (net deficits) continuously declined from 4.2 per cent of the GDP (1978) to 2.6 per cent (1981). Nevertheless there was no return to the original base line of the period prior to the massive deficit spending of 1975. In 1982 the budgetary deficit again increased, to 6.3 per cent of the GDP, reaching an all-time high. However, the extent of this deficit could only be partly explained by anti-cyclical policies of the government. In addition structural problems of state finance played a role (increased contributions to retirement insurance, service of the public debt, increasing wage costs, and so on). Between 1983 and 1986, the gross deficit was even higher (average 7 per cent of the GDP). But it had only a small stimulatory effect on the business cycle.

To finance the deficit, taxes had to be raised both between 1976 and 1978 and during 1980–1. The tax quota increased from 22.7 per cent of the GDP (1975) to 24.6 per cent (1981). In 1983 during the electoral campaign the government proposed new taxes in order to pursue an active economic policy. The subsequent (relative) defeat of the SPÖ, as well as the formation of a coalition government with the bourgeois FPÖ, meant that only a small and fiscally ineffective part of the originally proposed tax package could be introduced. On the basis of economic (reduced yield of the tax system) and political considerations in the mid-1980s all relevant political forces concluded that the limits of possible tax increases had been reached, particularly since the total net-quota of public taxes and charges of the GDP had increased from 38.2 per cent (1974) to 41 per cent (1985).

In addition to increased taxation, greater budgetary flexibility had also been achieved since 1978 by the reduction of governmental contributions to the social insurance institutions. These in turn had to either increase membership contributions or reduce benefits. This policy of budgetary restraint has been reversed, since 1982, by the independently increasing financial needs of the social insurance sector (Tálos, 1985). A third way of financing deficit spending was by increasing the public debt, which in 1986 was about ten times as high as in 1974. At the same time the amount of governmental liability guarantees increased enormously (from AS 120 billion in 1974 to AS 400 billion in 1982). They mainly concern financial guarantees for publicly owned companies conducting business for the government (for example construction) or guarantees for export credits. This activity constitutes a form of 'flight from the public budget' (Smekal, 1977): that is, expenditure that should be included in the federal budget are actually listed elsewhere.

Reactions of government, parties and the social partners

The *government*, as has been suggested, primarily reacted to the economic crisis with a number of expenditure-intensive special programmes. In an attempt to increase effectiveness the budget was divided into an 'ordinary' budget and a 'disposable quota' to be used flexibly for necessary anti-cyclical measures. Besides trying to speed up the business cycle, government also attempted to improve the industrial structure by selective measures. The public response to actions differed: anti-cyclical policies were broadly accepted, whereas structural policies usually encountered resistance from economic interest groups and from the opposition. Naturally, this resistance increased when specific groups of the population were forced to finance measures by higher or special taxes. Indirect taxes, however, were increased without serious resistance. In contrast to the immediate post-crisis period, the early 1980s were characterized by rather narrow limits to governmental action. This led to a gap between what the government could actually do and the level of expectation established in the early years of the crisis.

In policy areas not directly related to the realization of economic priorites and on issues which ran counter to merely materialist interests (for example in the field of energy and environmental policy) the government acted with less determination. In virtually all cases when faced with considerable resistance, the government was willing to abandon economic priorities, either by abandoning policies or at least by side-stepping the issue.

The *parties* at first did not develop substantially differentiated strategies for dealing with the crisis. Until the beginning of the eighties they decided instead to compete by emphasizing their different skills in managing the *techniques* of economic policy. Despite earlier doubts within the ÖVP, this political strategy did not change considerably until the early 1980s. The long consensus on basic orientations of economic policy broke down as the opposition then shifted its ground and proposed a partially neoliberal economic strategy. It is important to note that under Austrian conditions this by no means led to a real and complete break with past patterns. When the SPÖ changed Chancellors in 1986, nominating Vranitzky, a banker by profession, it soon adopted a good deal of the economic policy proposals previously promoted by the ÖVP, without losing its political credibility. Although the new neoliberally inclined economic consensus was not a complete one, it was sufficient to serve as a basis for the economic programme of the new grand coalition government.

The cooperation between the *social partners* so far has not been threatened by the economic crisis or its consequences. On the contrary the incomes policy of social partnership constituted an essential element of the 'Austro-Keynesian' policy mix. Nevertheless, the general dominance of the corporatist style of policy-making was somewhat reduced by the increasing relevance of party competition, particularly concerning issues that implied policy measures which would affect strategic parts of the electorate, for example within the area of social policy (Müller, 1985). The cooperation between social partners and government was less affected by the problems of the economic crisis than by the government's yielding to strongly supported post-materialist demands. In practice there was some pressure from economic interest groups upon the two big parties to again form a grand coalition government.

Prevailing policy patterns

It can be argued that there were, sequentially, four prevailing broad policy patterns during the period under review. At first the Social Democratic government tried to continue its policies of *liberal reform*, which it had introduced after assuming office in 1970. This included issues such as a new penal code or university reform or the establishment of the *Volksanwaltschaft,* a kind of ombudsman institution. Sometimes these issues were solved by consensus, sometimes at least formal conflict prevailed.

Because its original reform agenda was nearly exhausted by 1975, and under the impact of the somewhat belated consequences of the economic crisis, the government increasingly fell back upon the pattern of *consensual crisis management* by deficit spending, and lost its enthusiasm for reform politics. Eventually when more severe consequences of the prolonged crisis were being felt a more complicated pattern emerged: the government tried to continue with traditional forms of crisis management. Deficit spending was in this respect at first a politically rather comfortable strategy because no demands had to be frustrated. However, because of the high financial costs of this strategy during the crisis it was more and more difficult to maintain it on the basis of consensus. After the Kreisky era the initial tendency was to *ride out the storm.* The SPÖ-FPÖ government, handicapped by its coalition character and by its lack of money, refrained from actively carrying on with former strategies of crisis management (even if paying lip service to them). The government accepted the maintainance of a large budgetary deficit as well as an increase in unemployment and relied on the positive effects of the upward international economic cycle. Since Vranitzky became Chancellor a fourth pattern emerged which found its expression in rather rigorous reform measures of the nationalized industries, including sizeable lay-offs. It may be termed *doing the inevitable* even if it is unpopular. Then the opposition was again caught off guard when the government, as mentioned above, accepted its previous plans. The ÖVP was therefore even more willing to join the grand coalition.

Issues and policies

Economic problems were of course the most important issues during the period under review. They remained continuously on the political agenda. During the seventies the macroeconomic policy which we have described above was supported by a broad popular consensus. Even for the opposition, which of course criticized the government's economic measures, it was difficult to define what they would do differently. Kreisky's formula 'we prefer debt to unemployment', proposed in different versions, was generally accepted and as a rule determined the climate of economic policy-making. The achievement of full employment was clearly the most important goal of economic policy. The problem of inflation declined, the SPÖ could no longer be identified with an inflationary policy. On the contrary, in opinion polls its estimated competence at stabilizing prices even overtook that of the ÖVP (Ulram, 1985).

1975 was an election year during which the ÖVP opposition forcefully introduced the theme of the economic crisis. In doing this it tried to remind voters of its own old image as the party of economic efficiency (and of the special qualities of its leader, a banker) and thus attempted to gain an advantage over the SPÖ which so far had been identified mainly with welfare-oriented, economically expensive reform policies. The SPÖ won the election, since voters seemed to assume that the present government would continue to guarantee their economic security. The apex of social democratic crisis management was finally reached in 1979. The crisis and the way to manage it ('the Austrian way') were on this occasion introduced as a campaign theme by the government. Until then economic indicators demonstrated an undoubtedly impressive record for the government's economic strategies. While the strategy's costs were not yet visible, Kreisky became the incarnation of this 'Austrian way' and reached the peak of his popularity. In view of the objectively prevailing consensus among the population there was little with which the opposition could counter. It ran a somewhat unpolitical campaign of flowers and meekly demanded 'A new spring for Austria'.

At the beginning of the 1980s when economic success started to crumble, when outside Austria neo-conservative ideologies had succeeded or were on the upswing and governments of many important countries had given up Keynesian economic strategies (cf. Goldthorpe, 1984), even in Austria economic policy issues became more controversial. While the SPÖ government insisted upon the continuation and, as far as taxation was concerned, even intensification of its former policies, the ÖVP now began to try to articulate a clear-cut alternative (Chaloupek, 1985). It pointed out that an increasing degree of state intervention had always tended to contribute to stagnation. The ÖVP's favoured policy proposals included the neo-Conservative elements of flexibility, deregulation, budget cuts and shifts, tax reform, (re-)privatization and the promotion of private property. The electoral outcome of 1983 did not imply a clear choice between these differing policy options: although the Social Democrats lost their absolute majority they remained the strongest party, while the Austrian People's Party gained only marginally. However, when it became clear during the following years that the period of electoral success for the old economic policy had come to an end, as mentioned, the SPÖ demonstrated a remarkable flexibility. Although it did not accept the ÖVP's proposals in 1986 outright, it turned towards policy options which were based on the same principles, but softened by governmental responsibility and a pragmatic sense of the limits to what could really be done. Thus the Social Democrats shifted from Keynesianism and turned towards supply-side economics. The state sector is to be modernized and hence to be reduced in size. This, in particular, applies to the nationalized industries, which are to be at least partly privatized, partly closed down and partly modernized and reorganized in accordance with the competition-oriented principles of a market economy. Moreover, the state's role is to be reduced by deregulation.

In addition to the main macroeconomic concerns, the political agenda also had always included important specific measures as, for example, public subsidies for (mostly the nationalized) enterprises. These issues, until the beginning of the 1980s, reflected the general trend towards consensus. Until then such measures as, for example, the salvage of the Länderbank, one of Austria's largest banks, in 1981, were usually also supported by the opposition. However in this field too, the growing discrepancy of concepts of economic policy has emerged since the opposition, after 1983, refused to support the government in these matters. This in particular held true in 1985, when the nationalized industries, due to unsuccessful oil speculations and a series of failed investment projects, would have collapsed if the state had not provided billions in subsidies. This event was of crucial importance for the reorientation of the Social Democratic economic policy strategy described above (Müller, 1986; 1988b).

The development of the debate on economic policy found a parallel in the area of social policy. Until the end of the 1970s the governing SPÖ proposed expansive *social welfare policies,* which were, however, lukewarmly supported by the parliamentary opposition. In the 1980s the climate completely changed in this field as well: the SPÖ only rarely introduced new social benefits, while the ÖVP now invariably voted against them even though it continued to propose some of its own. The new policy consensus which emerged before the grand coalition was that an extension of social policy programmes would be inappropriate. Indeed, exisiting social policy programmes were to be reconsidered in terms of their necessity.

Since the mid-1970s *environmental issues* regularly appeared high on the political agenda. According to opinion surveys, environmental protection even sometimes replaced employment security as the most important political goal. The public generally believed that traditional parties have only a limited capacity for problem-solving in this area (cf. Ulram, 1985). Therefore it was not surprising that these issues were frequently connected with forms of unconventional participation. The first relevant case was the broad protest movement against the use of atomic energy in Austria. This ultimately led to the first general referendum in Austria in 1978, concerning the question whether the already completed nuclear power plant at Zwentendorf should go into operation. The government lost by a narrow margin, leaving it with what wits have called the world's largest museum of atomic energy. Ultimately this result can be traced more to the effects of the competition between the two big parties, than to the immediate effects of the protest movement itself. In principle this is equally true for later examples of successful unconventional participation. However, the strength of protest movements has increased steadily. The most recent example in the area of environmental politics was an unprecedentedly huge sit-in by conservationists against the attempt to begin clearing woods for constructing a new hydroelectric plant at Hainburg on the Danube, close to Vienna. The government called in the police, drew back following a public outcry and ultimately abandoned the project (Müller, 1985), at least temporarily.

Citizens' protest and unconventional participation was not limited to environmental questions: in 1976 many people protested by deliberately giving false responses to a census questionnaire trying to establish the size of ethnic minorities. In so doing they frustrated the original purpose of this government survey. In 1977 independently organized, that is non-union, truckers practically brought to a standstill all cross-border traffic by blocking major roads to protest against the introduction of a tax law. In 1979 a popular anti-centralist initiative was started in Vorarlberg, the most western province. In 1982 demonstrations caused the government to adopt an amendment bill prohibiting the export of arms into crisis areas. In 1984 civil servants protested against a reduction of their retirement benefits; also the governor of Salzburg openly defied orders of the federal government concerning shop closing hours. He was brought before the Constitutional Court, which held his action to be illegal. However he would have clearly won an election in his province, had he been removed from office by the court's judgment. Finally in 1986 authorities shrank from anticipated protest of farmers against the new wine law, which had been the government's reaction to a huge wine scandal, and it relaxed those rules to which the farmers were most opposed. Other decisions which might have caused popular protest and unconventional participation were postponed, for example the construction of a hydroelectric plant in East Tyrol. Even if these actions appear rather minor in a comparative perspective, no one would have considered this long list of popular protests possible in the subject-oriented political culture prevailing in Austria during the 1960s. However, some of this protest was not quite spontanous citizen activity, but was organized and directed by the opposition Austrian People's Party. When this party returned to government in 1987, as the junior partner of the Social Democrats, it realized that it could no longer control such protest movements, even with respect to subunits of the party itself, notwithstanding the requirements of a government party (cf. Müller, 1988a). For example, the province of Styria, led by its ÖVP governor, complained against the government's decision to station newly acquired jet fighters on its territory. Thus even for the grand coalition government the problem of governability exists.

One issue of central relevance which again and again appears on the political agenda is that of conflicts which concern the Austrian Radio and Television Company, the country's most important mass medium. Until the 1960s it was totally and jointly controlled by both parties, according to *Proporz* rules. In 1967 a reform instigated by the independent newspapers led to more autonomy and above all to a reduction of the influence of the SPÖ. This party therefore tried to increase its influence during the 1970s, by structural reforms as well as via personnel policy, while the ÖVP exerted every means to defend the traditional bourgeois dominance. Periods of 'media war' and 'media peace' between the two main parties therefore alternated, without ultimately leading to any major changes either in the basic outlook or the transmission policy of the radio and television company.

Finally, Austria was increasingly rocked by *political scandals*: cases of corruption, mismanagement of public enterprises and, to some degree, discussions over the past history (especially during the Nazi years) of some political leaders. More than a dozen major scandals arose during the decade after 1974. The most famous (or infamous) was that concerning illegal gains in connection with the construction of the huge new General Hospital in Vienna. As in other cases, the opposition tried to hint at a connection with members of the government, while the government argued that this was a politics of 'scandalization', because its successful policy could not be otherwise challenged. Moreover, the government tried to compensate for its own embarrassments by uncovering the ever available regional scandals involving members of the main opposition party. In a sense these cases may be considered as birth pangs of an increasingly open political system, since in the past the traditional broad consensus had often also served as a pretext for mutually covering up misuses of political influence (cf. Gerlich, 1981). However, the lack of real actions following these scandals contributed considerably to unease and to protest behaviour by an increasing proportion of the population.

Results of crisis management

Policy-making and leadership styles

In this final section we will first deal with the repertoire of concrete policy styles, that is, did the Austrian system develop new techniques for dealing with new challenges? We will then turn to an attempt at evaluation: how successful were Austrian measures of crisis management, concerning the economic as well as the political challenges?

As regards concrete policy styles, a distinction can be made between the pre- and post-1980 periods. As was pointed out above, Kreisky was able to exercise a considerable degree of leadership. Aside from applying the more general patterns of liberal reform and consensual crisis management, he exercised skilfully what could be called 'show politics', basically concerned with making use of his very personal media skills (he was sometimes called the journalist's chancellor). 'Show politics' meant announcing proposals, plans or reactions very effectively in public and thus commanding attention without worrying too much about implemenation or even consistency. In a sense he was the master of formal political conflict, although he could still rely upon a large amount of real consensus. 'Side-step' was just a variation of this style. The referendum on atomic energy in 1978 failed, but was still a success because (unlike in Sweden) the Social Democrats did win the next election, in which atomic energy no longer was an issue. His answer to scandals was to issue the so-called 'Chancellor's Ten Commandments' demanding anti-corruption legislation and so on, which in the event was only partially implemented. One may, in retrospect, sum up Kreisky's achievements as those of a mainly successful agenda managment. He would put on or remove from the political agenda issues as seemed appropriate to maximizing his own leadership reputation. He usually got away with that strategy quite successfully.

The 1980s were, as suggested earlier, basically characterized by 'riding out the storm' (or 'letting it stew') politics, which follows the Austrian tradition of 'therapeutic nihilism' (Johnston, 1972). During earlier periods of Austrian history the respective administrations often realized that they did not have the power to intervene effectively but that, at the same time, experience tended to show that finally and simply many problems would solve themselves. More specific techniques of the later period could be termed 'open the club' or 'deny access to it' respectively. It is remarkable that on the one hand the goals of big demonstrations were usually respected: both the anti-nuclear as well as the conservationist anti-Hainburg power plant initiatives were successful. But on the other hand established groups also tried to restrain alternative political parties from gaining too much access, for example to the state-controlled TV and radio, and subjected them to sometimes rather vicious defamatory campaigns – a strategy which has so far been rather successful but which shows signs of being less so in the future.

After Vranitzky took over as Federal Chancellor, a new pattern emerged. He tried to reintroduce more effective policy leadership as opposed to agenda management, even proposing unpleasant but necessary restrictive budgetary reforms, restructuring the economy and limiting subsidies. So far his personal style has been much appreciated by the general public, including his effective representation of the country's position at the international level.

An evaluation of responses to crisis

Let us now turn to the general evaluation of Austrian policy responses to the different aspects of the crisis. An international comparison of some basic indicators leads to a rather positive evaluation of Austrian economic policy. The absolute levels of these indicators seem quite acceptable and indeed impressive during most years of so-called crisis: inflation never reached double figures; unemployment remained, until 1986, below 5 per cent; there was no year with a substantial negative growth rate; and no substantial reductions of welfare took place. Even the deterioration of the unemployment figures during the 1980s by no means reached the much higher levels of the OECD averages. Growth during this period was likewise better than in most OECD countries. This implies that the relative lead of

Austria has been maintained in the 1980s notwithstanding the difficulties described above. The successes of the past are also relevant for the future because they imply a level of aspiration which can probably be achieved: Austria can already be satisfied if it manages to stabilize its economic position. The situation is not as difficult as in countries suffering from double-figure rates of unemployment, when a high political price may have to be paid for stabilization (Chaloupek, 1985, p. 342).

Yet apparent economic 'success' in Austria is counterbalanced by problems of the public debt (with its consequences for the reduced effectiveness of deficit-spending financed in this way). Even if the *economic* limits of the public debt have not yet been reached (Winckler, 1985, p. 311), the *political* limits have been. The new grand coalition government has made the reduction of the budgetary deficit its main concern. This was not only caused by an increasing public unease but also by the élites' consideration that any postponement of budgetary stabilization will eventually and automatically lead to more severe policy measures. Such a 'crash concept' might reduce the willingness of the big societal groups to accept immediate sacrifices, and thus might seriously endanger the political consensus. In principle the grand coalition is well placed to introduce these kind of stabilization (and possibly tough) policies. In practice it may turn out to be very cumbersome in doing so, since it is usually only able to achieve a kind of lowest common denominator compromise between the most powerful (and demanding) special interests.

Another difficult question concerns the structure of the Austrian economy. Do the good economic indicators show a true picture of the economy or do they hide severe structural deficiencies? Certainly the present-day range of Austrian industrial products is not sufficiently sophisticated. It is also doubtful whether the successful export rates would have been achieved without the comprehensive system of public subsidies (especially export liability guarantees). They must be increasingly called into question, because Austrian exports are increasingly absorbed by countries of high credit risk which would have difficulties in finding alternative suppliers and contractors. This in turn contributes to the maintenance of an inadequate industrial structure.

Similarly, independent technological developments, which in a long-term perspective are essential for structural improvements, are absent in many areas. Particularly, the 'sunrise industries' are represented in Austria only by production, and not by research and development. There is agreement that many pre-conditions for a successful solution to the structural problems have yet to be provided (Chaloupek, 1985, pp. 339f).

As regards reactions to the ecological movements and interests, the government's 'crisis responses' appear to be less successful. Surveys demonstrate repeatedly that there now exists an increasing and continuous tendency among the population to react negatively to the politics of the established parties. The picture is of course far from unambiguous. Some indicators, as well as membership figures, tend to demonstrate continuous support levels. However the clear and continuous rise of percentages favouring an expansion of the number of parties, that is, of the spectrum of choice open to the voter (from about 10 per cent in the early 1970s to almost 50 per cent in the mid-1980s) appears to present a clear message (Plasser, 1987).

The big parties have not been very successful recently in trying to convince the population that they know best how to deal with both traditional and new problems. At the 1986 election their combined vote was reduced to 85 per cent, the lowest level for thirty-seven years. Both the SPÖ, the main governmental party, and the ÖVP, the only opposition party, lost votes and seats (cf. Luther, 1987).

So the final evaluation remains ambiguous. Economic success now appears to be fragile and is counterbalanced by popular dissatisfaction. Future developments will of course be strongly influenced by international conditions. As long a the international economy maintains its present relative (if by earlier standards reduced) rate of development, Austria will certainly ride along and will continue to attempt a strategy of consolidation. Such an approach may possibly be successful in spite of increased social costs and political conflicts, as long as these conflicts stay within certain limits. If the international economy deteriorates again, and if the goal of economic consolidation is not achieved, three courses remain possible: a continued policy of muddling through by a grand coalition government; a renewed emphasis on symbolic and show politics (at least for a limited period); or (especially if fiscal developments force a show down), a true change of politics and shift to the right, for example by a small coalition between the People's and Freedom parties.

Notes

1 Chancellor Kreisky in parliament (Stenographische Protokolle des Nationalrates, XIV, GP, 16 July 1977, p. 5643; 5 October 1977, p. 6170).

2 The new Chancellor Sinowatz in parliament (Stenographische Protokolle des Nationalrates, XVI, GP, 31 May 1983, p. 29f).

References

Blaas, W., A. Guger (1985). Arbeitsbeziehungen und makroökonomische Stabilität im internationalen Vergleich, pp. 255–277, in: P. Gerlich, E. Grande and W. C. Müller (eds), *Sozialpartnerschaft in der Krise*. Vienna, Böhlau.

Bös, D., B. Genser, and R. Holzmann (1979), 'Die finanzpolitische Entwicklung in Österreich 1975–1978', *Finanzarchiv,* 37, pp. 485–510.

Butschek, F. (1981), *Vollbeschäftigung in der Krise.* Vienna, Orac.
Butschek, F. (1985), *Die Österreichische Wirtschaft im 20 Jahrhundert.* Stuttgart, Fischer Verlag.
Chaloupek, G. (1985), 'Sozialpartnerschaft in der Zeit des Übergangs', pp. 331–47 in P. Gerlich, E. Grande and W. C. Müller (eds), *Sozialpartnerschaft in der Krise.* Vienna, Böhlau.
Genser, B. and R. Holzmann (1982), 'Die finanzpolitische Entwicklung in Österreich 1979–1980, *Finanzarchiv,* 40, pp. 109–34.
Genser, B. and R. Holzmann (1983), 'Die finanzpolitische Entwicklung in Österreich 1981–1982', *Finanzarchiv,* 41, pp. 486–505.
Genser, B. and R. Holzmann (1986), *Die finanzpolitische Entwicklung in Österreich in den Jahren 1983 und 1984.* Vienna, Forschungsbericht 8603, Ludwig Bolzmann Institut für ökonomische Analysen wirtschaftlicher Aktivitäten.
Gerlich, P. (1981), 'Korruption im Systemvergleich', pp. 165–81 in Chr. Brünner (ed.), *Korruption und Kontrolle.* Vienna, Böhlau.
Gerlich, P. (1985), 'Ernstnehmen oder Augenzwinkern: Grün-Alternative Herausforderungen der traditionellen Politik', pp. 183–202 in F. Plasser, P. Ulram and M. Welan (eds), *Demokratierituale.* Vienna, Böhlau.
Gerlich, P. (1987), 'Austria: consociationalism to competition', pp. 61–106 in H. Daalder (ed.), *Party Systems in Denmark, Austria, Belgium, the Netherlands and Switzerland.* London, Pinter.
Gerlich, P. (1988), 'Deregulation in Austria', *European Journal of Political Research,* 16 (forthcoming).
Gerlich, P., E. Grande and W. C. Müller (eds) (1985), *Sozialpartnerschaft in der Krise.* Vienna, Böhlau.
Gerlich, P., E. Grande and W. C. Müller (1988), 'Corporatism in crisis: stability and change of social partnership in Austria', *Political Studies,* 36, pp. 209–23.
Gerlich, P. and W. C. Müller (eds) (1983), *Zwischen Koalition und Konkurrenz. Österreichs Parteien seit 1945.* Vienna, Braumüller.
Goldthorpe, J. H. (1984), 'The end of convergence: corporatist and dualist tendencies in modern western societies', pp. 315–43 in J. H. Goldthorpe (ed.), *Order and Conflict in Contemporary Capitalism.* Oxford, Clarendon.
Johnston, W. (1972), *The Austrian Mind.* Berkeley, University of California Press.
Lehner, G. (1982), 'Deficit-spending', in Österreich, *Wirtschaftspolitische Blätter,* 29, no. 3, pp. 24–35.
Lehner, G. (1983), 'Diagnose der Budgetprobleme', *Wirtschaftspolitische Blätter,* 30, no. 2, pp. 15–24.
Lehner, G. and A. Stanzel (1976), 'Wirtschaftsprognosen, Rezession und Budgetentwicklung im Jahre 1975', *Monatsberichte des WIFO,* no. 8, pp. 352–64.
Luther, K. R. (1987), 'Austria's future and Waldheim's past', *West European Politics,* 10, no. 3, pp. 376–99.
Müller, W. C. (1983), 'Parteien zwischen Öffentlichkeitsarbeit und Medienzwängen', pp. 281–315 in P. Gerlich and W. C. Müller (eds), *Zwischen Koalition und Konkurrenz. Österreichs Parteien seit 1945.* Vienna, Braumüller.
Müller, W. C., (1984), Politische Kultur und Parteientransformation in Österreich, *Osterreichische Zeitschrift für Politikwissenschaft*, 13, no. 1, pp. 53–76.
Müller, W. C., (1985), 'Die Rolle der Parteien bei Entstehung und Entwicklung der Sozialpartnerschaft', pp. 135–224 in P. Gerlich, E. Grande and W. C. Müller (eds), *Sozialpartnerschaft in der Krise.* Vienna, Böhlau.
Müller, W. C., (1986), 'Mikroökonomische Steuerung und Parteien-Konkurrenz in Österreich', pp. 160–208 in H. Abromeit, G. Himmelmann and U. Jürgens (eds), *Steuerungsinstrument öffentliche Wirtschaft?*, IIVG, discussion paper, pp. 86–214. Berlin, Wissenschaftszentrum.

Müller, W. C., (1988a), 'Conservatism and the transformation of the Austrian People's Party', in B. Girvin (ed.), *The Transformation of Contemporary Conservatism.* London, Sage pp. 98–119.
Müller, W. C. (1988b), 'The Politics of Privatization in Austria', *West European Politics,* 11, no. 4, pp. 101–16.
Nowotny, E. (1985), 'Beschäftigungsorientierte Wirtschaftspolitik und Strukturwandel – der Weg Österreichs', pp. 65–82 in J. Langkau and C. Köhler (eds), *Wirtschaftspolitik und wirtschaftliche Entwicklung.* Bonn, Verlag Neue Gesellschaft.
Plasser, F. (1987), *Parteien unter Stress.* Vienna, Böhlau.
Richardson, J. J. (ed.) (1982), *Policy Styles in Western Europe.* London, Allen & Unwin.
Rothschild, K. W. (1984), 'Politische Ökonomie in Österreich seit 1984', unpublished conference paper.
Scharpf, F. W. (1984), 'Economic and institutional constraints of full-employment strategies: Sweden, Austria and Western Germany 1973–1982, pp. 257–290 in J. H. Goldthorpe (ed.), op. cit.
Schmidt, M. G. (1983), 'The welfare state and the economy in periods of economic crisis: a comparative study in twenty-three OECD Nations', *European Journal of Political Research,* 11, pp. 1–26.
Seidel, H. (1985), 'Die Entfaltung der Produktivkräfte der österreichischen Wirtschaft', pp. 77–123 in E. Bodzenta, H. Seidel and K. Stiglbauer, *Österreich im Wandel.* Vienna, Springer.
Smekal, Chr. (1977), *Die Flucht aus dem Budget,* Vienna, Jupiter-Verlag.
Steiner, K. (1972), *Politics in Austria,* Boston, Little, Brown.
Tálos, E. (1985), 'Krise der sozialen Sicherung in Österreich', *Österreichische Zeitschrift für Politikwissenschaft,* 14, pp. 275–94.
Tálos, E. and M. Wiederschwinger (eds), *Arbeitslosigkeit. Österreichs Vollbeschäftingungspolitik am Ende?.* Vienna, verlag für Gesellschaftskritik.
Ulram, P. A. (1985), 'Um die Mehrheit der Mehrheit', pp. 203–37 in F. Plasser, P. A. Ulram and H. Welan (eds), *Demokratierituale.* Vienna, Böhlau.
Winckler, G. (1985), 'Sozialpartnerschaft und ökonomische Effizienz', pp. 295–312 in P. Gerlich, E. Grande and W. C. Müller (eds), *Sozialpartnerschaft in der Krise,* Vienna Böhlau.

10 Challenges confronting Swedish decision – makers: political and policy responses 1974 – 1987

GUNNEL GUSTAFSSON

Important dates

1970	The first steps towards a constitutional reform: a unicameral system replaced the two chamber system and elections to parliament, counties, and municipalities were held simultaneously every third year
1945--70	Social Democratic majority governments 1951–7 coalition with the Farmers' Party, which in 1958 changed its name to Centre Party
1970–3	Social Democratic government with relative but no absolute majority Social Democratic Party was the largest in the Riksdag and Social Democrats and Communists together held more than half of the parliamentary seats
1973–6	Social Democrats and Communists together held exactly half of the parliamentary seats this was the time of the so-called lottery Riksdag (the number of seats was 350)
1975	The constitutional reform was completed (the number of seats in parliament was reduced to 349)
1976–82	Non-Socialist majority in the Riksdag; coalition and minority governments 1976–8 coalition between Centre, Conservative, and Liberal parties 1978–9 Liberal minority government

	1979–81 coalition between Centre, Conservative, and Liberal parties
	1981–2 minority coalition between Centre and Liberal parties
1980	referendum on the energy issue (nuclear power)
	there were three choices and the middle or compromise line gained more votes than the others
1982–7	Social Democratic government with relative but no absolute majority
	as in 1970–3 the Social Democratic Party was the largest in the Riksdag; together with the Communists they held more than half of the parliamentary seats

Source: Birgersson *et al.*, 1984.

Perceptions and definitions of the post-1974 'crisis'

In Sweden the unfavourable developments during the early 1970s were, in the main, believed to be caused by high energy costs, especially for oil. Swedish industry had, at that time, tended to base its calculations on low energy costs. Therefore the rise in oil prices had immediate adverse effects on GNP.

The economic decline was also viewed in a broader perspective. Swedish exports correspond to approximately 30 per cent of GNP and the country is largely dependent on economic developments outside its borders. It goes without saying that what a small free-trade nation can do is partly to 'create a favourable climate' within the country and partly to counteract some imported developments if these are judged undesirable. The tendency in western Europe and the United States towards a combination of inflation in prices and stagnation of production was judged to be such an undesirable development, which could be counteracted, at least to a large extent.

However, a number of ill-defined challenges continued to confront policy-makers, although during the mid and late 1970s these problems were still considered to be temporary. It was believed that they could be overcome if suitable economic policy measures were taken. Unemployment was judged to be the most serious evil. Therefore there was agreement that every possible effort had to be made in order to avoid it, reflected by an underlying attitude that the difficulties could be ridden out via temporary measures, and that all efforts were to be made to keep unemployment low and to increase economic growth. It was assumed that external conditions would improve and that the old policy-making machinery would continue to work smoothly. By the end of the 1970s, however, 'the seriousness of the Swedish situation had become clearly visible and recognized as a more or less permanent fact of life' (Heckscher, 1984, p. 235).

General responses

Swedish policy-makers usually attempt to deal with problems before they reach the main political agenda, that is, before they become exposed to public debate and, eventually, conflict. Actions are often undertaken in order to *prevent* something which is otherwise likely to need future correction. This is a long-term agenda-management strategy. It means that future perspectives are part of the policy-making routines. This preventive or anticipatory attitude can be seen as a main ingredient in the radical/consultative policy style which has made Sweden a welfare-state 'model'.

Despite this anticipatory style, in a comparative perspective Sweden was slow to react to the new economic situation. One explanation for the delay is to be found in the fact that the radical-preventive policy style used to be so successful. The idea that it would not prove as instrumental in renewing the Swedish welfare society as it was in constructing it, simply did not occur to policy-makers. When the problems became more significant and it was clear that the old recipe no longer worked as effectively, there was great uncertainty about how to handle the new challenges. The task was both to deal with the actual problems and at the same time maintain existing values and policies. In order to gain trust from voters as well as time to 'research' how best to handle the new situation, decision-makers responded in accordance with the old cultural patterns, stressing consensus and common efforts to develop the welfare state further along traditional lines, that is, by using long-term measures which had worked well in the past.

Political changes

Prior to the crisis in 1970, the first steps had been taken towards a constitutional reform which was completed by 1975. A unicameral system of 350 members (in 1975 reduced to 349) replaced the old bicameral system. Elections to parliament, counties and municipalities were to be held simultaneously every third year. The previous voting system (which involved some over-representation for the largest party) was replaced by a system of complete proportional representation of all political parties which obtain either 4 per cent or more of the total number of votes or 12 per cent of the votes in a district.

The strong and stable multi-party system is, of course, an important part of the Swedish political system. For more than half a century representation has been confined to the same five parties: Conservative, Liberal, Centre, Social Democratic, and Communist. Between the end of the Second World War and 1970 the Social Democrats were able to form continuous majority governments. Since 1970 the situation has become more volatile. In the period 1970–3 Social Democrats governed with the support of Communists;

in 1973–6 the two parties together held exactly half of the parliamentary seats, and in 1976 the non-Socialist parties (Centre, Conservative and Liberals) gained a parliamentary majority. After the 1976 and 1979 elections the three non-Socialist parties formed coalition governments which on both occasions collapsed before the next elections. From 1982 onwards, as in the early 1970s, the Social Democrats have had a relative but no absolute majority. In parliament therefore they have to rely on support from other parties.

The post-1974 crisis period thus coincides with an unstable *parliamentary* situation. But there is no direct relationship between the two developments. Instead, the extremely stable party structure is an important factor in explaining why Swedish decision-makers, regardless of party, were slow to perceive the new circumstances and slow to take action to deal with the economic problems.

The declining support for the Social Democrats in the 1970s reflects a decline in the proportion of workers within the electorate (Berglund and Linström, 1978). As the party structure continues to reflect the composition of the electorate when the modern mass parties were formed originally, the transition from an industrial economy to a service economy had adversely affected support for the Social Democrats. When the political parties were originally formed, there was a small public sector and widely differing living standards. The successful development of the welfare society in Sweden, however, extended the public supply of goods and services to cover almost any human needs. The result is not a classless society, but a society with a very large middle class and few people who are extremely poor or extremely rich. In such a society, and especially within the large middle class, cleavages develop along new lines. Controversies such as between materialists/traditionalists on the one hand and environmentalists, feminists and representatives of the peace movement on the other, have developed. However, because of the stable party structure, these cleavages, have developed *within* the political parties, rather than *between* them.

Some of these newer concerns relevant to the economic crisis have been, since the early 1970s, an integral part of public debate in Sweden. Even so, such questions find difficulty in reaching the national political agenda. This gives rise to some mismatch between cleavages represented by the parties on the one hand and the electorate on the other. The tendency to vote for issues rather then for 'class' interests reflects these developments (Holmberg, 1984).

One can ask why the party system has not undergone bigger changes, and why it has not increased its responsiveness to the electorate. There are three main reasons why it is comparatively difficult for the Swedish multi-party system to renew itself. First, the 4 per cent hurdle means that small parties cannot achieve representation. Secondly the public party subsidy system, favours the larger parties in the financing of election campaigns (Gidlund,

G., 1983). Thirdly, the long period of Social Democratic governance, and the successful establishment of the welfare state through long-term preventive policy-making, is in itself an obstacle to radical changes of policy style within the Social Democratic Party. Thus there is a tension between the need to take new measures to deal with the crisis and the need to appear faithful to earlier ideals and actions. One of the consequences is that local and often temporary parties and interest groups are formed (Gidlund, Je, 1978). Another consequence is that unconventional participation, for example 'wild' demonstrations and similar actions, are more common. These usually concern newer issues – for example environmental protection.

One new issue which has managed to reach the national agenda, although not in the 'conventional' way, is the nuclear energy question. This issue is of crucial importance in terms of industrial renewal itself, as well of importance in the process of economic crisis management. In 1980 the nuclear energy topic became so politically controversial that a referendum had to be held in order to resolve it. This was very unusual – the previous referendum being held in 1957 concerning the introduction of a supplementary pension scheme. In the 1980 referendum there were three choices. In the event the compromise proposal won the day. A referendum, according to the constitution, is not decisive but is meant to advise parliament. After the 1980 referendum all parties agreed to accept the electorate's verdict, thereby hoping to avoid future conflicts.

The Environmental Party was formed in 1981 and first participated in a national election in 1982, gaining 1.65 per cent of the votes. Three years later the national support was somewhat lower, at 1.5 per cent, whereas local support had increased considerably (2 per cent for counties and 2.5 per cent for municipalities). The Chernobyl accident, not surprisingly, put the environmental issue back firmly on the political agenda. However, steps had already been taken to try to avoid further increases in local support for the Environmental Party (it being judged that the Environmental Party could, in the long run exceed 4 per cent in national elections). Thus in 1986 a new national authority with explicit responsibility for the environment was formed in attempt to head off further support for the movement.

Disagreements within the non-Socialist governments is, to some extent, also related to the developing crisis. In 1978, for example, the disagreement concerned the nuclear question, after which the smallest of the three non-Socialist parties, the Liberals, formed a minority government for a year. During the period 1979–81 the coalition split was caused by disagreement over tax policy, with the Centre and Liberals then forming a minority government. The return of the Social Democrats to office in 1982, as well as the 1985 election result, can be seen as an expression of trust for the old Social Democratic machinery. People then believed that Social Democrats were more able to deal with the crisis, not least because of their close connection to the blue collar trade union organization (LO).

Budgetary changes

There were three main budgetary developments during the 'crisis' period, namely growth of public expenditure in relation to GNP; increased state loans in order to finance public consumption; and increased local rather than national government expenditure.

However it is measured, the Swedish public sector is comparatively large and is growing. In 1981 public expenditure exceeded 65 per cent of GNP, compared with 45 per cent in 1970 (Lybeck, 1984, p. 34). An additional indicator of the size of the public sector is the number of public employees as a share of total employment. Thus in 1983 there were almost three times as many public employees as in 1960. During the same period total employment increased by 17 per cent (*Offentliga sektorn,* p. 21).

The use of loans to finance public expenditure coincided with the arrival of the non-Socialist governments. It could be argued that the non-Socialists were afraid of rising unemployment and therefore spent more than Social Democrats would have done in an attempt to reassure the electorate that the old values were still in place. Moreover there was a broad consensus that high GNP growth and low unemployment were the main means by which the difficulties presented by the world crisis could be met. In fact 1977 was the year in which a relatively large national debt emerged. The debt is still very large in the mid-1980s, in part because of the accumulated interest on earlier loans.

The view that lower labour costs could solve some of the problems is also broadly shared. But trade unions and parties have not managed to agree on how to achieve this goal. Even in Sweden there is insufficient trust between different groups in the labour market and an unwillingness to accept that one's own group's salary should be reduced or at least not increased. On the contrary both low and high income earners argue that it is their turn to get a rise.

An overview of the distribution of public expenditure illustrates the increased importance of interest paid on the national debt. It also shows that the patterns of distribution between different sectors such as defence, social welfare, labour, housing and so on, is relatively stable (Table 10.1). The main budgetary response to the unfavourable economic situation, which emerged during the mid-1970s, was in fact over-consumption and an inability to balance the national budget, either through increased taxes and other revenues or through decreased expenditure. During the 1980s, however, the budget deficit on the general government account has improved considerably. Thus in 1982 it amounted to 6 per cent of GDP whereas by 1986 it had fallen to 1.5 per cent (*OECD Economic Survey on Sweden 1987*, pp. 24–25). This favourable change can be partly attributed to budgetary benefits related to the devaluations of the Swedish crown (see below).

Table 10.1 Expenditure in billion crowns 1975–85

Department	1975–6 Expenditure Cr. bn	%	1979–80 Expenditure Cr. bn	%	1984–5 Expenditure Cr. bn	%
Interest on national debt	4.1	4.2	14.5	7.9	75.2	22.8
Justice	3.9	4.0	6.4	3.5	9.6	2.9
Defence	10.2	10.4	15.8	8.7	23.9	7.3
Social welfare	27.8	28.5	48.1	26.3	76.6	23.3
Transport	6.2	6.3	9.7	5.3	13.0	4.0
Finance	6.4	6.6	10.8	5.9	15.3	4.6
Education	13.6	14.0	24.1	13.3	37.8	11.5
Labour	5.4	5.5	12.0	6.6	20.8	6.3
Housing	5.9	6.0	12.0	6.6	25.2	7.7
Industry	3.8	3.9	12.8	7.0	14.4	4.4
Others	10.3	10.6	16.3	8.9	17.3	5.2
Total	97.6	100.0	182.5	100.0	329.1	100.0

Source: *Statens finanser 1985* (1986). Stockholm, Riksrevisionsverket, p. 53.

Another important trend is that local government consumption increased, whereas national government consumption has been relatively stable. The extension of the public sector in Sweden has therefore been in the main via a growth of service delivery through local government (Figure 10.1).

Decentralization

The size of local government expenditure is just one indication of the importance of counties and municipalities in Sweden. Another is that election turnout at county and municipal levels is more than 90 per cent and is as high as at the national level. There are a number of factors which contribute to the crucial role played by local governments in Sweden. The most important is the constitutional right for municipalities and county councils to levy income tax and charge fees for services and benefits. Municipal income tax is proportional, unlike the progressive national income tax. Taxation rates are decided by the elected councillors, and local income tax has increased continuously over the last twenty years. In 1987 it amounted to more than 30 per cent of a person's income (Table 10.2).

Several important tasks, which in many other countries are performed by national government, are the responsibility of local authorities in Sweden. Therefore the response to challenges is far from a purely national task. Although it is the Riksdag which formally has decisive power in most policy areas, increasingly parliamentary decisions are often of a framework character and the recommendations made by government and national bureaucracies are vague. In practice, local governments play a strategic role in the processes of collecting and distributing public funds, and their importance continues to increase.

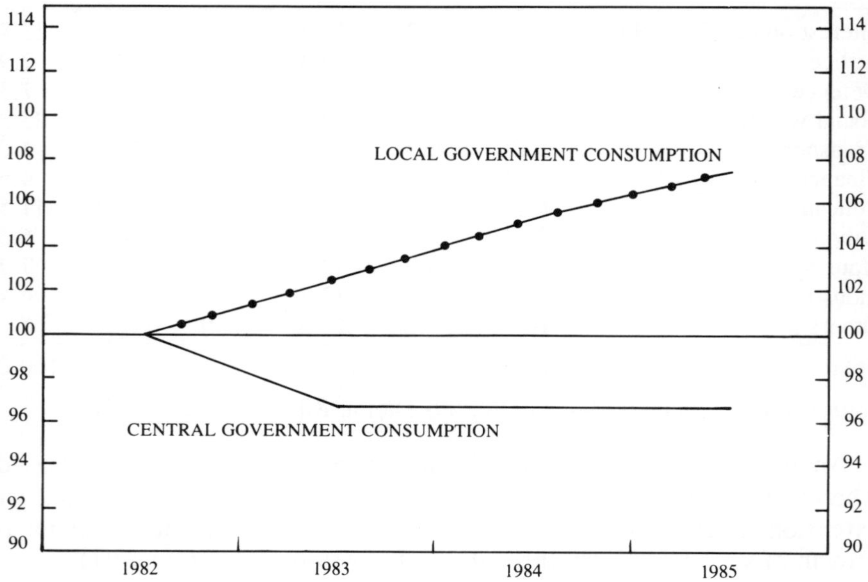

Source: National Institute of Economic Research, OECD, as referred to by the *OECD Economic Survey on Sweden 1987*, p. 26.

Figure 10.1 Public sector consumption 1982–5: volume index 1982 = 100

Local government reform, which between 1965 and 1973 reduced the number of municipalities, was the starting point for massive decentralization (Gustafsson 1980, 1987). The transfer of powers and responsibilities covers almost all policy sectors – for example education, social welfare, environment, and health. Making local governments more 'responsible' is, however, accompanied by a major effort to devolve and decentralize *within* national government, for example from a national agency to a regional or local branch of national government.

Table 10.2 Local government taxes 1955–87

Year	Municipal taxes Average	County taxes Average	Total local government taxes*
1955	8.93	3.75	12.24
1960	10.85	4.38	14.63
1965	12.18	5.95	17.25
1970	14.18	8.06	21.00
1975	15.23	10.21	25.23
1980	16.68	12.61	20.09
1985	17.20	13.30	30.38
1986	17.08	13.37	30.34
1987	17.07	13.50	30.44

Note: *the total sum of local taxes – because of some incongruity in the division of local governments – cannot be calculated just by adding municipal and county taxes.
Source: *Årsbok för Sveriges kommuner 1987*, p. 14.

When the decentralization movement started it was in no way caused by economic difficulties nor was it believed to be instrumental in the management of any future crises, should they occur. On the contrary it was part of a long-term plan to make the service delivery system more efficient and democratic. The considerations were based on a belief that GNP growth should continue and that the national long-term goals included further reforms of the welfare state. The assumption was that local action would be consistent with national goals but that many details could best be handled lower down the system.

When the new challenges finally emerged they became, because of earlier developments, as much a *local* governmental as a *national* governmental responsiblity. Thus, instead of one conflict over a given issue, there are often as many conflicts as there are municipalities and counties. At times this is convenient for national policy-makers, but it also presents obvious problems in handling the actual economic crisis.

The formal responsibiltiy still remains with national government, and voters thus demand some action from the governing party, which in many cases cannot control local government policies and/or expenditure. Therefore some national policies become part of the rhetoric and are never intended to be implemented (Gustafsson, 1983).

As suggested earlier, local government expenditure is to a very large extent based on local taxes. Somewhat paradoxically, however, there is a commonly accepted norm that all Swedish inhabitants, wherever they live, should have roughly the same service and welfare delivery. State grants to municipalities, by tradition, have therefore been distributed in order to guarantee the same minimum universal standard. Such transfers are either given for general purposes, that is, as compensation for unfavourable general local characteristics, or are given for specified purposes, that is, tasks which according to specifications made by national agencies have to be carried out by the municipalities or counties. Education, social welfare and child care are examples of such specific tasks (Table 10.3)

Table 10.3 State transfers to local governments 1970–83: billion crowns in current prices

To local governments	1970	1975	1980	1983
Municipalities				
General grants	1.0	2.4	5.8	4.3
Specified grants	5.5	11.2	24.2	31.5
Total	6.5	13.6	30.0	35.8
per cent of municipal income	21.9	25.9	27.7	24.4
Counties				
General grants	0.5	1.3	4.0	3.1
Specified grants	1.3	2.8	4.9	7.5
Total	1.8	4.1	8.9	10.6
per cent of county income	18.8	19.2	17.7	15.4

Source: Kommunernas finanser as reported in *Offentliga sektorn: utveckling och nuläge*, 1985, p. 52.

As is clear from data presented in Table 10.3, the relative importance of grants has begun to decrease. State grants to the counties had already started to decline during the mid-1970s. In the case of municipalities the importance of state grants began to decrease in 1980. It has to be noted, however, that there is a wide variation between local governments in this respect. In some municipal budgets the relative importance of state grants is still great and increasing, whereas the opposite trend characterizes other local government units.

Issues and policies

Swedish welfare policies have long since been based on a firm (and, in retrospect, possibly naive) belief in continuing GNP growth, as well as on the assumption of low energy costs. The main task has generally been perceived as formulating long-term goals, in close cooperation with all affected parties in society, and the implementation of these goals through highly efficient institutions. Procedural improvements such as the decentralization reforms described above, are part of the broadly supported strategy of further developing the welfare state.

Nevertheless, as suggested, there were already, prior to the mid-1970s, signs of conflicts concerning future policies. Consensus was still reached on the surface, but ideological controversies appeared concerning the principles according to which goods and services should be distributed between groups, as well as regarding more general 'lifestyle' questions. Sometimes this ideological debate has been quite lively at lower levels in the system. When the country's economic situation definitely became less favourable, these underlying differences became more visible.

The most dramatic conflict surrounded the nuclear issue cited earlier. Other aspects of public policies of relevance in a crisis perspective have experienced difficulty in reaching the national agenda as coherent issues. This is partly a consequence of the fact that many conflicts are appearing *within* the parties rather than *between* them. In addition the highly specialized or sectorised bureaucracy, which occupies most of the organizational space, makes it difficult for cross-sectoral issues to reach the agenda. Regional authorities, for example, concerned to improve the labour market conditions in their area, sometimes succeed in doing so by presenting what they are doing as policies concerning health, education or communication. The sector 'label' in such cases means that the issue does not reach the agenda in its own right. On other occasions the well-organized policy community is a real hindrance to action.

Irrespective of whether or not decentralization is meant to cause substantial changes, it has actually moved much of the policy-making from parliament to other areas of society. Therefore potential conflicts which in the past could not reach the national agenda, now to some extent manage to do so at the regional and local level, although sometimes under a 'false' label.

The formal decentralization of transfer of power in the political/administrative system has also affected interest group activities in Sweden. Thus there are now more diversified trade union activities. The unions' concern is not just with wage bargaining but with representation at all stages of policy-making – from policy formulation to implementation. They are often successful in preventing employers' attempts to limit public expenditure, for example.

The combination of decentralized negotiations and the absence of central decisions regarding the total wages bill has resulted in difficulties in reaching agreements about the criteria by which wages should be set. As a consequence strikes and lock-outs have become relatively common during the 1980s. It cannot be argued that the more conflictual situation in the labour market is entirely due to the economic crisis. Its background is of a much more complex nature and in the main reflects structural economic developments – such as the shift to a service-orientated economy. The slow or non-existent GNP growth, however, does make peaceful agreements more difficult to reach.

Labour market and industrial policies

Labour market policy was immediately affected by the economic challenges which appeared in the mid-1970s. As mentioned, the employment issue was judged crucial, as the political commitment to full employment has always been extremely strong in Sweden. Even though the rate of reported unemployment remained low (3 per cent), the rates were increasing especially in some regions – for example in the inland areas of the north as well as among some groups, especially the young. In addition to the reported unemployment there is some hidden unemployment. Even when these figures are estimated and added to official figures, the unemployment rates are still comparatively low, however.

Youth unemployment rates are difficult to measure. Even so, it was clear at the end of the 1970s that these rates had increased to a politically unacceptable level. In 1980 parliament decided that municipal authorities had to provide unemployed young people who had not yet reached the age of eighteen, with a job or some form of education. In 1984 this municipal youth employment guarantee was extended to everyone under twenty (SFS 1983:1070, pp. 2855–8).

During the 1970s the main labour market goal had shifted from full employment to 'work for everyone', and specific policies were introduced in order to assist groups who appeared to be less able to enter the labour market. There was an increasing tendency to consider work as a social right, not merely as an instrument through which material welfare is increased (Henning, 1985). The old commitment to keep unemployment rates at a low level, and the new high aims set for the policy area, coincided with the international recession in the economy and this resulted in some fundamental changes in Swedish industrial policy.

Until 1976 the old-fashioned but sophisticated industrial policy instruments dominated. A dramatic change occurred when the shipbuilding and iron industries experienced a rapid worsening of their already problematic situation (Lundmark, 1983; Bill 1983/84:135; SOU 1981:72). Signs of crisis, under the impact of the world recession, were also reported from the other sectors – for example textiles and wood pulp. Severe regional imbalances arose due to these problems. Instead of the traditional state support – based on long-term considerations aiming at modernization and increased production – temporary subsidies were generally given to crisis-ridden sectors, companies and regions. During the whole non-Socialistic period of government, industrial support continued both to increase and to be focused on rescue operations (Figure 10.2) Why then, was there this enormous increase under the non-Socialist governments? The explanation is that: 'When the government was suddenly faced by a number of crises that affected whole sectors as well as individual firms, it dared not risk the higher unemployment that would have resulted if the market had been left to its own devices. Hence the government was predisposed towards crisis interventions by a mixture of structural and electoral factors' (Lundmark, 1983, p. 240).

When the Social Democrats returned to power in 1982 strong efforts were made to achieve economic recovery. The so-called 'third way' economic policy included a reduction of subsidies to industry, especially of temporary support. The Social Democrats were convinced that there was a real need for industrial restructuring and for less industrial reliance on government. This policy has reduced direct subsidies, and the share of temporary support dropped considerably after 1982–3., when it reached its peak. As is clear from Figure 10.2, a shift from 'defensive' to 'offensive' measures occurred in 1983–4.

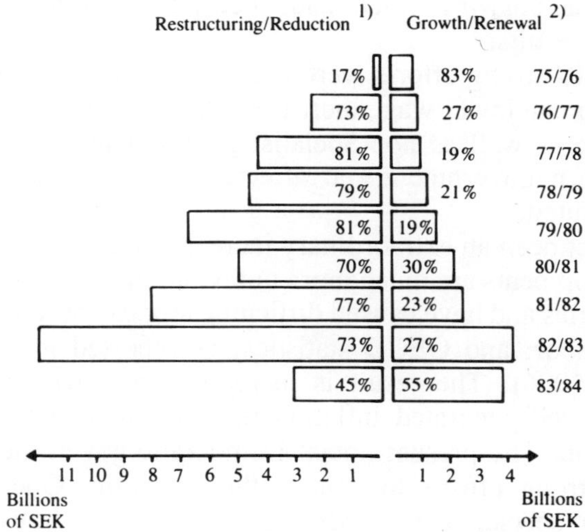

Notes:

1 Restructuring/Reduction = temporary support + sectoral support

2 Growth/Renewal = Technological Development including tax deductions for research and industrial funding + regional policy support + export support + small business support

Source: Swedish Industry and Industrial Policy 1985, p. 15

Figure 10.2 Support to Swedish industry 1975/6–1983/4 allocated according to restructuring/reduction and growth/renewal

The first step in the new Social Democratic policy was the 16 per cent devaluation of the crown, a few weeks after the 1982 election. The emphasis was put on a revitalization of the economy through a package of measures. Some measures, such as the devaluation of the crown, were meant to improve the situation for exporting industries, whereas others were meant to combat inflation and reduce real individual incomes. The introduction of the much debated wage earner funds was one way of maintaining the loyalty of trade unions.

Compared with other countries, Swedish industrial development was very weak for a ten year period beginning around 1974 (Swedish Industry and Industrial Policy, 1985, p. 4). By 1984 industrial production returned to its 1974 level and industrial employment increased somewhat (ibid. p. 4). This may have been partly the result of the new policies. However it coincided with an international upswing which made it easier for the new measures to 'produce' desired results.

During the 1980s strong efforts were made to encourage employers and employees to negotiate lower wage increases. The main instrument used by Social Democratic as well as non-Socialist governments was round table discussions between government and affected parties. The success has, however, been limited.

There has in fact been an extraordinary increase in labour costs via wage drift. These developments are much more unfavourable for Sweden than for comparable countries and have caused difficulties for export companies (US Department of Labor, and OECD statistics, as reported in 'Reallön och Inflation', SAF, 1986). The result is increased costs without increased productivity, and self-generated inflation in addition to the considerable 'imported' inflation. The present Social Democratic government (1985–) has made very strong efforts to control this situation. One sign is the appointment of a special Wages Minister. There are, however, many obstacles to be overcome. One problem is the creation of 'incentives' for employees to agree to lower wage increases and another is internal opposition within the Social Democratic party itself.

Another trend in labour market policy can be characterized as a greater concern over the location of jobs. At the beginning of the mid-1980s many Swedish municipalities had reached a reported unemployment rate of approximately 8 per cent (DsI 1984:25, p. 33). This rise is partly due to the high female economic activity rates in Sweden. As both the man and the woman in a family are active in the labour market it becomes increasingly difficult to create effective incentives for labour mobility. In the absence of well coordinated long-term regional and labour market policies, the response to this situation is more direct support to companies in trouble.

Not surprisingly the increased emphasis on local markets also means a degree of transfer of responsibility from national to local governments, administrations and networks (Lindmark and Lundmark, 1983). The well established labour market bureaucracies operate together with trade unions, local governments and other interested parties. Construction Labour Market Boards constitute a good example of the tendency towards a mixed regional labour market economy (Winoy, 1980). Local employer associations and unions, municipalities, as well as the regional labour market agencies, are represented on each of the sixty-eight boards located throughout the country. The purpose of these bodies is to adjust seasonal fluctuations in unemployment rates in the local construction market. As a consequence of the difficulties in finding and using instruments which work in a situation characterized by international recession, by ambitious labour market goals, and by more local demands, the costs of unemployment insurance have increased considerably during the last decade (Gustafsson, 1985).

Comparing Sweden's labour market policy with those of other countries, it must still be judged successful. The rescue operations, and gradual switch to more local and regional activities, have contributed to the low unemployment rates. Despite such efforts, the less favourable international environment means that since the 1970s Sweden has nevertheless faced similar problems to those of other countries.

Thus the question of unemployment is constantly on the political agenda, and the ideological solutions to the present problems differ somewhat (though predictably) between parties. Non-Socialists generally stress freedom for the market, more than Social Democrats do. Privatization of some public services, lower income taxes, and much more freedom of companies, are suggested by the Conservatives, for example. The Liberal and the Centre parties want to move in the same direction but not as quickly as the Conservatives. Social Democrats too are willing to reconsider at least some parts of 'their' welfare prototype. There are clearly ideological conflicts relating to the future of the welfare state. Issues which reflect such conflicts concern, for example, how to govern the now existing Wage-Earner Funds, 'waiting days' for sickness benefits, and provisions of public child care versus more support for parents who stay at home and take care of their own children and thereby 'save' public expenditure. These disagreements have not so far proved to be of fundamental importance for the issues considered by parliament and the government, and the differences appear to be even smaller at the implementation stage. This is both because all interests in the field are well organized and tend to defend the status quo and because of difficulties in identifying a new rationale which is both politically and economically realistic. In that sense the ideological cleavages have not proved to be of more than marginal importance in actual policy-making and implementation.

Expenditure on social security and welfare

It has already been pointed out that the increase in public expenditure from the middle of the 1970s on is, to a very large extent, a local government phenomenon. In addition there has been an increase in costs for services delivered through social security institutions, that is, quasi-governmental bodies which are 'collective or juridical persons under public law', from approximately 4 per cent of the GNP in the mid-1970s to 8 per cent in 1983 (Gustafsson, 1985, p. 8).

Sweden's social security and welfare programmes are designed to meet almost any eventuality for the citizen. Naturally they cover old age pensions, sickness and unemployment benefits. A large battery of measures is used. The stress is on provision of services without means-tests. The main increase in expenditure has been on old age pension schemes.

'Social assistance' is given by municipal Social Welfare Boards in order to help individuals and families who cannot manage, despite the general social security and welfare measures. After contacts with the client, a sum of money (usually a small amount of cash which is intended to cover specific needs) is paid. Before the introduction of general social insurance, social assistance used to be of great importance. Nowadays, however, it is marginal in relation to other measures, and 'social assistance' expenditure is almost negligible in relation to GNP – 0.3 per cent of GNP in 1983 (Gustafsson, 1985, p. 8). However there has been a slight increase in 'social assistance' costs during the 1980s and this is a fact of great importance in the political debate. It is considered to be an indication of emerging social problems of a new type. What is new is that normal employees, in increasing numbers, need 'social assistance'. This 'new-poverty' is considered to be a bad sign of the effectiveness of the Swedish welfare model as it has not, despite expectations, been prevented by the general measures.

Another social question which has caused political debate concerned sickness benefits. In 1982 the non-Socialist government proposed a three-day 'waiting period' for such benefits, after reported sickness. This suggestion however met strong opposition not only from Social Democrats and trade unions, but also from supporters, and even MPs, of the governing parties, particularly the Centre Party. This was because such a reform could be seen as governmental intervention in the free negotiations between employers and employees and because white-collar workers had already negotiated an agreement exempting them from a new proposal. If this agreement had been upheld, the manual workers would have been the only group to be affected by the new policy. Such potential differences of treatment caused great bitterness, and public debate took place in an emotional atmosphere. This is despite the fact that, like social assistance, sickness benefits are not significant in expenditure terms. Sickness insurance benefits' share of GNP increased slightly during the late 1970s, but had already decreased again by the time of the 1982 proposal.

Despite the criticism, the government managed to obtain a parliamentary majority for its bill. The Social Democrats, during the 1982 election campaign, promised to abolish the 'waiting days'. They also said they would guarantee the old age pension system and the national government grants for municipal child care activities. The Social Democratic victory of 1982 in practice meant that the social security and welfare system remained largely intact despite the economic problems. Instead of cutting social expenditure the emphasis, as suggested, was placed on revitalizing the economy. In addition, there were some attempts at small annual budget reductions.

The results of crisis management

The economic policies adhered to since the change of government in 1982 have continued to stress GDP growth and full employment. (See economic indicators in Table 10.4.) The programme includes repeated devaluations of the Swedish crown, a radical restructuring of the industrial sector, and stimulation of growth in the private sector through deregulation measures. The Social Democratic governments during the 1980s have been determined to formulate economic policy programmes, which are supported as much by non-Socialists as by Social Democrats themselves. It could be argued that the economic adjustment policies, in terms of ideological content, is as much characterized by non-Socialist ideas as it is by Social Democratic principles. Through the still *relatively* good (in comparative terms) relationships between trade unions and Social Democrats, however, the Social Democrats are generally thought to be able to implement this policy more strictly than the non-Socialists would have been able to, had they been in office.

For the time being, external economic conditions have improved and the policy is judged successful by most groups. Sweden's economic performance has thus improved during the 1980s. GDP growth amounts to approximately 1 to 2 per cent, inflation has fallen, the balance of payments has improved, and the public sector deficit has recently been cut back significantly. Moreover this has been achieved without a rise in general unemployment, which is still below 3 per cent and one of the lowest in Europe. A recent (1987) OECD report on Sweden, however, suggests that:

> economic progress has relied substantially on improvements in the external environment . . . while certain domestic developments have been less favourable:
>
> – Labour costs rose much more rapidly than in other countries, and Swedish industry has been losing market shares both at home and abroad;
> – Probably related to this, growth of business fixed investment (fairly strong in 1985) slowed down. The expansion of activity therefore relied essentially on higher private and public consumption;
> – Although the share of public expenditure in GNP has been reduced, the level is still high, as is the level of taxation (OECD, Economic Survey on Sweden, 1987, p. 58).

Table 10.4 Sweden: economic indicators 1970–83

Year	Unemployment[1]	Inflation Index; 1980=100[2]	GDP at constant prices[3]	Budget Deficit Billion crowns current prices[4a]	Money borrowed abroad in % of GDP[4b]	Public expenditure[5]	Total Tax revenue percentage of GDP[6a]
1968	—	—	—	—	—	42.8	—
1970	1.5	42.1	6.3	—	3.7	—	40.23
1971	2.5	43.3	.9	—	4.5	—	41.06
1972	2.7	46.1	2.3	—	4.9	—	42.47
1973	2.5	48.9	4.0	—	6.8	44.7	41.63
1974	2.0	55.6	3.2	—	5.3	48.1	42.83
1975	1.6	60.7	2.6	3.7	2.9	48.9	43.88
1976	1.6	66.9	1.1	10.4	0.9	51.7	48.19
1977	1.8	74.0	1.6	25.2	−1.1	57.5	50.46
1978	2.2	82.3	1.8	38.6	−2.2	59.2	50.87
1979	2.1	89.1	3.8	50.0	−5.2	60.7	49.54
1980	2.0	100.0	1.7	60.0	−9.5	61.6	49.36
1981	2.5	111.0	−.3	68.1	−14.5	64.6	51.21
1982	3.2	121.7	.8	86.6	−22.1	66.6	50.26
1983	3.5	132.6	2.5	77.1	−22.3	66.2	50.50

Notes:
— indicates that data are not available
1 *Source*: *Main Economic Indicators 1964–1983* (1982). Paris, OECD, p. 555.
2 Inflation is measured by consumer prices, excluding direct taxes; 1980 = 100. Source: ibid. p. 561.
3 *Source*: *International Financial Statistics. Yearbook 1985* (1985). International Monetary Fund, Washington DC, p. 131.
4a These figures are calculated for budget years running from 1 July one year to 1 July the next. The year 1975 as presented in the table thus really means 1 July 1975 to July 1976, etc.
Source: *Statens finanser 1985* (1986). Riksrevisionsverket, Stockholm, p. 52.
4b *Source*: Finansräkenskaperna as referred in 'Fakta om Sveriges ekonomi' (1984). SAF (The Swedish Employer's Association), Stockholm, p. 66.
5 Total outlays of government as a percentage of GDP. *Source*: *Historical Statistics 1960–1984* (1985). Paris, OECD, p. 64.
6a *Source*: For the years 1970–82 A) *Revenue Statistics of OECD Countries 1965–1983* (1984). Paris, OECD, p. 85; for 1983 B) *Revenue Statistics of OECD Countries 1965–1985* (1986). Paris, OECD, p. 82.

Year	Personal income taxes as percentages of GDP[6b]	Taxation on corporate income % of GDP[6c]	Social security contributes % of GDP[6d]	Property taxes % of GDP[6e]	Consumption taxes % of GDP[6f]	Taxes on specific goods % of GDP[6g]
1972	19.75	1.69	6.75	0.53	12.01	5.92
1973	18.60	1.80	6.53	0.52	11.62	5.62
1974	19.29	1.47	8.31	0.43	10.47	4.91
1975	20.25	1.91	8.55	0.49	9.95	4.70
1976	20.81	1.72	11.23	0.51	10.85	4.87
1977	21.01	1.43	12.84	0.45	11.10	4.72
1978	21.50	1.56	13.64	0.42	11.14	4.43
1979	21.03	1.53	13.45	0.45	11.02	4.40
1980	20.26	1.21	14.12	0.46	11.14	4.54
1981	20.42	1.48	15.13	0.45	11.55	4.63
1982	20.50	1.68	14.03	0.51	11.54	4.91
1983	19.65	1.72	13.60	0.84	11.75	4.91

6b *Source*: ibid. A) p. 89 for the years 1972–1982; ibid. B) p. 87 for 1983
6c *Source*: ibid. A) p. 90 for the years 1972–1982; ibid. B) p. 88 for 1983
6d *Source*: ibid. A) p. 91 for the years 1972–1982; ibid. B) p. 89 for 1983
6e *Source*: ibid. A) p. 95 for the years 1972–1982; ibid. B) p. 93 for 1983
6f *Source*: ibid. A) p. 97 for the years 1972–1982; ibid. B) p. 95 for 1983
6g *Source*: ibid. A) p. 99 for the years 1972–1982; ibid. B) p. 97 for 1983

It is fair to conclude that Swedish developments present two constrasting pictures. On the one hand there are political demands for further social welfare reforms, and on the other, economic commitments to limiting both public and private spending. One of the conclusions in the OECD Report is that local government consumption has to be restricted, and that wages have to be kept low (OECD, 1987, pp. 58–60). Both of these suggestions may, however, be hard to implement. The long tradition of local autonomy, together with the strong and recently increased legal and economic power which rests with local government, means that national government decisions on, for example, the introduction of spending ceilings for municipalities, are simply politically unrealistic. It is almost equally difficult to make the trade unions listen to government declarations on the need to keep wage negotiations below the rate of GDP growth. Thus over the two years 1986 and 1987 wages increased by 13.9 per cent some 4.8 per cent above the level agreed upon by LO and SAF for 1986–7 wage contracts. LO's claim, presented in November 1987, was for a further 10 per cent increase in 1988. Not surprisingly Sweden's inflation rate has begun to reflect the pressure of rising wages. Thus the Price and Cartel Office's figures in November 1987 showed that inflation was 4.6 per cent in the period January to October 1987, compared with 2.5 per cent in the first ten months of 1986. The inflation rate at the end of October 1987 was in fact 5.7 per cent (reported in S.I.P. *Newsletter*, November 20, 1987).

Low income earners, for example nurses, employed by the public sector, argue that their turn for a pay rise has now come. The same view is put forward by relatively well-paid groups, usually employed by successful private companies. This cleavage between public and private employees and between high and low income earners has a gender dimension as well. It is mainly women who have low-paid public jobs, whereas men are often highly-paid private employees. This multitude of potential conflicts makes the now decentralized wage negotiations hard to steer centrally. The tradition, among labour market partners, of sharing responsibility for the economy may, however, still prove to be sufficiently strong to support the general political and economic goals of high employment, low inflation and GDP growth, although strikes and lockouts continue to take place.

Demands for improvement of public services, especially health and day care, are still strongly articulated. At the same time there is no willingness to increase taxes or limit costs for other public services. So far the policy-responses to such demands are changes in policy delivery procedures, which are meant to improve efficiency and thereby result in better services produced without an increase in public expenditure. It is sometimes even argued that the consequences of such decentralization will make it possible to reduce rather than increase costs. The policy responses have been partially successful in two ways. Firstly the efforts have dispersed – if not eliminated – both the conflicts and the possibilities for their solution, and have thereby improved the democratic machinery somewhat. Secondly, as a result of the decentralization of authority in the system, the actual problems are to some extent made visible through the redefinition of old issues. Procedural efforts, however, have also resulted in increased fragmentation of authority, and the positive effects of decentralization in terms of crisis management still remain to be seen. Because of the improvements in the Swedish economy, the *immediate* pressure for cutbacks in public expenditure is not as strong as it was in the early 1980s. However if Sweden's international economic situation becomes less favourable, the present economic policy and other measures undertaken will probably not prove to be successful in 'riding out the storm'. In such a situation the crucial internal factor will be the ability to reach wage agreements which neither cause costly strikes nor severe political conflicts nor give rise to rapidly rising labour costs.

References

Berglund, S. and Lindström, U. (1978), *The Scandinavian Political System(s)*, Lund, Studentlitteratur.

Birgersson, B. O. *et al.* (1984), *Sverige efter 1900.* Stockholm, BonnierFakta Bokförlag AB.

Gidlund, G. (1983), *Partistöd.* Lund, CWK Gleerup.

Gidlund, Je (1978), *Aktionsgrupper och lokala partier.* Lund, CWK Gleerup.

Gustafsson, G. (1980), *Local Government Reform in Sweden.* Lund, CWK Gleerup.

Gustafsson, G. (1983), 'Symbolic and pseudo policies as responses to diffusion of power', *Policy Sciences*, 15, pp. 269–87.

Gustafsson, G. (1985), 'Swedish social security and welfare', *Research Report*, 1985: 10. University of Umea.

Gustafsson, G. (1987), *Decentralisering av politisk makt: en studie av svensk byrakrati i kontakt med sin omvärld.* Stockholm, Carlssons Bokförlag.

Heckscher, G. (1984), *The Welfare State and Beyond.* Minneapolis, University of Minnesota Press.

Henning, R. (1985), 'Industrial policy or employment policy? Sweden's response to unemployment' in Richardson, J. J. and Henning, R. (eds), *Unemployment: policy responses of western democracies.* London, Sage.

Holmberg, S. (1984), *Väljare i förändring.* Stockholm, Liber Förlag.

Lindmark, L. and Lundmark, K. (1983), 'From central steering to local resource mobilization: a study of small firms in a mixed economy', *Research Report.* University of Umeå.

Lundmark, K. (1983), 'Welfare state and employment policy: Sweden' in Dyson, K. and Wilks, S. (eds), *Industrial Crisis.* Oxford, Martin Robertson.

Lybeck, J. A. (1984), *Hur stor är den offentliga sektorn?* Malmö, Liber Förlag.

S.I.P. (1987), *Newsletter*, November 20.

Winoy, L. (1980), 'Public policy and the Swedish construction labour market', *Research Report.* University of Umea.

Statistical and other reports

Historical Statistics 1960–84 (1985). Paris, OECD.

Main Economic Indicators 1964–83 (1982). Paris, OECD.

Revenue Statistics of OECD Countries 1965–83 (1984). Paris, OECD.

Revenue Statistics of OECD Countries 1965–85 (1986). Paris, OECD.
International Financial Statistics. Yearbook 1985 (1985). Washington DC, International Monetary Fund.
OECD Economic Survey on Sweden 1987. Economic Surveys 1986–7. Paris.
Offentliga sektorn: utveckling och nuläge (1985). Stockholm, Statistiska centralbyrån (SCB).
'Fakta om Sveriges ekonomi' (1984). SAF (The Swedish Employers' Association).
'Reallön och inflation' (1986). Ekonomiska fakta från SAF (The Swedish Employers' Association).
Statens finanser 1985 (1986). Stockholm, Riksrevisionsverket (RRV).
Swedish Industry and Industrial Policy 1985 (1985). Stockholm, Ministry of Industry.
Årsbok för Sveriges kommuner 1987 (1987). Stockholm, Statistiska centralbyrån (SCB).

Government statements and Royal Commission Reports.

SOU 1981:72, *Att avveckla en kortsiktig stödpolitik (1981).* Betänkande av industristödsutredningen. Stockholm, Industridepartementet, LiberFörlag/Allmänna Förlaget.
SFS 1983: 1070 (1983), *Lag om arbete i ungdomslag hos offentliga arbetsgivare.* Stockholm, Allmänna förlaget.
Bill 1983/84:135 om industriell tillväxt och förnyelse, *Industripolitiken i Sverige och vissa andra länder* (1984), Bilaga 2. Stockholm.
DsI 1984:25, *Regional utveckling och mellanregional utjämning* (1984). Bilagedel V till regionalpolitiska utredningens betänkande. Stockholm, Industridepartementet, Liber/Allmänna förlaget.

11 Policy change, ideological change and the persistence of problems

Introduction

The foregoing chapters clearly demonstrate that all countries under study were indeed affected by the economic crisis initiated by the oil price shock. In view of the close interdependence of the industrialized countries, no country was safe from the consequences of the crisis: reduced growth, inflation, unemployment as well as budgetary problems caused by the attempts to overcome the crisis by traditional means. Differences of degree are apparent, but ultimately no country was spared the moment of truth. Perceptions differed, and in many cases differing perceptions of the crisis and of possible solutions delayed decisive policy changes. Also other political problems pushed economic difficulties lower down the political agenda to some degree, and for some time.

Our main expectations were outlined in Chapter 1. Thus we expected perceptions to differ according to existing political configurations; we expected a great variety of political responses ranging from institutional reform to changes in policy style and leadership patterns, including changing relations between government and interest groups; finally we expected differences in the *results* of crisis management. These results could point towards creative new approaches – particularly in terms of leadership styles – and might suggest more effective styles of political action in the future. It goes without saying that not all our expectations have been fulfilled.

While perceptions did indeed differ, there also seemed to be a much greater variety of policy-making (both in style and content) at the beginning, a divergence of approaches in which each country attempted to fall back upon its specific policy styles and policy traditions. Later, as the crisis persisted the countries converged in their approaches, each in turn moving towards austerity, more conflict, and stronger leadership. This was in part due to a realization that the separate economies were linked – thus reducing the capacity of any one national government to affect the development and outcome of the crisis – and in part due to an imitation or learning process. The results of both the old and the new policies and styles are mixed. In varying degrees Sweden, and to some extent Belgium, Holland and even Britain, appear to have achieved some of their own policy goals. In the rest of the countries there has been some improvement in certain respects, against which have to be set continuing or even worsening problems in other areas. Moreover, the economic indicators can change rather rapidly. As we write (January 1988) Sweden's rising wage costs appear problematic, Denmark faces difficult problems, and the West German economy begins to look very sluggish and inflexible, facing mounting internal and external criticism. On the other hand Britain, once the 'sick man' of western Europe, suddenly looks healthier – with one of the fastest growth rates in Europe – than seemed possible only a few years ago. One thing is, however, very striking: the surprising degree of general *political* stability in the face of the severe economic crisis.

The most difficult question is how to evaluate the limited economic successes. Looking into the future, one might well conclude that political complacency – now so widespread – may indeed be premature and that more difficult problems may lie ahead as the world tries to adjust to the new problems caused by the crash in the world's stock markets and the continuing problems of the imbalances in world trading patterns.

This concluding chapter will take up our main questions in turn: it will start by discussing perceptions of the crisis and will then take a more detailed look at reactions to the crisis. Finally the results will be analysed within a broader perspective.

Perceptions of the crisis

Since there is no objective indicator of 'crisis', much depended on how developments were perceived and interpreted within each political system. Indeed,what may have been seen as a major problem in one country could be regarded as a success in another. Thus, unemployment levels varied considerably across western Europe, yet all countries perceived it as a very serious problem. Perceptions were determined by political constellations: some countries could not avoid facing the problems immediately, others were preoccupied with other problems and still others tried to ignore and implicitly deny or belittle difficulties as long as possible.

The United Kingdom and Belgium belong to the first category. In both countries economic decline was on the agenda long before the world economic crisis set in. Politicians could not avoid addressing the crisis.

Indeed, they seized the post-1974 crisis as an opportunity to be exploited. It was almost as though the new crisis was seen as a last opportunity to take some long overdue tough decisions for those societies. Other countries had other concerns which delayed a full perception of the new economic difficulties. In this category belong Spain, attempting to create a viable democracy out of the remnants of Franco's dictatorship; Denmark, which experienced a disintegration of its party system at about the time when the crisis started; and France, where the left wanted to make use of its historic chance to introduce new policies despite the more immediate pressures of the crisis. Finally, some countries tried to postpone the moment of truth as long as possible: the Netherlands; West Germany; Austria; and Sweden, which, perhaps, still do not recognize a fully-fledged crisis and prefer to talk only about 'economic difficulties'.

Although variations in perceptions did occur, there was a general tendency towards recognizing the crisis as a more relevant problem. Initially, even if the crisis was not ignored, it was interpreted as only a cyclical phenomenon. That is why many countries continued with well-established policy patterns and styles. As soon as the interpretation changed to one of a structural kind, a more basic policy change came to be recognized as necessary. The same applies to interpretations which stressed, usually later in the crisis, the *internal* causes of the problems, in contrast to earlier views that the difficulties were only external, or 'imported' difficulties. The German case illustrates these shifting interpretations quite well.

The German case also underlines the extent to which political controversy coloured interpretations of the crisis. If parties, more particularly government and opposition, differed widely in their interpretation of the situation, the latter of course painting it in darker colours, the tendency to change policies became stronger. If there was a political consensus on the interpretation of the economic situation, as for example for long periods in the more corporatist and consensual systems of Austria and Sweden, this tended to postpone major policy change. Where a broader spectrum of political opinions is available, as for example in Denmark or Belgium, the heated discussions provided by the more extreme parties tended to force the moderates into a more 'sensible' consensual position which nevertheless provided the basis for common political action to tackle serious problems.

It is also important to note that external initiatives could strongly increase awareness of the economic crisis. This holds especially true for real or threatened intervention by the IMF. This is mentioned or implied in the chapters on the United Kingdom, Belgium and France, for example, and underlines a factor which was probably underestimated in the design of our comparative project – namely – the relative *lack* of autonomy for national governments, in some cases.

An important question is whether differing perceptions really affected behaviour in the end. Since all countries eventually adopted austerity policies, it could be said that the relevance of awareness, concern and interpretation with respect to the crisis did not matter very much in the long run. Intermittently it did matter, as has been pointed out above: perceptions determined the speed or time-lag with which countries reacted. Those more concerned naturally acted much faster, while those initially less interested took more time to adapt to the new reality. Thus in autumn 1987, Sweden, for example, announced that it would for the first time introduce cash limits for wage increases in the public sector, whereas this system had been tried many years earlier in Britain.

Reactions to the crisis

Political reactions to the crisis can be observed on different levels: first, there are structural responses: to what extent has the crisis led to reform of structures and institutions? Secondly, it might be possible to observe attempts to change the policy style, that is, the dominant patterns of policy-making. Thirdly, it might be useful to examine leadership patterns and possibly new methods applied by politicians in order to govern within a more difficult environment. These leadership patterns include relations between governments and the main interest groups. Finally, there is a need to analyse policy change, that is, changes of policy *content*. This might be done on the general level of ideology – and such changes of basic political philosophies are indeed the most outstanding tendencies of political change within the timespan and countries we have looked at – or on the concrete level of actual policies by which such ideologies are, or are not, implemented in practice. We placed particular emphasis on the analysis of budgetary policies, but we also examined other policy issues which had become salient in particular countries. While ideological change was in some respects followed by at least attempted radical policy change, this did not hide the fact that, in all countries, radical change was also accompanied by much 'business as usual' in many policy sectors.

In contrast to what had happened in the 1930s or 1950s and 1960s European countries did not, in the 1980s, choose to combat the economic crisis by major institutional reform or rearrangements. On the contrary, existing political institutions appeared to work with surprising efficiency despite the special difficulties. For example, the break-up of the Danish party system did not seriously damage the decisional efficacy of the Danish system – on the contrary it worked rather well. The same applies to the theoretically much feared experience with 'cohabitation' in France. Where institutional change did occur, it happened independently of the economic difficulties, such as in the cases of the development of a democratic constitution in Spain or of constitutional reform in Belgium. Decentralization where it occurred especially in France, Belgium and Sweden, was initiated independently of the economic troubles, even if it presented political benefits by devolving responsibility for some of the unpleasant austerity policies. The other countries did not follow the British example of actual 'institution bashing' – on the contrary institutions appeared to be taken for granted. Deregulation (now fashionable) may appear to be an exception, but when practised it often included some form of reregulation, introducing new rules which benefit groups other than those benefiting before. Institutional stability may have been a characteristic in industrial structures too: there appeared a reluctance to introduce major innovative reforms in this area with the exception of the ill-fated plans of Mitterrand's early years, or the major structural change which the crisis brought to British industry. This very fact may be the reason why economic conditions have not seen a major improvement in most of the countries analysed here. The very resilience which western Europe's *political* institutions have demonstrated has not been able to induce the major structural changes in industry which may well be necessary.

It is interesting to note that the institutional complexity of political systems did not seem to be as great an obstacle to reform policies as might have been expected. While it is in theory true that a fragmented governmental structure, a fragmented party system, as well as a fragmented system of organized interests would tend to make policy change difficult, it is remarkable that those countries which might have been expected to suffer most from cumulative problems of this kind did not perform any worse than countries with more concentrated structures. The challenge of complex circumstances perhaps made an active leadership style more possible. But also, citizens were more ready to accept tough measures once they too perceived that there was indeed a very real crisis.

In practice, most countries ultimately moved from a pattern of rather reactive and consensual politics, to one of innovation and conflict. This constitutes the major *political* change in western Europe. This change in pattern occurred especially in the United Kingdom, but also in Belgium, Denmark and Spain. Less distinct versions of this development occurred in Germany where more conflict is accepted, but the tendency is to adapt rather than to innovate, and France, which tended to fluctuate within an innovative conflictual pattern throughout. Other countries tried to maintain consensus – at least on the élite level – even if moving towards policy innovation (the Netherlands and Austria). Sweden, though still characterized by a pattern of innovative but consensual policy-making has also seen increased conflict, in the labour market for instance. Once again we observe the distinction between the old corporatist and the more pluralistic or less corporatist systems. As a rule, however, the changes in the basic policy style also coincided with an ideological change, even if concrete implementation did not always reflect the intentions.

The change in concrete leadership patterns can also be seen in this context. While politicians under the impact of the crisis often initially tried to maintain appearances by 'placebo politics', 'symbolic politics' and 'showmanship', they generally switched to a more active leadership style, disregarding protest or criticism, with a greater inclination to 'tough it out'. It is remarkable how many politicians made use of the opportunity to exercise leadership, expressed by a different leadership pattern and advocating a different ideology which a crisis situation provided (see Gourevitch, 1986). Gonzales, Lubbers, Vranitzky, Schlüter and Mrs Thatcher are obvious examples. In spite of the difficult conditions they encountered, they managed to mobilize support and at least in part implement quite difficult policies, no doubt assisted by a more compliant citizenry, as suggested above.

In terms of government/interest group relations, in the case of the trade unions, there has been a general tendency to sever links, to reduce the role of unions in national policy-making and to impose new restrictions on union activities. This applies in all countries with the possible exception of those with a more corporatist tradition. But even there, the unions have had to aquiesce in austerity measures or, as in Belgium, even relinquish the initiative to the government altogether. On the other hand, even if it cannot be exactly measured, we now appear to live in a business-oriented world in which enterprise and entrepreneurship are the predominant cultural values. Deregulation, tax cuts for business, privatization, are being either advocated or actually carried out in practically all countries, although capital has not been immune from tough governmental action or, of course, from the effects of the crisis.

As mentioned above, the big change, the 'Wende', sooner or later did occur everywhere. Ideology changed from welfare state/Keynesianism to austerity/Reaganomics, budgetary priorities followed suit and all this was accompanied by specific policies, by a changed policy style and by new leadership patterns. Practically all countries now accept, at least as goals for policy-making, cutting the budget deficit, restricting the growth of the welfare state, learning to live with unemployment, initiation of deregulation and privatization, restricting trade union rights and powers, and introduction of measures to assure wage discipline. There is , however, less emphasis on a *determined* restructuring of industry, or even on an effective technology policy and economic innovation, although these goals are also espoused and subject to some policy innovation. In true *laissez-faire* fashion, governments appear to assume that market forces will introduce the necessary developments automatically and hence they place greater emphasis on affecting market conditions. Indeed, this might be the main thrust of policy innovation, namely to institute policies which allow market forces to operate more freely.

Most countries perhaps rediscovered traditional patterns of policy-making after finally adopting the new orthodoxy. Belgium, as on occasions in the past, gave the government greater independence, Austria reintroduced grand coalition government, Spain reconstructed a strong state, France entered a period of experimentation. On the other hand there was, naturally, a desire to continue traditional policies before finally making the jump. Germany tried to continue its West German Model, and Austria, Denmark and the Netherlands tried first to stick to traditional policies; the French socialists tried to implement their grand design when they finally gained office. Sweden seems to be the only country to follow fairly continuous and consistent policy-making patterns while being, in some policy terms, more 'Thatcherite' than Mrs Thatcher.

It has to be stressed that the ideological change has by no means led to a general shift in all policy areas and in actual politics. Even in the United Kingdom (the 'lead' state in this respect) the government selects a few central issues such as union deregulation, privatization or educational reform in which to determinedly push new policies. Elsewhere much policy-making and policy administration is carried out as usual. This applies – and again all other countries follow suit – to the main elements of social programmes. Although cutbacks of some welfare programmes do occur, the essentials of social policy, including unemployment benefits, are not questioned. Indeed, this may be one of the main reasons why governments do, unlike in the 1930s, enjoy considerable mass support for the new orthodoxy. The 'Wende' is in part possible because the state already has a reasonably acceptable safety net in place, to take care of the casualties. The thirty years spent building welfare systems has acted as some kind of effective insurance in times of crisis. In this respect the Labour or left parties did not lose the battle caused by the economy crisis. The welfare state rather proved to be robust in difficult times.

We have argued that, although a new orthodoxy has developed, it took hold at differing rates in different countries. It is not possible to be very precise in terms of timing, but Table 11.1 gives a rough approximation of what we see as the time-lag involved. For example, in the United Kingdom Labour moved towards austerity in 1976 even before Thatcher took over three years later. Similarly, the German Social–Liberal coalition had, by 1981, acknowledged the failure of its West German Model, and changed its approach before Kohl became Chancellor. In Denmark the big change occurred in 1982, when Schlüter replaced Jorgensen. In France, Mitterrand had to abandon his plans for industrial socialism in 1983, by introducing austerity measures. As a final example, Austria experienced a U-turn in 1986 when Vranitzky shifted over to a rigorous policy and abandoned politics in the 'traditional' Austrian way. Only Sweden has moved along more consistently, possibly because it had long embraced some of the new orthodoxy, being a rather open and competitive industrial economy more used to an innovative policy style. In most cases it was the political left which took the first big step, or at least tried to do so, but it was usually the Conservatives who ultimately took the plunge. The conservatives usually benefited politically from doing so while the left tended to attract the electoral blame (with three exceptions: Spain, Austria and Sweden.)

Table 11.1 Time-lag of big policy change after 1973 (in years)

UK	B	D	DK	NL	F	E	A	S
3	8	8	9	9	10	10	12	15+

More generally, four groups of countries can be distinguished: the United Kingdom and Belgium come first – with a long tradition of political discussions about economic decline. The next group is Germany, Denmark and the Netherlands following suit after some hesitation, and attempts to apply traditional remedies. France and Spain, preoccupied with political problems follow later. Austria and Sweden – the most corporatist systems in our sample – come last. Sweden has so far never introduced a 'big bang' change in policy style, but has applied the new orthodoxy nevertheless, albeit in the context of long-standing labour market policies which have still avoided high unemployment. On the whole this development is compatible with the conclusion reached by Keman and Whiteley (1987, p. 211) that the various strategies of state intervention to cope with the crisis are strongly influenced by specific political and social factors, which also must be understood in an historical perspective.

Three main explanations can be given for this development, which prima facie do indeed suggest a diffusion of innovation processes. One is economic pressure for change. Thus there appears to be some correlation between wealth, as measured by GNP per capita, and time-lag, as expressed above. Within the economic laggards, forces to finally do something seem to be relatively strong. On the other hand, the degree of corporatism appears to be related to this time-lag also, but in the opposite direction. The least corporatist states move first and the most, last – this does not only apply to the two most corporatist countries, Austria and Sweden. Corporatism organizes forces of defence against basic policy change. Finally, one might mention foreign or international influences. IMF intervention is the most obvious example. But the international environment, especially on the economic level, exerts all kinds of influences, as we saw in the stock market crashes in 1987. Nevertheless, it appears that countries can still make choices, in terms of how to react to the international environment, particularly in a period of crisis. At least some countries, particularly the smaller ones, appear able to remain unaffected for longer (see Gourevitch, 1986).

Consequences of policy change

The *effects* of the political reactions of European countries can be evaluated on at least two levels. First, what have the *political* consequences been? Has the stability and effectiveness of political systems suffered? Has their legitimacy declined – in other words has the *economic* crisis also been transformed into a *political* crisis? In this context one can also assess the extent to which there were losers and gainers in society, following the crisis. Which leaders and which interests made use of the opportunities offered by the economic crisis and who suffered because of it? Secondly, one could review purely economic developments: have the new patterns of politics and the new policies contributed to a solution of the crisis or at least to a lessening of the economic difficulties created by it?

At about the time of the first oil price shock, when the crisis started and the good times seemed to be over for good, C. Offe sketched a model of crisis politics which tried to connect both the economic and political aspects and outlined a dilemma for the state which it could probably not really solve. Consequently, Offe expected a breakdown of traditional politics and its replacement by a better system via revolutionary means. Offe saw the political environment in two parts. In his model, the state or political system proper was confronted by the economic system on the one hand and by the social system on the other (Offe, 1973). It services the one by economic policy, the other by social policy, and receives resources for its operation and for financing policies, as well as general support. In a crisis, that is, in the case of a declining economy, financial restrictions would, according to the logic of the model, lead first to rationalization within the state, then to cutbacks of social policy, because of fiscal requirements and the overriding priorities of economic policy. That in turn would lead to delegitimization of the government, revolt against it, and its breakdown.

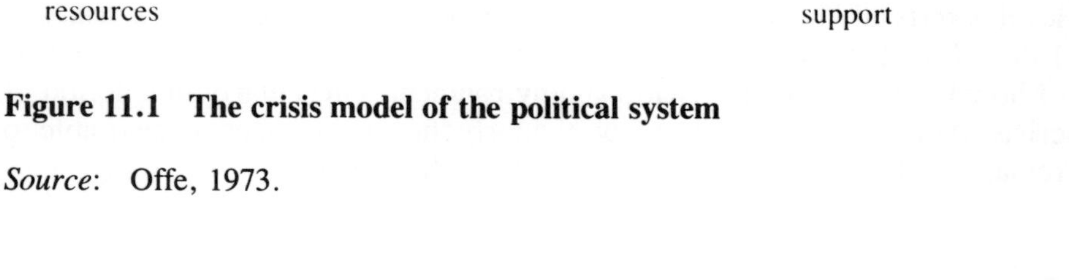

Figure 11.1 The crisis model of the political system

Source: Offe, 1973.

In the real world, matters have turned out rather differently. One of the most remarkable results of the country studies is the high degree of *political* stability maintained in spite of the very real difficulties. These difficulties corresponded to those expected by Offe and necessitated restrictions in the development of social policy. In practice, the basic elements of the welfare system have generally not been affected, but enough limitations and rationalizations have occurred to have caused some of the delegitimization expected by analysts of revolutionary change. However, almost the opposite developments have occurred. Most governments seem more secure rather than less and have increased rather than decreased in their popularity and legitimacy. It is true that some governments have suffered, especially those of the left. In general, they have neither been able to successfully challenge the spirit of the times (or the new orthodoxy) nor succeed by jumping on the Conservative bandwagon. This appears to be the case for the United Kingdom, France, Germany, Denmark and the Netherlands. On the other hand the Conservatives (as well as the Social Democrats in some cases – possibly in countries where they in some sense constituted the truly 'Conservative' broadly-based party) have benefited from the crisis. They have introduced the great political change and at the same time have usually increased their political status. The same difference holds true for interest groups. Business influence has increased, its values dominate the policy process; Labour has been reduced in influence, and has been subject to regulation, sometimes even excluded from the councils of government. The explanation for these developments may lie in other than political decisions or political leadership – such as the changing structure of industries and world trade or the universally high levels of unemployment. But the decline of the political influence of labour is remarkable nevertheless, although other interests and protest movements have declined also. These interests have not faded away, but governments have learned to live with them and no longer feel profoundly challenged or threatened as they might have done in the 1960s and early 1970s. The United Kingdom, Belgium and Denmark illustrate this trend. Times of crisis have indeed presented political opportunites and have led to some changes in the informal political rules governing the relationship between governments and interest groups. Crisis has also changed the expectations of citizens – both in relation to what can be achieved by governments and in terms of the expected style of governance – in essence, governments have often, by their own citizens, been given scope to govern notwithstanding the institutional and process changes of the 1960s designed to facilitate greater citizen participation.

The economic achievements are less impressive and much more mixed, in comparative terms. Rates of inflation and budget deficits have been reduced in many of the countries under study. However, growth rates remain disappointing and unemployment figures remain persistently high for most of western Europe. There is little doubt that the political efficiency of western European systems has not generally been matched by their economic efficiency, although significant adjustments have been made. This should not surprise us perhaps, because as Keman and Whiteley concluded: 'the correspondence between policy intention and economic performance is on average rather low' (Keman and Whiteley, 1987, p. 209).

The very fact that political stability coincides with serious economic problems in contemporary Europe need not necessarily be seen as either failure or success. In spite of outward appearances Europe has not really risen to the economic challenges posed by the crisis. Maybe it has taken the easy way out, adjusting itself somewhat economically but rather well politically. Thus Europe is settling down into a new kind of complacency. As long as governments appear reasonably popular, only lip service need be paid by them to more strenuous policy options despite a general acceptance, in principle, of the new orthodoxy; symbolic politics can once again replace actual initiatives, much business of government may be carried on as usual in conjunction with its 'clients'. Possibly Europe's capacity for political management, as seen approximately a decade and a half after the first oil shock, has simply been too sucessful. Evaluated within a democratic perspective, however, one should not underestimate the maintenance of political stability despite the persistent economic problems. After all, we are dealing with countries in western Europe, the citizens of which have, and freely use, the constitutional right of political expression.

None the less the new political complacency can be criticized both from the right and from the left. It can be argued on the one hand that the necessary structural adaptation to world markets has often been avoided, and on the other that unnecessary and ultimately unproductive social hardship are much too readily accepted. The criticism from the right has been concentrated in the diagnosis of so-called 'Eurosclerosis' (see Giersch, 1985; Olson, 1982). While other countries, particularly Japan and the United States, have been rapidly advancing into areas of new and technologically advanced industries, Europe has not really kept pace and will ultimately be overtaken by these more efficient economies of the Pacific region. That market forces alone would lead to a restructuring of industry, that new foreign markets would materialize out of the blue, seem to be the assumption in some countries. There is remarkably little reference to major industrial restructuring, technological change and aggressive foreign market strategies in the country reports. The ill-fated first strategy of Mitterrand, or the fairly determined efforts of Swedish industrial policy and Britain's willingness to see an accelerating de-industrialization, seem the only major exceptions.

The new political complacency can, however, also be criticized from the point of view of its social costs. To accept high levels of unemployment constitutes not only social waste, but also an expensive burden upon the welfare system and a large amount of economic inefficiency. It is less the traditional left than the alternative movements which have tried to raise this issue, although with limited political effect.

It is remarkable that so many groups and parties have accepted the so-called divided or 'two-thirds' society. Only Sweden has so far managed to combine a fairly determined austerity policy with an imaginative and successful policy of retraining and re-employment. Perhaps that country succeeded because it reached beyond the new complacency in both the technological and the social dimensions? But then even the Swedes worry about the question of whether the modern welfare state can handle the problems generated by future structural change (Geer *et al.*, 1987).

The future is hard to predict. Three possibilities stand out. First, economic recovery might emerge if the imbalances in world trade can be corrected. Secondly, we might see a continuation of the present form of political management – a politically successful strategy which may imply a rather civilized administration of economic decline and social decay. Thirdly, one should certainly not exclude the possibility of more serious challenges in the future. These might be external, originating from competition in the world's markets, or internal as dissatisfaction of the disprivileged groups ultimately challenges what currently seem very legitimate governments. In this case politics will not, as some observers rather prematurely suggest, become obsolete, but on the contrary will be *more* important. Policy-makers are constrained by their environment but, as Peter Gourevitch has pointed out, no country is *forced* by the crisis to react in a particular way (Gourevitch, 1986). Those who do not pay attention to the possible challenges may eventually be punished. Political initiative and leadership will be more necessary than ever in order to rise to such challenges.

References

de Geer, H. *et al.* (1987), *In the Wake of the Future.* Aldershot, Avebury/Gower.

Giersch, H. (1985), *Eurosclerosis.* Kieler Beiträge no. 112, Kile.

Gourevitch, P. (1986), *Politics in Hard Times: comparative responses to international economic crises.* Ithaca, Cornell University Press.

Kemen, H. and P. F. Whiteley (1987), 'Coping with crisis: divergent strategies and outcomes' in H. Keman *et al.*, *Coping with the Economic Crisis* (London, Sage, 1987), pp. 205–14.

Olson, M. (1982), *The Rise and Decline of Nations.* New Haven and London, Yale University Press.

Offe, C. 'Krisen des Krisenmanagements, Elemente einer politischen Krisentheorie' in M. Jaenike (ed), *Herrschaft und Krise* (Opladen, Westdeutscher Verlag), pp. 197–223.

Index